T0366613

Is College Worth It?

Class and the Myth of the College Premium

Richard Ohmann and Ira Shor

 JOHNS HOPKINS UNIVERSITY PRESS   BALTIMORE

Johns Hopkins University Press
2715 North Charles Street
Baltimore, Maryland 21218
www.press.jhu.edu

Library of Congress Cataloging-in-Publication Data

Names: Ohmann, Richard M. (Richard Malin), 1931–2021 author. |
    Shor, Ira, 1945– author.
Title: Is college worth it? : class and the myth of the college
    premium / Richard Ohmann and Ira Shor.
Description: Baltimore, Maryland : Johns Hopkins
    University Press, 2024. | Series: Critical university studies |
    Includes bibliographical references and index.
Identifiers: LCCN 2023030023 | ISBN 9781421448800 (hardcover) |
    ISBN 9781421448817 (ebook)
Subjects: LCSH: Commercialism in schools—United States. |
    College costs—United States. | Education, Higher—Political
    aspects—United States. | College students—United States—
    Finance, Personal. | Universities and colleges—United
    States—Sociological aspects.
Classification: LCC LC1085.2 .O37 2024 | DDC 378.3/80973—
    dc23/eng/20230718
LC record available at https://lccn.loc.gov/2023030023

A catalog record for this book is available from the British Library.

*Special discounts are available for bulk purchases of this book. For more
information, please contact Special Sales at specialsales@jh.edu.*

Contents

A Note on the Making of This Book vii

Preface. *"Beauty of an Implied Collaboration,"
or How Dick Ohmann and I Made This Book* ix
IRA SHOR

Introduction. *The Myth of the College Premium
and Other Truisms of American Culture* 1
JEFFREY J. WILLIAMS

1 The Costs and Benefits of College Education 20

2 Does Going to College Raise Lifetime Earnings? 58

3 What Makes People "Well-Off"—or Not? 98

4 Education for Jobs and Careers 127

5 The Payoff of College Education for the United States 162

6 At the End of the College Rainbow 190
IRA SHOR

Notes 229
Index 263

A Note on the Making of This Book

This book, alas, is posthumous. Richard Ohmann was working on it from 2015 until his death in the fall of 2021. Although the first four chapters were drafted, they were not yet in final form, and chapter 5 was still in progress, so Ohmann asked Ira Shor to complete it, as Shor recounts in his preface. Thus, Shor brought the book together, revising what was there, finishing chapter 5, and writing chapter 6, adding his own analysis of the mercantile imperative enforced on higher education, particularly in the form of occupational badges, a recent development that breaks education down into component parts for a job. After Shor's essential work, I helped ready the manuscript for publication and composed an introduction. Ohmann asked big questions about culture and society and always looked at how education furthered or impeded equality, and this book continues that effort, holding a glass to the commonplace of the college premium and asking who actually benefits from college, and who doesn't.

Jeffrey J. Williams, Series Editor,
Critical University Studies

"Beauty of an Implied Collaboration," or How Dick Ohmann and I Made This Book

Ira Shor

For Dick Ohmann's ninetieth birthday on July 11, 2021, old friends, students, and colleagues planned a Zoom celebration. Some composed comic limericks, while others wrote or selected poems and excerpts to read. I was much looking forward to singing happy birthday to Dick that day. We had met nearly 53 years earlier, at the raucous 1968 conference of the Modern Language Association (MLA), when I was 23 and in grad school. He spoke there on a panel, urging academics to risk opposing the status quo and join the mass movements of that time against racism and the Vietnam War. I had never encountered a professor who spoke like him: strikingly tall and handsome, he was poised, plainspoken, and persuasive in his oppositional appeal. Doubtless, I wanted to be like him when I grew up, to become as smart, knowledgeable, and fluent. A year after, I spoke with him at the equally raucous MLA of 1969. Some weeks later, I sent him an essay for the journal *College English,* which he was then editing.

Dick rejected my paper, which I titled something like "The Relevance of Literature in a Time of Radicalism." However, I was not dismayed. His rejection letter was kind, encouraging, and helpful. I took seriously his invitation to write more and send him new material in the years following. In short, from that letter on, Dick became an early mentor as I wrote about teaching for critical literacy. In those years, I was among the new doctorates fortunate enough to find an academic job and, as I was caught up in transitioning from "student" to "faculty," the political climate was transitioning to the right, from opposition movements on the wane to conservative authorities on the offensive.

In that difficult time for activist faculty, the 1970s, Dick published my earliest essays on critical teaching. Even more supportive, he invited me to guest edit materials for two special issues of *College English*, one about the experimental basic writing program I helped build at the College of Staten Island, CUNY. During a turbulent period, his support and tutelage helped steady my attention on the work at hand. Another influence was *English in America* (1976), his remarkable book providing a big picture in which to situate the work of writing teachers. In addition, at Wesleyan University in Middletown, Connecticut, Dick hosted editorial meetings of the *Radical Teacher* collective, a journal on which I worked in that decade with older luminaries such as Louis Kampf, Florence Howe, Paul Lauter, and Adrienne Rich.

In debt to Dick for crucial help when I started out, of course I looked forward to his ninetieth birthday party. I logged on to my computer that Sunday, but, instead of an affectionate revel under way, I received a shocking email that Dick had been rushed to the hospital and the party was off. Two days later, Dick's longtime friend and collaborator on *Radical Teacher*, Susan O'Malley, sent around a missive from Dick himself:

> Thank you for your limericks, poems, tributes, and love that you have sent to commemorate my birthday. The morning of my 90th birthday I was sent in an ambulance to Baystate Franklin hospital emergency room in Greenfield for three blood transfusions because my hemoglobin count was very low. This was the third time that this has happened. The following day [the doc-

tor] told me I had a serious blood infection in my heart and he did not foresee my making a full recovery from it. It was then that I decided to go into hospice. . . . [T]his is a difficult decision, but I believe it is the right decision for me given the circumstances.

These words drove the air from my lungs as I stared at the screen; my old mentor was dying, with little time left. I wanted to see him as soon as possible.

Dick began hospice at his nineteenth-century farmhouse in small-town Hawley, deep in the beautiful Berkshires of western Massachusetts, a place whose history figures into his narrative in this book. In his hospice message, Dick invited friends to visit him at the farm, so I called his daughter Sarah, who was there with him, and she said it was OK to come that first weekend. When I asked what treats Dick liked that I could bring, she told me he favored chocolate, and that people in hospice can eat anything they want. With a full box of Italian chocolate and cream pastry, my wife, Maryann, and I drove four hours north to see him on July 17, 2021.

In rural Hawley, his farmhouse sat high up a long, partly paved road, bordered on both sides by fields and pastures, some strewn with rock outcroppings and boulders, some overgrown with tall oaks, maples, and pines, others partly cleared for small homesteads. We parked by the barn a short way from the house, where Sarah greeted us at the door, took the box of pastry, and welcomed us into the kitchen with its nineteenth-century walk-in hearth. Dick joined us at the kitchen table, wheeled in by a home hospice aide. He was thinner and paler than before but still sociable. I introduced Maryann and asked him how long was good for him to talk; he spoke softly, saying "about an hour or so," occasionally short of breath as we conversed.

Dick asked what I had been working on. I told him that with the COVID-19 lockdown, I had stopped traveling and was giving Zoom interviews, talks, and seminars to folks in Europe, Turkey, South America, and the United States. I was unsure about asking him about his illness, so I risked inquiring about any new thoughts or material he had in mind. He took an audible breath and said, "I've been writing a new book," pausing momentarily before adding, "but I'll never get to finish it." When he ended with, "I'll never get to finish it," his voice lowered, and his eyes fell into a sadness I had never seen in them before. My chest tightened as I stared at those eyes.

After a brief pause, I ventured uncertainly, "What is the book about? Can I have a look at it?" He turned to me and suddenly blurted out, "How would you like to finish the book for me?" I was taken aback by this out-of-the-blue proposal. His demeanor brightened as he uttered it, his face lifting and eyes widening. I could see his sudden invitation cheered him. Of course, I was completely unprepared for such an overture, but intuited a chance to be of use to a dying mentor for his generous attentions 50 years earlier. So I said, "Yes, I think so, but can I read the draft? What is it about?" For the next hour, Dick spoke about his unfinished book as we ate Italian pastry.

Dick explained the argument he pursued across the first five chapters. I much liked what I heard. We had long agreed on the politics of education, and we had been working, as he put it, in "the same problematic," namely, critical university studies, though from different locations—he in the academy and I in mass colleges and critical pedagogy. Dick told me his five chapters needed finishing and asked if I would "curate" them. He also wanted me to compose a concluding chapter, in my own voice, to summarize the first five, to bring the narrative up to date vis-à-vis the direction of higher education, and to propose a democratic agenda for opposition. Dick urged me to profile ideology, power relations, and working-class perspectives in curating his chapters and writing my own. As we spoke and ate pastry, the conversation changed Dick's mood; he became livelier and more engaged, encouraging me to push ahead into a daunting task I had never done before. For the moment, his pending death no longer filled the room but was temporarily shelved out of sight. For my part, I was happy to be of use in some way at this terrible time, while I worried that I had bitten off far more than I could chew.

Back home the following week, I received five chapter files from Dick, as well as the following note: "It was a pleasure to see you and Maryann, and an astonishing stroke of helpfulness on your side to say you'd have a look to see if you could curate it in some way that would make it part yours and part mine. I see a beauty in the idea of our completing the implied collaboration of our careers." His words propelled me. I read each chapter twice, made preliminary notes, and emailed him a first overview of my thoughts. I also ordered a few texts he mentioned to prep me for close reading of the chapters. Then I returned to the chapters for a third time, learned how to edit the manuscript with the program he had been using, and began several months of close attention to each line. I discovered that "curating" these unfinished chapters involved a number of tasks besides adding missing punctuation marks and letters or words. I recorded every change, edit, and addition I made and emailed them to Dick for his approval. Dick thought some paragraphs were "clunky," so I rewrote sentences and transitions to see which smoother wordings he preferred. Some places lacked citations, and some had references in the text without notes. Other places could benefit from citations to sources I knew of. I "cured" all these spots by adding necessary text, missing citations in the paragraphs, and notes, consulting Dick as I went. If I thought that a paragraph needed more explicit commentary on a point or claim, or distinct reference to an aspect of ideology, power relations, class, race, or gender, I would compose text and seek Dick's concurrence before adding the new material. Through it all, I did my best to copy his style and kept Dick's first-person voice. In the concluding chapter, which I wrote by myself, I use the "I" to indicate this narrative is in my voice.

I kept busy curating like this for two months. In early August, I visited the farm a second time to work directly with Dick. At the end of this second visit, Dick gave me a large file box filled with research materials he had gathered as background for what would have been his final chapter, which he never wrote and asked me to compose. When I finished his chapter 5 in late September 2021, I opened the big box and began studying the wealth of sources in it to see how Dick himself was preparing to do the conclusion. The prominence of occupationalism and badge programs encroaching on higher education was a central theme here and became central to my chapter 6. We had been emailing back and forth since July, chapter by chapter, when, at the end of September, I noticed that Dick's replies to my messages would stop sometimes for two or three days. The delays worried me. Often I was on the verge of calling the farm to see how he was. I dreaded hearing that he had again been rushed to the emergency room or, worse, that he had died. Twice, just as I couldn't wait another day and was about to call Sarah at Hawley, a new email from Dick suddenly appeared in my inbox; I finally exhaled and went back to work. But then, on October 8, a message arrived from Sarah that Dick had died.

Though not unexpected, the loss of an old friend, mentor, and collaborator left me grieving for some days, unable to work. I was honored to have received his trust and attention while working on the book, and fifty years before, so finishing it was my final tribute to him. I resumed work, diving into the large box of research items he gave me for chapter 6, and spent the ensuing months completing it. The book that follows is the result, and it continues in the critical spirit that both Dick and I shared in looking at American education and hoping for a more just and equal society.

Introduction

The Myth of the College Premium and Other Truisms of American Culture

JEFFREY J. WILLIAMS

The Myth of the College Premium

What's gained by going to college? And who gains it? We hear all the time that there is a $1 million premium added to your income over the course of your lifetime if you go to college and get a bachelor's degree. That's over and above what you would earn with a high school degree, and the amount would be even more extreme if you didn't attain that diploma. You'd be hard-pressed to find a professional or an executive who does not have a college degree. A fixed idea of contemporary American culture is that college is the main path for people to get ahead; more generally, it is the institutional motor for equality. In some ways the college premium has updated the Horatio Alger story: no matter where you came from, as long as you do your work in school, you can climb. The implication is that if you fail to get a college degree and make less, the lower earnings are a direct result of that choice. Thus, the college premium is not only an economic tally sheet but a social imperative.

This book deflates the myth of the college premium. In it, Richard Ohmann unpacks what we think we know about the premium and shows that what it reflects is a *wealth premium* or *class premium* in the United States. The standard commentary confuses the effect for the cause, arguing that the college premium causes a class rise, as if the game starts on "Go" and college helps one advance around the board. Rather, much of the premium results from class position already in place. As Ira Shor remarks in the final chapter, the college premium pays off—for a select few. If you start with a hotel on Boardwalk, you have a substantially better chance to prosper. In other words, instead of a path to social equality, the college premium testifies to the way that class tends to reinforce itself in the United States. Yet we still repeat the commonplace of the college premium as a remedy to inequality.

However tonic in deflating that myth, the book is not cynical and Ohmann is not attacking higher education, as many conservatives have done lately. Rather, he's presenting a corrective to the false bill of goods we're sold, as well as to the claims of many educational pundits who should know better. Ohmann goes to first principles, analyzing the assumptions and commonplaces that are bandied about regarding college and teases apart the web of cause, effect, and ideology so that we have a clearer picture with which to figure out what to do. Ohmann calls us to consider what college actually does and whom it is for. If anything, he is attacking the way capitalism inevitably causes inequality and how it governs our lives, and he points out that college is a ground of class struggle. What would college look like if this were a more equal world? If we hold to the American value of equality, how might we attain it?

The book brings out a number of corollary points about the college premium. Ohmann underscores that, compared to average high school graduates, those from the wealthiest classes have much better preparation, many more life opportunities, and other advantages, and they have greater access to elite higher education and opportunities attached to it, like potentially lucrative internships and other doors of entry into the VIP lounge of US society. So the process is largely closed and self-confirming. It's like saying that princes have royal accents because they earned them, rather than because they grew up in royal households. In other words, whereas most people might acknowledge that the wealthy might have a small advantage, discourse on college tends to discount or minimize that advantage; in contrast, Ohmann, backed by data on social mobility, holds that the wealth advantage is in fact determinative.

A further point is that what the college premium actually measures defaults to the simple base of income. Strangely, commentators rarely ask what people actually learn in college, much less see the purpose of college as something other than a job and its salary. Again, this perspective registers, to a large extent, the class advantages that put one at a winning position in the game of contemporary life.

Who, then, is actually served? Along with the wealthy, Ohmann shows that college more generally serves the market and the businesses that participate in it. For instance, college serves corporations that hire people with computer science or engineering or other STEM (science, technology, engineering, math) degrees. The college premium, in other words, operates as a premium to businesses in many respects, subsidizing training and sorting, while transferring the cost to public funds and to students themselves, as they pay tuition and accrue debt for the chance to work.

Thus, another corollary of Ohmann's argument is that in holding onto the college premium, we unthinkingly subscribe to the ideology of the market, assuming that the primary purpose of our society is the profiting of businesses. If the goal of college is simply to enable people to get jobs, then college is merely a conveyor belt for the market. This line of criticism is furthered by Ira Shor in the final chapter, where he unpacks the rise of the new credential: "badges," or certificates, for certain skills. These also reinforce the idea that college serves businesses and the training they want. As Shor suggests, badges seem to be the way of the future, feeding directly into the segmentation of educational tasks to more exactly serve job training.

Finally, Ohmann's argument is undergirded by the idea that we could create a society different from the one we have, a society that goes beyond serving the imperatives of capitalism and corporations. He doesn't work this out in the book—his analytical approach sifts the facts and related commentary in order to debunk falsehoods that commentators and policymakers endorse—but Ohmann's insights give us clearer knowledge on which to base action. Ohmann's is not a nostalgic view of higher education, as some criticism of the university, especially from those in the humanities, hearkens back to. He does not yearn for a halcyon past when the university was pure; in fact, Ohmann points out the injustices of, say, the Vietnam War–era university. Instead, the book unwaveringly calls for struggle to attain social equality.

Though already a professor in the 1960s, Ohmann took some lessons from the resistance to the draft and the Vietnam War. In chapter 2, he discusses the draft system instituted in 1969, a lottery according to one's birth date. It was installed because it seemed to be unbiased, based on just the luck of the draw and thus equal for everyone, but in reality it heavily favored those with wealth—who could obtain deferments in various ways, most notably via medical exemptions and college enrollment. In practice, college admissions operates much like the draft lottery: although everyone presumably has an equal chance, the sorting mechanism gives people with wealth crucial advantages and leaves those without for conscription—into debt instead of the military. So much for the idea of a meritocracy: again, the fortunate few start on Boardwalk, while everyone else starts at the first square or not even on the board.

Ohmann also notes that scholarly commentary on higher education tends to repeat many of these skewed, sometimes mistaken, and often harmful ideas about college. In a sense, he performs a critique of education studies similar to what Edward Said performed with "the Orient" and Orientalism. Ohmann illuminates tacit "educationalism" and how it supports existing structures of power and capitalism. (While Ohmann analyzes "discourse" on the university, as Said does discourse on geopolitics, Ohmann's diagnosis looks more immediately to the effects of capitalism than Said does.) Ohmann calls out a few of the main educational commentators who extol the virtue of the college premium, when they in fact are reproducing its harm.

One striking consequence of this argument bears on the progressive slogan "College for All." Gaining traction from Bernie Sanders's campaigns, the slogan brilliantly conveys the idea that college should be free or for minimal charge—that is, publicly supported—rather than a cash machine for the banking enterprise and for corporate–theme park universities. And it responds to the student loan debt debacle by cutting off the travesty of student debt at the source. But, in chapter 5, Ohmann questions whether the many "College for All" avowals feed into the assumption that the purpose of college is to obtain a job and gain a wage premium. That might be a reasonable, pragmatic position—I would prefer than my students can get good jobs, if they aim for them—but Ohmann shows that we should be careful to look beyond the loop of job success in measuring the value of education. He reminds us that our slogan should be "Equality for All," putting the horse before the cart.

Even if we resist cynicism, it's tempting to be fatalistic about what is going on in higher education. The system's massiveness and complexity make finding a solution hard, and it seems as if the institutional juggernaut can only lumber on. But one key step is to start with the kind of cold-eyed intellectual resistance that Ohmann offers.

Unpacking Other Myths of American Culture

Richard Ohmann was one of the most probing American-ist critics of the past half century and had a singular voice. Besides the college premium, he unpacked other mythologies of our culture, particularly in his major books, *English in America: A Radical View of the Profession* (1976) and *Selling Culture: Magazines, Markets, and Class at the Turn of the Century* (1996), and in a number of remarkable essays, such as "The Shaping of a Canon: U.S. Fiction, 1960–1975." His work overall shines light on our cultural institutions—the ground beneath our feet, as it were, in higher education, literature, and publishing—and how they interweave with capitalism and class. And it does so in a plainspoken, narrative voice, scholarly but without the laboriousness of much academic writing.

In *English in America*, he turned a gimlet eye on the pieties of literary training in the university, showing how it does something other than its advertised purpose. A typical assumption is that literature and culture improve us, conferring cultural enlightenment, refining our taste, or spurring critical thinking. They convey the best that is known and thought, which presumably uplifts us. But Ohmann looks under that gloss and points out that university English also furthers the march of modern business, training the professional-managerial class and separating it from lesser classes. For instance, almost every English department in the United States teaches composition, and what is composition for? For clear reasoning and expression, one hopes, but it also teaches a number of social lessons. As he puts it, English comp instructors and professors

> train young people, and those who train young people, in the
> skills required by a society most of whose work is done on paper

and through talk, not by physical labor. We also discipline the young to do assignments, on time, to follow instructions, to turn out uniform products, to observe the etiquette of verbal communication. And in so doing we eliminate the less adapted, the ill-trained, the city youth with bad verbal manners, blacks with the wrong dialect, Latinos with the wrong language, and the rebellious of all shapes and sizes, thus helping to maintain social and economic inequalities. (230)

The book was a promising one in bringing into focus the social function of humanistic learning and the university, and also in comparing the work that we, as professors, actually do to the conventional rationales for what we do. That approach inspired me when I started writing about student debt in the late 1990s: we tell ourselves that higher education inculcates humane values, or forges critical thinking, or simply helps one get a job, but if two-thirds of students carry an average of $40,000 in student debt on graduation, we are also teaching them another lesson. For all too many students, especially those borrowing larger amounts, we deliver a *pedagogy of debt* that subsequently permeates their lives, shapes their career and life choices, inflects their understanding of social institutions, and tones their feeling in the world.[1] While the effects of this lesson are often delayed, they have proved long-lasting for at least two generations of contemporary Americans.

In some ways, *English in America* aligned with a wave of criticism during the 1970s and '80s that looked critically at social institutions, including the radical pedagogy movement that Shor, Henry Giroux, and others developed. One wing of that movement, led by Samuel Bowles and Herbert Gintis, posited the "reproduction theory" of education—that is, the idea that one of the main tasks of education is to reproduce the power structures and class order of capitalist society. Bowles and Gintis were primarily talking about grade school education; similarly, the British cultural studies critic Paul Willis, in his book *Learning to Labor*, examined the reproduction of the working class in secondary schools in England.[2] Ohmann shared the spirit of that critique, but looked beyond grade school to higher education, focusing on the gateway of literary training. In some sense, reproduction is enforced in high schools through mandatory attendance and disciplinary structures like bells between classes. These structures segue to the punch-clock parameters of many working-class jobs. Higher education presents a different case: it assimilates those selected, presumably with merit, for professional jobs, people who stand between the working class and owners. It produces the "professional-managerial class," or PMC, as Barbara and John Ehrenreich named it, or the professional-middle class.[3]

In his scrutiny of higher education, Ohmann served as a beacon for the generation of critics and activists who came onto the scene in the 1990s, coalescing around the field of critical university studies, particularly those critiquing the ways higher ed serves corporate capitalism and exploits academic labor. Ohmann was one of the few models who turned to the institutional situation we encountered—and that has become even more severe for subsequent generations, particularly in the humanities. While theory of the past half century has forged many critiques of society, they have tended to be abstract, for instance in employing overarching concepts of discipline and power or of ideology. Ohmann brought the critique down to earth, to our concrete workplaces, holding a magnifying glass to the ways our departments operate and we work. Few critics looked at academic jobs and what students were experiencing regarding debt, as well as exorbitant work hours (students at public colleges and universities work an average of 30 hours a week). But Ohmann did—in

English in America, as well as subsequent essays, such as "Graduate Students, Professionals, Intellectuals," collected in his 2003
book, *Politics of Knowledge*.

English in America marked a departure from criticism as it
was typically practiced at that point, and often still is. He
moved from a focus on formal matters, notably style, to a kind
of sociology of literature, looking at its institutional channels.
(His first book, appearing in 1962, examines the stylistic habits
of George Bernard Shaw and pays close attention to language
and syntax.) Along with the university, Ohmann looked at the
channels of editing and publishing, magazines and advertising, and book reviewing and distribution, all of which shape
literature. In general, he mapped how modern industrial capitalism makes culture, both high and mass culture.

One essay that stands out for me, especially as a critic of
contemporary fiction, is his "The Shaping of a Canon: U.S.
Fiction, 1960–1975" (1983), a rich examination of the literary
field of that moment that traces how particular works might
attain nascent standing of a classic. We tend to assume that
quality shines through regardless of its circumstance, but, like
academic merit, material conditions have a formative hand, and
the value of a book rarely starts from zero; rather, Ohmann
unpacks the stages through which novels attained their meri-
torious position. For one thing, critical acclaim usually starts
with a significant push from the enterprises producing and
distributing them, in the form of advertising and promotion
in influential places, like the *New York Times Book Review*.
And Ohmann sketches the various hands that go into the
production of a work: agents, editors, marketers, reviewers,
academic critics and teachers who might put the books on
syllabi, and finally professional-managerial-class readers, who
might find similar values that they hold in the fiction and who
read the kinds of magazines that advertise it. In other words,

instead of bearers of pure aesthetic merit, works of literature are shaped and given provenance through their institutional circumstances and tend to express PMC values. While the essay makes its case with empirical facts, such as the correlation of ad pages with the frequency of discussion of particular works, it also quietly makes a larger theoretical point about aesthetics: contrary to the idea that aesthetic value is timeless and universally recognized, Ohmann shows how it is class driven and informed by its social conditions. This was Ohmann's response to the controversies over the canon; against the idea that the canon is an ineluctable measure of merit, he essentially argues that it expresses its own class premium, inflected by the PMC values.

"The Shaping of a Canon" and other essays that Ohmann wrote in this period are gathered in his *Politics of Letters*, which still bears rereading. The title and perspective resonate with the British critic Raymond Williams's *Culture and Society* and *Politics and Letters*, which emphasize the social conditions of culture, in contrast to an emphasis on literary language or its deconstruction. Ohmann's approach also had affinities with the Birmingham School of cultural studies, albeit reset for American culture. This focus on culture and society, or literature and capitalism, undergirds Ohmann's masterpiece of Americanist cultural studies, *Selling Culture: Magazines, Markets, and Class at the Turn of the Century*. The book shows how modern US culture entwined with late-nineteenth and early-twentieth-century capitalist industry. It examines the way national magazines arose in conjunction with mass production and the nationwide transport of goods that developed in that period. This new, commercial culture fueled advertising, which effectively made those magazines possible, and in turn was the seedbed for turn-of-the-century American literature.

Whatever else culture does, it offers the attention of an audience to capital markets.[4]

The book animates the culture of the time, opening with a brilliant vignette of a person in Cleveland around the end of the nineteenth century and how they might have perceived, read, and used literary works—for example, as an activity of the new mercantile class, which could afford nonessential goods like novels, had leisure to read them, and had comfortable spaces like parlors to read them in. Many of these new readers were middle- and upper-class women, freed from conventional work by the new business wealth. *Selling Culture* links these books and readers to the emergence of national brands like Pears soap and Quaker Oats, which pumped funding and pages into magazines such as *McClure's*, *Century*, *Atlantic Monthly*, and *Cosmopolitan*. They all expanded as they gained ads, from a handful of pages of them in 1880 to around 100 pages of ads in each issue by around 1900. It was a golden age of magazines—in their prominence as well as their revenue—that in turn pumped up American literature.

Sometimes it seems as if the connections among economic and cultural events is indecipherably complex, but Ohmann doesn't hedge his bets in attributing a chain of causality: "The real causes come first . . . [and] have to do with big capital, factories, machines, products, and profits; secondary causes include the labors of middlemen to move products about and win over consumers; farther downstream are the projects of writers and editors, then those of the new middle class that bought magazines and the commodities advertised there; and at the end of the causal flow come representations, meanings, ideology" (340). In the era of high theory, especially in the wake of the Nietzschean suspicion of causality, we are often shy about attributing cause and effect. Or cause disperses to the ethereal force of "power." In contrast, Ohmann traces how modern culture is not a separate sphere but is materially entwined with the particular moments of the history of capitalism Still, he makes clear that he does not subscribe to a rigid determinism; rather, he finds that the process takes shape in a web involving big factories along with representations. Antonio Gramsci's concept of hegemony is one of the few technical concepts that Ohmann invokes—much as Raymond Williams does in understanding the relations of culture to material conditions. For Ohmann, in charting the formation of modern American culture, capitalism holds a hegemonic position: like a river current that moves ever downstream but has bends, swirls, and eddies along the way, it might move unevenly but it still is shaped by the dominant class. In naming the cause, Ohmann also evokes a politics: the modern stream of capitalism engenders substantial inequality, which yields a problem similar to the one created by contemporary higher education. This analysis begs the question of how to resist or change that stream. Indeed, what would culture look like in a more genuinely equal society?

A Career against the Grain

With the kind of critical work I've described, Richard Ohmann cut a path against the grain. *English in America* stepped off the conventional path of criticism to take to task the profession of literature itself. Biting the hand of the profession was not a way to earn the favor of those at its center. *English in America* was attacked by Steven Marcus, for instance, a major critic at the time, who wrote in *TLS* that it was a "deficient and inapplicable . . . irrelevant . . . collection of tendentiousness and claptrap."[5] One might think Marcus would have been more sympathetic, given that his first book was a study of Friedrich Engels in Manchester. But, as a longtime professor

at Columbia, he had probably not presided over many composition classrooms, and few outside the Ivy League. In a
different vein, Stanley Fish criticized *English in America* as expressing a kind of self-hating anti-professionalism.[6] The book
is certainly ambivalent about professionalism, but I think it
more accurate to say it expressed anti-classism. The real nub
was the question of politics: Fish has long held that criticism
should deal only with literature and keep in its lane,[7] whereas
Ohmann came to believe that criticism should do more than
that and could be a form of social and cultural critique, not
just an intraprofessional practice. Indeed, criticism has had a
role in bringing social issues to the public sphere since the
eighteenth century. This debate over the purpose of criticism
continues today, of course—and obviously ties to the concern with higher education.

   To see in perspective Ohmann's choice to do a kind of
oppositional criticism, I find it particularly striking that he
had been on the fast track of the profession and among its
anointed during higher education's post–World War II boom.
Born in the 1930s, he went to a widely respected liberal arts
college, Oberlin, and then to graduate school at Harvard in
the 1950s. Harvard (and Yale and other Ivies) were the major
conduits for the profession at that time, and his cohort included,
at points, Paul de Man, Edward Said, and Noam Chomsky.
That cohort went on to forge what came to be known as
theory and to seed Ivies and major state universities as graduate programs expanded through the 1960s, from producing
about 300 PhDs a year in 1960 to 1,100 in 1970.[8] (Fish benefited from this boom, down the coast at Yale in the late 1950s
and early 1960s.) While in graduate school, Ohmann held a
vaunted fellowship in the Harvard Society of Fellows, which
typically supports the recipient for a term of three years while
they think and discuss with others so tapped. (Chomsky had

one as well.) During that respite, he spent two terms at Oxford studying with J. L. Austin, the progenitor of speech act theory, who was finishing the material for his foundational book, *How to Do Things with Words* (1962).[9] Ohmann next worked on "stylistics," publishing essays in some of the main journals of literary studies, speaking at the prestigious English Institute, and writing his book on Shaw. In other words, he was a major player in the new realm of theory, introducing the developments in speech act theory, as well as Chomskian linguistics, to literary criticism. Yet he walked away from much of that work when he turned to examining the way literary studies, and more generally universities, aid and abet inequality.

Walking away had costs. Ohmann had considerable standing in literary studies during the 1970s. For instance, a significant portion of Fish's *Is There a Text in This Class?* a major announcement of reader response theory, discusses and argues with Ohmann's version of stylistics.[10] Or the introduction to Paul de Man's *Allegories of Reading*, perhaps the most influential critical statement announcing deconstruction in the US, cites only two critics, one of them Ohmann, very favorably on the difference between ordinary statements and performative speech acts: "whereas the rules of grammar concern relationships among sound, syntax, and meaning, the rules of illocutionary acts concern relationships among people."[11] De Man uses Ohmann's distinction to show the deconstructive dissonance of grammar and rhetoric. As speech acts and performance became central terms in literary theory, Ohmann was positioned as a prime theorist. It's not that he could've been a contender; he was one.

To be sure, Ohmann held a good academic job at Wesleyan University in Connecticut throughout his career, so he was not on shaky employment ground, like those now who have adjunct, nontenure track, or other precarious jobs. But he stood apart from mainstream academic practice and ambition. I think his choice was remarkable not only in staking out different and more politically pointed topics but also in forgoing the rewards that many of the best and the brightest from his era received. It no doubt took some moxie to walk against the mainstream and oppose the powers that be. Ohmann stood apart in other ways, which I'll highlight, but first, what prompted this change?

Ohmann attributed part of his turn to the events of the 1960s and '70s, most obviously the American War in Vietnam. He was more a preppie than a hippie, but he came to politics by changes like the US Defense Department's growing influence on campuses and the draft, which loomed over students. It's little remembered now, but in many ways colleges and universities were part of the military infrastructure and fed into the war in Vietnam, and higher ed after World War II was pumped up as an arm of national defense, with many developments in weapons and technology coming from university research, most infamously Agent Orange at the University of Illinois. (The concluding chapters of *English in America* cover the military-industrial complex; in some ways, this book updates that analysis by looking at the corporate-financial complex.) Moreover, college ROTC programs supplied the officer corps, and male college-age students were issued draft cards, placing the sword of induction into what many considered a heinous war over their heads. As Ohmann told me in an interview, "I was increasingly discontent and uneasy with what we were doing in our own rush toward fuller professionalism and specialization in the early 1960s, and I was angry about race and militarism and class in our country, and those two strands fused for me."[12]

Ohmann found and worked with some like-minded people through the Modern Language Association (MLA) and other organizations, as well as with draft resisters on campus. Joining Louis Kampf, Florence Howe, Paul Lauter, and others, he participated in protests at the 1970 MLA convention that led to the collection *The Politics of Literature: Dissenting Essays on the Teaching of English*.[13] They and others formed the Radical Caucus, which has been a gadfly of the profession ever since, and they put out the journal *Radical Teacher*, which has marched on, now in an online incarnation. Unlike a mainstream academic journal, *Radical Teacher* deals with more practical matters of pedagogy and out-of-the-way kinds of institutions, as well as critiquing repressive policies inflicted on education and advocating more progressive policies and practices.

Another part of his turn was taking on the editorship of *College English*, which he steered from 1966 to 1978. The journal, published by the National Council of Teachers of English, looks at the fundamental curriculum of its name, particularly freshman comp and the other basic courses that form the aquifer of literary studies in most of our universities. And it gave many critics a start in publishing, as Ira Shor recounts in his preface to this book. In the interview I did, Ohmann mentioned that he had looked at copies of the journal while he was in graduate school, so his subsequent attention to teaching and more practical matters might have been less of a conversion than a consolidation of purpose. I think his service as editor for more than a decade and his concern with basic teaching and what students encounter are remarkable, as most of his cohort has tended to stay in their lane of scholarship and theory, leaving these less prestigious realms to the service workers in writing programs.

Ohmann stands apart in a couple of other ways that I think are worth thinking about. First, he relocated his professional focus from British literature to American, from literature to mass culture, and from stylistics to social and cultural history. In this last change, he developed his own version of cultural studies, which one can see especially in *Selling Culture*. From our prospect, it's no longer a surprise or a lesser pursuit to center on American literature, but in the late 1970s, as Bruce Franklin remarked in 1978, "we still consider[ed] American literature as a mere colonial implantation" and an "offshoot of European culture." Indeed, American literature was a kind of poor cousin of British literature; it shared a language but was a subsidiary, following in the wake of the British canon. Starting around 1970, Ohmann moved to make his focus American culture, which included politics and the criticism of capitalism.[14]

Second, I think that Ohmann has stood apart simply in terms of his writing. In contrast to most academic criticism, the style Ohmann developed was plainspoken and direct, with flashes of irreverence. "Accessible" sometimes implies "watered down," but his style is not intellectually lite. Ohmann leads the reader through facts and argument like a tour guide, pointing out one thing of note here, another twist there, reinforcing the basic point overall. It is a style that has influenced, for instance, the disability studies critic Lennard Davis, who identified Ohmann as his prime model in learning how to write criticism, and it was also a model for me.[15] You can see this style at work in this book, which seeks to decipher the truth and lies of the college premium by taking readers on a crisp tour through the mist of recent news reports about the return on investment in college and through the policy mud about things like student debt. Like his other books, *Is College Worth It?* avoids the technicalities of theory, but if we mean by theory an attempt to explain phenomena in the world, it helps us understand the phenomenon of college in contemporary American culture. *Is College Worth It?* continues Ohmann's project to call out inequality wherever we find it, and thus to try to change it.

A Richard Ohmann Checklist

1958	"Prolegomena to the Analysis of Prose Style." *Style in Prose Fiction: English Institute Essays, 1958*. Edited by Harold Martin. New York: Columbia University Press, 1959. 1–24.
1958	*Inquiry and Expression*. Coedited with Harold C. Martin. New York: Rinehart, 1958; rev. ed., 1963; 3rd ed., 1969.
1962	*Shaw: The Style and the Man*. Middletown, CT: Wesleyan University Press, 1962.
1962	Editor. *The Making of Myth*. New York: Putnam, 1962.
1966–1978	Editor, *College English*, 1966–78.
1972	"Speech, Literature, and the Space in Between." *New Literary History* 4 (1972): 47–64.
1975	*Ideas for English 101: Teaching Writing in College*. Coedited with W. B. Coley. Urbana, IL: NCTE, 1975.
1976	*English in America: A Radical View of the Profession*. New York: Oxford University Press, 1976; rev. ed., Middletown, CT: Wesleyan University Press, 1996.
1983	"The Shaping of a Canon: U.S. Fiction, 1960–1975." *Critical Inquiry* 10, no. 1 (1983): 199–223.
1986	*Politics of Letters*. Middletown, CT: Wesleyan University Press, 1986.
1996	*Selling Culture: Magazines, Markets, and Class at the Turn of the Century*. New York: Verso, 1996.

1996   Editor. *Making and Selling Culture*. Middletown, CT: Wesleyan University Press, 1996.

2003   *Politics of Knowledge: The Commercialization of the University, the Professions, and Print Culture*. Middletown, CT: Wesleyan University Press, 2003.

Chapter 1

The Costs and Benefits of College Education

This book is about whether college pays off for individual students and the related question of whether the United States benefits when more Americans go to college. While some conservatives have recently questioned its value, isn't "yes" the well-established answer to both questions? Our fellow citizens believe—five to one, among those with an opinion—that getting a BA or BS pays off. Most economists believe so as well, on the basis of much empirical study within a well-developed theoretical framework. Pundits and journalists generally take "yes" for granted; as I began to write this book, the *PBS NewsHour* (June 7, 2017) started with the premise that the "meaning" of a college education is "marketable skills." It said that employers couldn't learn enough about job candidates from their college records; maybe digital "badges" for mastery of particular skills would be handier.

By 2021, digital badges were emerging as a challenge to the college degree. In the midst of COVID, PBS broadcast a series called "Rethinking College" as some 560,000 students left their campuses. Two mainstream spokespersons initiated the PBS series: a high-level Democrat matched with a high-level Republican, both reiterating that college remains a path to success.[1] Politicians continued sharing the conviction that college pays off for students, families, and the nation, a theme opined on by several US presidents:

Barack Obama played hundreds of variations on this theme, bluntly stating in 2012 during a speech at the University of Michigan in Ann Arbor: "A higher education is the single best investment you can make in your future."[2] One of his stated goals for the United States was that it again become first among nations in the percentage of college graduates among adults.

Bill Clinton, in urging that more people undertake college education, called it "the fault line, the great Continental Divide between those who will prosper in the new economy and those who will not."[3]

George H. W. Bush, in sending his main educational proposal to Congress, listed four claims about "greater educational achievement"; number three was that it improves the national economy, and number one that it "leads to higher incomes for everyone."[4] Neither Bush nor the other presidents cited citizenship, national culture, or any non-economic reasons for supporting education.

Donald J. Trump, who showed more interest in privatizing K–12 than in public or higher education, and less interest in the payoff on college than in disorder on campus, talked the talk: "There's nothing more important to the future of this country than our colleges and universities, so college loans should be viewed as an investment in" that future, as well as in the financial success of the individual student, who will increase their lifetime earnings almost 50 percent by adding a college degree to their high school diploma, and so on, repeating the usual credo of conservatives and liberals alike.[5]

Joe Biden promoted the college premium on wages even before assuming the presidency in 2020. In 2012,

speaking at Florida State University, he dismissed those
who doubted the payoff of a college degree. "I'm here
to tell you it is well worth it," he said.[6] Later, as vice
president in 2015, he declared "We need to commit to
16 years of free public education for all our children."[7]
After his inauguration, Biden sent to Congress his
"American Family Plan," a $3.5 trillion omnibus pro-
posal with $109 billion for free community college
and preschool, but this entire bill and its higher education plank had to be erased because two Democratic
senators opposed it, one of them (Joe Manchin) killing
the slim Democratic majority needed to pass it.

I challenge the confidence accompanying the beliefs of
Biden and other presidents regarding the college payoff, especially when they are presented as common sense in the media
and in political discourse, not to mention in the work of public relations departments at colleges and universities. I question
the clarity of the ideas: what is it, precisely, about college that
pays off? And how can the payoff be measured? I question the
wisdom of basing individual choices about higher education
on the dependability of the college premium, and the wisdom
of making broad political and social decisions about investment in higher education on straight economic grounds. Not
that there's any doubt about the higher lifetime earnings,
on average, of college graduates in comparison to high school
graduates. I agree with William G. Bowen and Michael S.
McPherson, who between them have presided over Princeton University, Macalester College, and the Mellon and Spen-
cer foundations, that "there is probably no better-documented
finding in the social sciences." But the clause with which they
finish their sentence, "than that education pays,"[8] blurs correlation with cause. Yes, people who finish college earn more on

average than those who stop with high school diplomas. But "education pays" is a claim about both cause and effect—quite another matter, which I discuss at length in chapter 2. An army of scholars have labored to prove it and thus to end doubt about whether a family can know that investment in college will turn out well for their 18-year-old. Still deeper doubt attends the question of whether increasing the proportion of citizens with bachelors' degrees will increase the wealth of the nation. To promote clear thought about such questions is my main purpose.

These issues have figured prominently in public talk and political deliberation for decades. As the conversation progressed, its emphasis shifted; in fact, the very subject has changed. The phrase "college wage premium" came into use in the early 1980s and has been common since then.[9] The change it marked in how politicians and educators discuss the value of college occurred more gradually; those who see education as its own reward opposed the shift. But now, the idea of a college premium—more formally, a return on investment in college—dominates the conversation, weighs heavily in students' educational choices, and drives the making of educational policy. It seems obligatory now for those advocating more college education (or less of it) to talk about its economic consequences. They might prefer to cite civic or cultural or personal benefits, but they must at least acknowledge the economic ones: that college education increases the earnings of individuals and drives American prosperity; in both cases the benefit is greater than the cost. This gradual change of subject marks a deep change in the politics of American education—another reason for clear reflection, now.

To be sure, broad claims for the power of education have long been staples of official doctrine in this country, from Jefferson's belief that a free society depends on wide diffusion of knowledge and skills, through the assertion of Horace Mann— foundational to our public school system—that republican government succeeds only where joined to good education for citizens, to the still grander sweep of Lyndon Johnson's rhetoric: "The answer for all of our national problems, the answer for all the problems of the world, comes down, when you really analyze it, to one single word—education."[10] No doubt, Jefferson and Johnson would have endorsed Mann's collateral proposal that education enables its beneficiaries "to turn a wilderness into cultivated fields, forests into ships, or quarries and clay-pits into villages and cities,"[11] but none of the three thought to measure its value by how much it contributed to the monetary payoff of those ventures, as did Johnson's successors over the following five decades. The way important people praise education has changed.

To be sure, Mann did expect the common school to help reduce inequality by opening the development of national resources to anyone who could acquire the skills and knowledge required and join them to his or her own ingenuity and drive. And many US leaders have followed his example, seeking, like Johnson, to find in education an "answer for [one or another] of our national problems." The "GI Bill" (formally known as the Servicemen's Readjustment Act, passed August 1944) addressed, among other problems, that of reintegrating 12 million World War II veterans into civilian society. *Brown v. Board of Education of Topeka, Kansas* (1954) addressed the problem of racial inequality by remixing school children. The National Defense Education Act (1958) responded to the problem (the threat) of Soviet superiority in applied science. The aim of the No Child Left Behind Act (2001) was intended to solve the problem that not all children had an equal chance at education of high quality.

The Trouble with "Problems"

I use Johnson's word "problem" as a drumbeat because it captures a persistent habit of US politicians and intellectuals, originating well before they began focusing on the monetary payoff: to cast almost any social crisis, conflict, difficulty, or failure as a problem to be solved by adopting new policies or amending old ones. That approach makes sense for many situations—too much traffic in the city center, perhaps, or limited internet access in rural areas. It may have made sense as a way to think about demobilizing at the end of a war. Certainly, unemployment and disaffection among veterans of the First World War had been a problem, which exploded into a crisis in 1932, when more than 15,000 veterans and family members camped and marched near the Capitol in the (derogatorily named) Bonus Army.

But the term "problem" is a poor fit for conditions such as historically entrenched white supremacy, US insecurity in the Cold War struggle for world domination, and economic inequality in the twenty-first century, when the rich are systematically distancing themselves farther from everyone else. Unsurprisingly, school desegregation (after 1954), the National Defense Education Act, and No Child Left Behind failed to set things right. The "things" were embedded in centuries of racial oppression, a potentially apocalyptic clash of political systems, and an upheaval in the terms of class conflict. Such situations differ from problems in important ways. They have deep historical roots. They involve dense relations among individuals and groups. They rise out of fraught social change. And—critically—they put some people's interests in opposition to the interests of other people. To cast a situation as a problem is to see it as unwelcome to all or injurious to all. A recurring icy patch on the front stoop may cause injury to any resident of the building, any visitor, the postman, the meter reader, even the landlord, who must worry about being sued, not just about bruising his hip. The clogged gutter that overflows onto the stoop is a problem whose fixing will benefit all.

Not so for a national system of public schools that range from excellent to terrible. That's a problem for parents and teachers in North Philadelphia and Detroit, but not for their counterparts in Scarsdale or Brookline; for employers who need more low-paid workers with STEM skills, not for those who want to hire contingent workers at the minimum wage; for realtors in East St. Louis, not those in Palo Alto; and so on. What would it take to make such a school system fair? For starters, a radical redistribution of wealth and leveling out of income. But short of revolution, some good first steps toward equality across K–12 schooling would be to divorce school funding from property taxes and from corporate or philanthropic support; to make for-profit schools illegal; to end the segregation of neighborhoods by class and race; to raise and equalize teachers' pay; and to replace decrepit schools with attractive, well-equipped ones. Two consequences of such a plan are obvious: first, it would change many social arrangements beyond those for educating children; and second, it would set the interests of the minority who benefit from inequality against the interests of the majority who do not. The former group has much more clout than the latter, so this strategy is out of the question, absent a profound political realignment. The realignment of forces in recent decades has been profound, but in the direction of plutocracy. So it has put ever more obstacles in the way of democratic schooling.

In this predicament, philanthropists and political leaders have tried one fix after another to address the "problem" of poor schooling: break up large schools; toughen curriculum through state and then federal intervention; install high-stakes tests to turn diplomas into credentials for employment or college; put teachers and public schools into test-based competition with each other; fire "bad" teachers and close schools that do not show "adequate yearly progress" (i.e., higher test scores); expand school choice, largely by freeing charter schools from democratic control and letting them compete with traditional schools for students and public funding; facilitate that competition with vouchers; allow corporate and philanthropic funding for charter schools; outsource the management of K–12 schools or of whole districts to for-profit companies.

The list is long enough and familiar enough to show how habitual the problem-solution approach is among leaders and policy intellectuals in the educational sector, as well as among the general public, and how ill-suited it is to addressing a major social need. Hence, the depressing repetitiveness of efforts to find the right fix for elementary and secondary schooling. Furthermore, the problem-solution approach has failed again and again and again, for at least one obvious reason: that in recent decades it has been put to work with the explicit and urgently announced aim of making schools cure inequality. Leave no child behind. Give each a fair start in racing to the top. Close the achievement gap between white and nonwhite students. Those are grand results to expect from patchwork reform of public schools. Inequality has been rising since the 1970s. The recession of the early 1980s and then the crash and recovery of 2008–16 made inequality worse, as did the pandemic of 2020–23. The vast wealth gap between the very top and the rest is now as bad as in 1929, worsened by Trump's 2017 tax cuts for the wealthy and major corporations, as well as support for privatizing the school system. Faulty schooling did not bring on the rise of the billionaires or the reduction of the bottom 50 percent to a precariat with little or no wealth. School reform has not slowed the rise of the 1 percent, much less of the billionaire class. The historic high in the achievement of college degrees has not led to the equalizing of wealth and income. More "accountability" in schooling and more college degrees among adults can't return inequality to the flatter levels of 1945 or 1970.[12]

I flesh out these assertions and apply them to higher education in the course of this book, arguing that the premise of a college wage premium is more an ideological tool or rhetorical claim than an empirical finding, more a dominant cliché that became a commonsense myth than a delivered promise. I see the tool or myth of a college premium as a special case of the problem-solution paradigm, which blurs social relations in ideological fog, underwriting denial of (or blindness to) inequality, power relations, conflicting interests, and antagonisms among groups, classes, and races.

What Do You Mean "We"?

I allude to a joke from the 1950s or before: The Lone Ranger and Tonto are surrounded by hostile Indians. "What shall we do, now, Tonto," the Lone Ranger asks. "What do you mean 'we,' paleface?" Tonto replies. The homogenizing "we" haunts the paradigm of problem and solution. To say "We need more investment in college education" implies commonalities among investors and beneficiaries that derive from wishful thinking, not from reasoned analysis of who might win and who might lose by a particular rearrangement of the educational system. Sometimes, to be sure, those who celebrate such commonalities do so in cynical efforts to enrich themselves by deceiving the likely losers. The swindle of mortgage-backed securities has parallels in higher education—most notably in recent schemes of for-profit universities to bury students under impossible loads of debt as they pursue never-to-be-realized returns on misinformed investments in college.

Although the political and educational landscape is littered with sad ruins of such schemes (including the briefly famous Trump University), and although new ones are doubtless in preparation, I do not see fraud as the main threat to sane educational planning. Nor would I chiefly blame privatization on the boost it has received from forty-plus years of "activist" philanthropy by families that have lavishly funded the conservative resurgence of these past several decades. My argument does not focus on their instrumentality, but I hasten to acknowledge its historical leverage. The Coors, Mellons, Broads, Waltons, Scaifes, and so on did clear the way for putting higher education on the market, though K–12 schooling (four times larger in the number of students served than postsecondary education) was under more direct assault. The main threat, however, has come from legal and open privatizing schemes— for example, those encouraged by the Bayh-Dole Act of 1980 to help universities profit from government-funded research, in partnership with corporations seeking to turn new knowledge into profit. Such projects are often well intended, supported by elected officials and mainstream institutions, backed by reputable academic research, and nested in ideologies of free market wisdom. The college premium is one synapse in this web of ideological faith that social domination and structured inequality have market solutions which do not threaten the market system and its winners.

Representing the college premium as a cure for inequality is a prime example. To decode the ideological magic, start with the fact that people with college degrees earn more money than people who did not go past high school. Then read this indisputable correlation as causal—as proof that going to college brings a big boost in income. Simply put, investment in college by an individual or their family pays off. In chapter 2, I'll explore some difficulties with this line of thought. Those difficulties deepen if the next steps in the chain of reasoning are (1) that everyone who is able would be well advised to get a bachelor's degree; (2) that government programs can make that choice possible for most people; and (3) that, given the proper financial boost and good information, most people would in fact choose college. If accepted, this argument would justify confidence that public support of college education for all who want it will guarantee the virtual elimination of poverty, and thus of inequality, within a few decades; that the cost will be modest; that there will be no ideological battle (who's not for more education?), no taking from one class to benefit another, no political winners and losers. In short, a simple, friendly, practical cure for a profound social disorder: irresistible.

Yet, on reflection, absurd. Turning absurdity into common sense is a major task of ideology. Ideology is often manipulative but not always conscious, or intentionally deceptive. It smooths the work of politicians and planners to imagine systemic unfairness as a collection of problems that can be solved by legislation, with malice toward none. The homogenizing "we" is a big help. Note how often commentators in the media use it even when assigning the blame for a social mess of some kind: "We don't talk to people in the other camp; we don't even acknowledge the existence of displaced coal miners; etc." Of course, the speaker knows that he (usually he) is not guilty, but his "we" is generous, conciliatory, irenic. When you hear this "we," get your hand on your wallet.

Time versus Common Sense

For some years before the Great Recession (2009 and after), a guarantee of a college premium, supported in part by problem-solution thinking, looked like common sense to policy experts, politicians, corporate leaders, educators, journalists, aspiring parents and their children, and, with caution, many economists. Then the recession landed many recent graduates in un- or underemployment, moving back into their parents' homes with degrees in hand. Also, both before and after the crash of 2008–9, the cost of investing in college rose rapidly, calling public attention to scary tuition rates and accumulations of debt on student loans (about $1.6 trillion in 2021, according to Educationdata.org). For a while, skepticism about the college premium spread, threatening one key pillar of the status quo: higher education as a path to upward mobility.

In response, economists and research centers undertook new studies and interpreted most of the results as showing that college was indeed still a bargain. Sampling the educational press and mainstream media in 2016–17, I saw a restored consensus about the payoff of education beyond high school, qualified this time by more careful differentiation of colleges, programs, majors, degrees, and credentials from one another (see chapter 2). But, although refinement of the hypothesis increases its usefulness to young people wondering which educational path will be most likely to bring them prosperity later on, fine-tuning the theory cannot turn today's common sense into a guarantee for tomorrow. The way education articulates with jobs and production now won't necessarily hold still even for the time it takes to earn the chosen degree or credential.

Take the kind of challenge posed by globalization. If the salary of a beginning engineer in South Asia is one-sixth the starting salary of a new engineer hired in Dallas, employers

will soon find a way to take advantage of the disparity: by setting up shop in India; by subdividing tasks for South Asian
engineers to do as piecework, online; by offering them jobs in
Texas (at lower salaries than native-born); and so on. In the
time it takes a high school graduate in Texas to finish the engineering degree in which they have invested, reckoning that it
will yield a starting salary of $60,000 or more, the best actual
offers may have dropped into the $40,000 range, and there
may not be nearly enough such offers for new graduates of engineering programs in Texas.[13]

Also, globalization threw into overdrive the standard capitalist practice of moving production to where labor is cheap,
unorganized, and unprotected. Through the first half of the
twentieth century, the textile industry left New England for
the American South. In the last quarter of the twentieth
century and into the twenty-first, not only did labor-intensive
textile and garment production move offshore to cheap-labor
nations but so did capital-intensive automobile production,
which shrank in the United States and vastly expanded in Asia,
Mexico, and elsewhere. To be sure, Volkswagen did build a
plant in Tennessee and Volvo built one in South Carolina, in
this dominantly deindustrializing trend (taking advantage of
declining domestic wages as once-powerful auto unions weakened in the United States, as well as shortening automakers'
delivery line to North American markets)—evidence that
capital migrates in pretty much all directions. Upheavals in the
auto industry and elsewhere took place through a variety of
globalizing metamorphoses—plant closings, bankruptcies, ac-
quisitions, outsourcing, corporate deals with foreign governments, trade agreements such as NAFTA, differential wage
scales designed to disfavor young new hires, downward global
harmonization of wages—but always disturbing old pathways
from education to work. Rage at the disappearance of indus-

trial jobs has become an explosive force in national politics: "Bring back coal." "Make America great again."

The slogans refer to well-paid, secure work for mostly white and male people with high school diplomas or less. But a shrinking of that job market is certain to affect the job market for college graduates, too. With influential voices proclaiming that a bachelor's degree will raise your lifetime earnings by 60 percent or more, young people who would otherwise have gone from high school graduation straight to factory or trade jobs may begin college instead. And that reasonable choice, by eventually producing more college graduates than employers need, could substantially lower the return on investment in four years of postsecondary education. Or high school seniors could look around, see college grads trying to keep up with their loan payments by waiting tables, and decide to forgo the risks of investing their money and five or six years of their lives seeking a bachelor's degree. There is much debate on what mix of such processes is at work now. My point is that the return on investment in college took high school into account during the period when college was still an insignificant part of the picture. Economists have so far not much studied the possibility that the return on college education might be substantially altered by a tectonic plate shift in the economic order—say from Fordism to neoliberalism— so severe that recent changes in the wage premium might leave it on a lower plateau, rather than return it to its prerecession path.[14] Hiring in the late pandemic, when cities first reopened then abruptly closed as mutated strains of COVID reinfected the population, created a sudden demand for noncollege labor to fill service positions in retail, food service, entertainment, reviving factory production, and supply chain movement of goods, forcing a sudden lift in wages to attract needed workers. At that golden moment for noncollege labor, the college premium took a back seat to the nonpremium job market, while the demand for graduate labor remained generally flat.

A crisis-based leveling of this kind, historic even if modest because the bottom of the labor market finally closed some of the 50-year increasing gap with high-wage tiers, may change the prominence of the college premium if graduates remain unable to negotiate higher salaries for themselves. When a corporation moves production from one place to another, it changes the job market in both: if Carrier had closed the plant in 2019 that employed 1,000 people in Indianapolis, rather than yielding to President Trump's blandishments, 750 or so workers would have become unemployed there, few of them college educated. Most technical, engineering, and management employees would have remained in Indianapolis. That would have decreased the return on a high school diploma in the area, but not on a BA or BS. Multiply the effects of that hypothetical move to industrial areas across the country, and a lowering of average wages in response to global economic forces, large and small, including the decisions of 18-year-olds to seek jobs or more education: this is a complex example but one that follows basic principles of supply and demand. The transnational mobility of capital, which has been relocating high-wage factory jobs to lower-wage areas, will also undermine the ability of North American working-class families to afford college educations for their children, thus complicating the intergenerational mobility that is such a familiar part of the American Dream. The rise in wages for service jobs in the later pandemic, even should it continue, does not elevate family incomes to levels enabling parents to pay for college for their children, especially as tuition and costs in higher education have risen steadily in the past few decades. The college premium as a road to the American Dream of upward mobility is largely out of reach at the low wages structured into the economy.

Economists recognize that the college premium changes over time in response to rational decisions of consumers; they have done many studies of why and with what effect. But most economists also see the monetary value of education as having risen dependably over the long run—since the middle of the nineteenth century if we take grade school into account, resulting in immediate measurable benefits for the United States. (Of course, advocates of free trade predict happier consequences in the long run.)

The flow of capital is multidirectional. Companies from other countries build plants in the United States, too, and can change the relation of college education to earnings in various ways. Volvo's deal with South Carolina to make cars in Ridgeville promised many jobs whose titles suggest applicants might need college degrees: Senior Manager Outbound Logistics, Purchasing Program Manager, Industrial Engineering Manager, Production Supervisor, Dimensional Engineer, Security and Risk Manager, and Geometry Technical Equipment Specialist are a few that the company listed in 2017. Many applicants will doubtless have some college study on their résumés, but those hired, whether college educated or not, will receive specific training for the work they are about to do, through a program run by the state's technical college system. In effect, South Carolina has dedicated part of its higher education system to giving them just that portion of college-level study that will prepare new workers for specific jobs at Volvo. Such an arrangement subsidizes the costs of a private company's training needs with public tax funds, enhancing the revenue stream captured by the private sector at public expense. In addition, such targeted occupational preparation is sure to lower the return on investment in traditional college study, as it allocates public funds to corporate uses, thus draining the state funds available for general education.

Mazda, Kia, Hyundai, Mitsubishi, Honda, Nissan, Subaru, Volkswagen, Toyota, BMW, Mercedes, and other foreign manufacturers have, like Volvo, built plants in the United States. Their main goal has been to reduce transportation costs on vehicles to be sold here. (There is also a "branding" bonus insofar as foreign companies poach the "Made in America" label, whose nationalist appeal animates sectors of the consumer market to reject imports.) More important, individual deals that car companies make with state and local governments include (in addition to the inevitable tax incentives) a variety of arrangements to secure a workforce that matches company needs. Education and training are always involved. A critical precondition for such deals in the domain of labor, however, is not one cemented in a deal; it is the carmaker's choice of a location, usually in the South, where unions are weak, historically suppressed, or nonexistent. Nationally, this development is one among several that have brought on the long decline in union membership among industrial workers—thereby reducing the number of highly paid American jobs with no educational requirement beyond high school and, as a further consequence, boosting the college premium while reducing the ability of working-class families to afford college for their children.

That a key practice of neoliberalism—the free and nimble movement of capital—affects workers' educational chances and aspirations, as well as their pay and the conditions of their labor, should surprise no one. To generalize: in any society, the making of goods is integrated with a system of making new generations of people who will produce and consume those goods now and into the future. Changes in production are sure to change social reproduction, too, including who gets the necessary knowledge and skills, and how. In short, an economic relation of the Fordist era, such as the college wage premium, may modulate or disappear as Fordism gives way to a more flexible kind of capitalism.

"May." To argue that the premium will shrink or vanish is beyond the scope of this book and of the author's competence. But still more powerful changes are at work in that direction than the global movements of capital I have touched upon. Although the three most prominent candidates in the 2016 election—Trump, Clinton, and Sanders—blamed recent trade agreements or rogue nations like China for the loss of American factory jobs, in 2020 Trump escalated his criticism of foreign trade agreements into an "America First" nationalism, while Biden, a longtime advocate of NAFTA, proposed only modest changes and focused public attention on his plan to rejoin the Paris Climate Accord and the World Health Organization, which Trump had left while in office. Once in office, Biden kept his promises concerning Paris and the WHO but has lived with Trump's United States, Mexico, and Canada Agreement (USMCA), which tinkered modestly with the NAFTA it replaced despite Trump's robust posturing on this issue. Those who were paying attention (and who were not wooing angry voters) know that automation, not the flight of jobs to other countries, has brought about the sharp decline in US factory work since 2000.

While US manufacturers in recent years were cutting their workforce by 5 million, the value of what they made actually rose more than 2 percent a year on average. Productivity increased; the labor force decreased. To put it more crudely, robots do a lot of the work that people used to do. If there had been no change in productivity between 2000 and 2010, manufacturers would have had to add 9 million jobs, not cut 5 million, to achieve the higher output they managed with robots. Experts forecast that automation will proliferate even faster in the years leading up to 2026.[15] Robots around the globe may then do a quarter of the tasks now performed by people.

Further social transformation along these lines would be far more disruptive than the movement of jobs from Indianapolis to Mexico, Chicago to China, and so on. It would result in fewer and fewer jobs for more and more people, worldwide, if population continues to grow. However, some demographic trends in the United States and other advanced nations—among them China, Japan, Russia, France, and Germany—indicate stagnant or declining populations as young people, especially young women, choose to have fewer or no children, or to have children later in life, nearer to their aging out of fertility, which lowers their potential number of childbirths, as they pursue higher education and career options and as the burdens and costs of family life, housing, and childcare become harder.[16] Barring profound adjustments in the distribution of labor, a reserve army of the un- and underemployed would grow vaster than anything that Engels and Marx imagined or that the Great Depression produced. Automation may reach physical limits, but since it is impelled by basic corporate motives and needs (profit, fewer workers with less power), it will be irreversible, short of revolution.

It is easy to imagine this dire narrative leading to a utopian future in which everyone works 20 paid hours a week producing what everyone needs, and the rest of human effort goes to music, laughter, good health, self-development, social action, and, sure, video gaming, too, if that's what the people want. But since the revolution required to get there, peaceful or not, would have to abolish the profit motive and class power, hard times seem more likely than socialized leisure, for some time to come.

What standard economic remedies might help avert the dangers implicit in neoliberal principles of efficiency and rule by markets? One answer already heard in the public arena, and sure to be heard more loudly as neoliberal labor strategies heat up, is of course education: ever more job listings, these voices say, will call for applicants with college degrees or higher. But if my prognosis turns out to be correct, such forecasters will be wildly off the mark, having mistaken a historical upheaval for a problem with a neat solution. This issue is a main topic of chapter 5. In advance, it is intuitively clear that combining more college grads with fewer jobs will produce either a large increase in the mass of high school graduates without jobs or with poorly paid, now-and-then work (an already-large class formation referred to as the "precariat" by David Harvey)[17] or a large population of college graduates doing work for which high school would have been preparation enough (an effect of too few jobs for college graduates who must accept lower-wage employment beneath their training and degrees, called "credentialism" when first critiqued as a phenomenon in the 1970s).[18] Add into the imagined mix people in their seventies and above still working because of a ruined pension system and grossly inflated costs for rent, food, and medical care, and you are looking at a disturbing and plausible vision of our emerging future. For an extra dash of distress, note that robots do not consider buying education: with the loss of them as potential student customers, today's chief justification for formal learning loses some of its persuasiveness; and of course, if the pandemic turn to virtual instruction settles in as a tech-driven answer to reducing education budgets, and robots as well as prerecorded modules take on some of the present tasks of teaching, the already-large reserve army of un- and underemployed would-be schoolteachers and college professors will continue to grow. Along with this machine replacement of human teachers, whom Foucault placed in the large social class of "relays" (middle-management deliverers and enforcers of mass discipline),[19] authorities delivering lower standards of living to the majority will produce growing disorder from the bottom up.

Finally, a "problem" for the whole society that an increase in college graduates is supposed to help solve is that of economic inequality, which has severely worsened through the neoliberal period. The cure is unlikely to succeed (see chapter 5). The automation of work promises to make clear that the widening gaps between the rich, the middle, and the poor is more like a war than like a problem, with the winners all on one side. Kai-Fu Lee makes this case with respect to the artificial intelligence "revolution," which—unlike the industrial revolution—is destroying millions of jobs while making billionaires out of AI innovators. The United States (and the world) "are thus facing two developments that do not fit easily together: enormous wealth concentrated in relatively few hands and enormous numbers of people out of work."[20] Lee proposes a bundle of remedies, including a universal basic income (a plank in Andrew Yang's brief presidential campaign in 2020). They could narrow the gap but will surely fail to bring it back to what it was in, say, the 1950s. The extremes of wealth and poverty in American society result from a conscious revolt of the upper class from the 1970s on against government regulation of business and against taxation on their wealth and income, measures that had limited the degree of inequality.[21] Will rich people, in an excess of altruism or enlightened self-interest, undo their own neoliberal revolution? The chances for such a change of heart and mind look meager.

In any case, more government investment in college education is, on the face of it, a terrible way to depose an oligarchy. Like most other Fordist institutions, public higher education has been reshaped in the interests of the upper class and, until recently, of its unreliable allies in the professional managerial class—not just their interest in holding wealth and power but also their interest in making the division of labor and privileges in generations to come look much as it does now. College has assumed a key role in reproducing inequality. Fifty years ago, it seemed likely that the university would be an agent not just of racial and gender diversity but of liberty, equality, and solidarity too. That's one reason neoliberal intellectuals, organizations, and politicians took early aim at higher education: think William Bennett, Lynne Cheney, the culture wars of the 1970s–1990s, and the continuing war of the right on what it calls "political correctness" and "critical race theory." The American university system—underfunded and vocationalized as it is already and moving further in that direction—serves the interests of corporate employers and rich people well enough. Why would they voluntarily return to the format of the postwar university, centered in liberal arts, sponsoring critical thought, and hosting democratic uprisings?

Here, I leave this speculative track and head back to the main topic: how to think about the costs and benefits to individuals and to US society of investing in college education. By bringing history, class, power, and conflict into the discussion, and by putting in doubt the problem-solution approach, I mean not to have proven anything but to have shown why it's important to weigh the value of higher education on grander and also more finely calibrated scales than that of lifetime earnings as the return on investment in college.

So, Is This a Time of Educational Crisis?

For certain, successive cycles of COVID-19 constituted a general and global crisis that of course affects education at all levels, though the worst effects in school and society accumulate from the bottom up. Great inequality has grave consequences in "normal" times but graver consequences during pandemics for schools, colleges, and communities with lower family incomes. Those social classes best organized and best resourced to deal with COVID are of course the upper layers of society whose privileged position enables them to come out ahead. While the pandemic is indeed a crisis, the college premium is not a solution. Nor is college-for-more-people an instrument to avert civilization-ending threats such as nuclear war and runaway global warming.

Between the apocalyptic and the quotidian, there's a wide range of troubles, concerns, difficulties, and (yes) problems: unwelcome situations that many people wish could be ended or improved. Consider, again, crises. The term "crisis" suggests severity, danger, persistence, urgency. It comes up a lot in talk about education, as in the "literacy crisis" of the mid-1970s ("Why Johnny Can't Write," as *Newsweek* alarmingly declared in a 1975 cover story) and numerous other echoes.[22]

Another crisis from that period was the collapse of the job market for new PhDs. In my field it manifested abruptly in 1969: hundreds of graduate students attended the annual convention of the Modern Language Association, hoping to be interviewed for several assistant professorships, as had their predecessors during the long expansion of the university system. As that hope faded, an angry "job seekers' caucus" sprang up alongside anti-war, civil rights, and other protest groups. The moment marked a crisis, no question; but to call the continuing shortage of academic jobs a "crisis" now, some fifty years later, as many have done, is to overlook the deep historical change, including the emergence and domination of neoliberalism, that brought permanent austerity to most academic fields and to other professions, to the welfare state, and to much else, ending the postwar boom and its customary relations of employers and employees.

Crisis rhetoric is usually deployed by those losing out in the historical shift rather than by those who engineered and profited from it. As ideology, it makes a nice gift to the latter. For example, the billionaires who have benefited most spectacularly from the global reorganization of production benefit from having the MLA and its peer groups blamed for overproducing PhDs and thus bringing on the immediate crisis, rather than understanding it as one small, natural outcome of a long campaign to make labor cheap and contingent, including the kinds of labor around which professions have built their market havens. Just so, neoliberal titans benefit from having politicians blame the disappearance of good working-class jobs on bad trade deals or on China or on illegal immigrants. And, of course, the ideologies of "problem" and "crisis" play a small part in making it less likely that former steelworkers bagging groceries and PhD candidates teaching part-time for low pay will join forces to challenge the global division of labor.

Those who follow news and debate about higher education will have run into the urgent rhetoric of crisis in the framing of many situations. Some instances include:

> Closely related to the shortage of tenure-track jobs for new PhDs is the fact that about three-fourths of the faculty members at nonprofit colleges and universities are not tenured or candidates for tenure. That's up from fewer than half forty years ago. (Not to mention for-profit universities, whose number has grown from a negligible proportion of all college students in 1990 to 13 percent in 2009, and where close to 100 percent of teachers are contingent workers.) The change has landed many who aspired to rewarding careers into tough, poorly paid jobs. Whether the steady degradation of

academic labor across four decades qualifies as a "crisis" is another matter.

The same scruple should encourage caution in analyzing and labeling a broad range of troubles in the academic profession. A fund-raising letter from the American Association of University Professors (AAUP) asked support for "our profession" because "threats to higher education are numerous, severe, and increasing daily" (July 10, 2017). Yes, indeed, the right is emboldened now to subvert tenure, put down faculty unions, condemn Black Lives Matter protests, launch "attacks on academic freedom," and spread bogus alarms about "critical race theory" invading classrooms, or to block appointments or promotions of those who write impolitely about Israel. It's hard not to see this parade of threats as a crisis, especially at a time when most members of one major party think that colleges and universities are bad for the United States. But less abrupt threats than those cited by the AAUP have evidenced the weakening of the academic profession (and most others) for decades. That long decline may be a more clarifying context for present difficulties than the four-year-mayhem of a Trump presidency, which morphed into outright insurrection on January 6, 2021, with continuing parliamentary and extraparliamentary right-wing insurgency leading up to the crucial mid-term elections in 2022.[23]

Another broad area of disruptive change, closely related to the troubles of the professions, is the funding of higher education.[24] Among many ways to depict the decline in public support of public colleges and universities, a couple of snapshots: The percentage of all state and local expenditures that went to higher education, nationwide, dropped by almost half in forty years starting from 1975. And in a much shorter period—2000 to 2012—state support per college student fell from about $7,000 to about $4,400, adjusted for inflation.[25] These cuts made for larger classes, fewer faculty appointments, more adjuncts, reduced student services, less financial aid, and so on. State funding rose in 2021, but the increase did not cover the losses from two recessions in the previous decade, 2009 and 2021.[26] Did leaner universities mean watered-down education? Another crisis if so.

Of course, as public funding declined, universities scrambled to increase revenue from other sources. Most notoriously, they hiked tuition and fees. From 1992 to 2022, tuition and fees increased from $2,310 to $3,800 within district at public two-year, from $4,160 to $10,740 in state at public four-year, and from $19,360 to $38,070 at private nonprofit four-year colleges, in constant dollars. Add on room and board, supplies, transportation, and the like, and the three figures jump to nearly $18,830, $27,370, and $55,800, respectively.[27] Financial aid helps many students, but such expenditures are daunting or prohibitive for many students and their families.

But even at that level, college education is supposed to bring a high return on investment, so students and their families that lack the resources to pay out of pocket have a strong incentive to borrow. As states cut their funding of higher education, and as universities raised tuition and fees to make up the shortfall in revenue, students took out more and more loans to cover their shortfall. The results are well known: more than 40 million students and grads are now carrying nearly

$1.6 trillion in debt, an amount that now exceeds the
total of all credit card debt in the United States.[28] Banks
and private loan companies lobbied their way into this
field and profited greatly. Collection agencies and even
the federal government are making money. Despite
President Biden's (temporary) moratorium on student
debt repayment during the pandemic, many indebted
students face financial ruin.

The mass media have told harrowing stories: a nurse who
borrowed $128,000 and, despite monthly payments
of $1,200, is losing ground; she now owes $152,000.
"I feel like I kind of ruined my life by going to college,"
she says. A salesperson for a company that packages
vacations owes 25 percent more now than she did when
she finished college; she worries not only about her
own future but about the real possibility that collection
agencies will pursue her aunt and mother, cosigners on
some of her loans.[29] Bankruptcy laws offer no protection for student debtors. Their plight has been treated
widely in mainstream media as a "crisis" and was
brought to public attention also by the Occupy Wall
Street protest movement in 2011. It is a disaster for
many students but not a sudden crisis: it has been
building for 30 years, a predictable result of turning a
public good into a private investment.

Another predictable result was the rise and (maybe) fall
of for-profit universities. Their enrollment was about
400,000 in 2000, peaked at 1.7 million in 2010, declined
to 1.1 million in 2015, then fell continuously in the years
leading up to 2021.[30] I say "predictable" because, so
many students were borrowing to cover the high cost of
college education, the federal government was backing
the process, and students could use loans to attend

for-profit institutions. The for-profits recruited aggressively and often deceptively; the crash of 2008 provided a further incentive for students; speculators founded hundreds of new universities to take advantage of the chance for easy profits (80–90 percent of their revenue came from the federal government via student loans); enrollment boomed. Then regulation tightened as abuses became a scandal; the government disqualified one-fifth of the for-profits from receiving federal financial aid;[31] families grew skeptical about the value of a college credential, especially one from a for-profit institution; the Great Recession eased; and the pandemic began in 2020. In retrospect, this looks series of events less like a crisis than an investment bubble. Investors took advantage not of a crisis in higher education but of opportunities for profit opened up in higher education by the decades-long rise of neoliberalism, one of whose primary features is the aggressive expansion of the private revenue stream at public expense.

The list could easily be extended. For instance, advocates for one or another subject area have in recent years nominated more specific candidates for crisis standing—the humanities, the STEM fields, the liberal arts as a whole, and so on. But these will suffice to clarify three generalizations that are important to the approach of this book. First, as with using the word "problem," calling something a "crisis" usually masks one or more conflicts. One group's crisis may be another group's boon. The reassignment of teaching from tenure-track faculty members to temps and part-timers has weakened the academic profession, driven many young people out of it, and landed others among the working poor, but has helped administrators cope with reductions in government funding, which in turn helped state legislators cope with tax revolts inspired by the conservative movement. For example, the demonization of professors—the "academic elite"—serves the interests of conservative leaders who launched a long-term culture war in the 1970s and then morphed into Tea Party radicals, followed by Trump insurgents and insurrectionists overtaking the GOP to defund higher education, weaken the power of its workforce, and fuel right-wing populist resentment. The rise in college tuition has enriched money lenders while impoverishing students in public campuses and enhancing richly endowed selective universities whose degrees still matter in the job market.

The second generalization is that each of these particular troubles, shortfalls, and failures is closely linked to the idea of the college wage premium. And third, each is part of the broad transformation of the economic and political system that has given us the neoliberal university.

To back up those claims and see what insight they afford into the politics of higher education is one task of this book. Thus, although the discussion sometimes runs to close reading, semantic analysis, and logical critique, its scope is broadly historical, and its context is a web of intense conflicts about which principles and whose interests should have the most weight in shaping the future American society.

A couple of polls from 2017 afford a striking snapshot of such a conflict. First, the Pew Research Center found that in just two years the percentage of Republicans who thought colleges were good for the country had dropped more than one-third, from 58 to 36. (The percentage among Democrats rose from 65 percent to 72 percent.) To put it the other way around, 58 percent of Republicans now thought college a target for privatization because they no longer generated enough good for the country to justify subsidizing them. It might be accurate to say that coverage in right-wing media of Black Lives Matter and other, campus outbreaks of "political correctness" was largely responsible for the shift in opinion, with a big boost on the negative side from the Trump campaign and administration.[32] (Mainstream media coverage was fairly unsympathetic, too.) But how did the college premium figure in this picture? What about the prevailing view that college education leads to higher individual incomes and greater national prosperity?

Well, a poll three weeks later showed that most white working-class voters (Democrats and Republicans) thought a college degree "would result in more debt and little likelihood of landing a good-paying job" (57 percent) and that it was "no longer any guarantee of success in America." They also favored job training over limiting imports of foreign goods to help Americans in international competition.[33] These findings suggest dissent from the standard view of a college wage premium. Respondents answered explicit questions about investment in higher education. When they rejected the idea that college is a dependably good financial choice, were they obliquely rejecting the faith in free access to college professed by Joe Biden in his "Build Back Better" omnibus bill for 2021, by Bernie Sanders in the 2020 campaign, and before that by both Sanders and Hillary Clinton in 2016—not to mention liberal economists, academics, and policy makers? Were they joining the Tea Party–Trump populist revolt against elites and experts? Does their endorsement of job training signal a belief that education beyond high school should be, above all else, utilitarian? Even more obliquely, were they signing on for privatization and the rule of the market? Possibly all of the above. For sure, they and the Republicans polled by Pew were jumping into the swirl and clash of political parties, economic interests, and ideological campaigns that has been the air we breathe for some time now.

This book elaborates my claim that the idea of the college premium is not a tidy hypothesis that can be abstracted from social process for scientific study but is, rather, whatever the intent of its academic proponents, entangled in conflict, politics, and historical projects.

The Education Market

Neoliberalism, the broadest project of development in our day, has brought ever more areas of human activity into the market: preventing and healing illness, traveling, exploiting natural resources, pursuing recreation, communicating, providing for old age, and so on. Educating the young is now high on the list of family endeavors, even though a century ago, by 1910, over 90 percent of K–12 students went to public schools, an arrangement that has held (roughly) ever since, except for a few years after 1954, when the Supreme Court ordered desegregation of public schools and many southern states replaced them with all-white, private academies. In the past 20 years, a less bluntly political scheme of privatization has won ground under the banner of school choice. More than 6 percent of children now attend charter schools, which are publicly funded but run outside the system of rules that govern public schools, often by independent groups.[34] Many charters have been run by for-profit companies such as Edison Schools, which for a while was considered as the possible savior of the whole Philadelphia school system and did in fact take more than 20 schools into its fold (with dismal results). School vouchers are another instrument for privatizing K–12. A growing number of students in the fourteen states with voucher laws now pay part or all of their private school tuition with public money. Private and corporate donors have also contributed major funding to charter schools, including the $20 million to Geoffrey Canada's Harlem Children's Zone from Wall Street's premier investment bank Goldman Sachs, which built a new high school for the Zone's project, though Canada "fired" the first student cohort supposed to inaugurate the ninth grade at the new school, because he considered their achievement inadequate.[35] Favored by both major parties, charter schools were avidly pushed by Trump and his secretary of education, Betsy DeVos, whereas, after Biden took office, the Democratic Congress passed $440 million in aid to expand charters. This amount was dwarfed by former mayor of New York City Michael Bloomberg when he announced a $750 million fund to expand charter schools by 150,000 seats.[36] Such largesse from billionaires as well as government has fueled a surge in charter schools, draining district budgets while producing student outcomes in the range of traditional schools.

There is a small flow in the other direction, too—from private donors to public schools. "California K–12 foundations, PTAs and booster clubs," the *Huffington Post* reported in 2012, raised about $1.3 billion in 2007, . . . up from $70 million in 1989."[37] Such fund-raising accounts for maybe half a percent of the $600 billion tab for public schools in the United States, but that $3 billion (and rising) far exceeds the returns from old-time PTA bake sales for school supplies, or the redemption of can and bottle deposits to support high school sports teams, as in my rural district. And predictably, such well-meaning efforts give school inequality an extra boost. Donors give more than $1,000 per student to some wealthy school districts (e.g., Coronado, California), but about $30 per student, on average across the nation.[38] The border between public and private good had been merely porous in K–12 schooling until billionaire-financed charter schools opened a major breech in the past decade.

In the postsecondary domain, public higher education, driven by the repeated cuts in state and city funding noted earlier, has moved perhaps farther down the privatization road than has primary and secondary schooling. As with K–12, the privatization of college has advanced gradually and erratically—not according to a master plan but through a hodgepodge of often desperate strategies. Chief among them, as every prospective college student and their parents know, is raising tuition and fees. Universities have also sought new revenue from many other, more novel sources. For instance, the Bayh-Dole Act of 1980 made it legal to patent knowledge developed with government support in university labs, then sell the patents to corporations. Or universities themselves act as entrepreneurs, turning faculty research into for-profit startups, some in commercial parks adjacent to the campus.

Another source of income: deals in which a corporation gains the exclusive right to sell a line of products on campus. A war between Coke and Pepsi to win soft drink franchises has gone on for years, with special appeal to universities struggling with austerity caused by loss of public funds. A telling example: Pepsi-Cola paid $21 million to the financially strapped City University of New York for a ten-year monopoly on beverage sales at all 24 CUNY campuses.[39] In fast food, Subway, Domino's, and other familiar brands have franchises on hundreds of campuses; but the appeal of selling to students is perhaps more evident in the smaller, regional, and newer companies entering that market. The Pita Pit, Baja Fresh, Espresso Royale, Bruegger's Bagels, Tropical Smoothie Cafe, and Moe's Southwest Grill are among the many that pay colleges for the chance to entice hungry young people who have disposable cash or credit and supposedly bright futures, deploying ideals of heath, urbanity, hipness, machismo, and so on. Another lucrative practice is to make deals with banks (more than a thousand universities have done so) providing ID cards that students can use to access their loan accounts and various banking services, for husky fees.[40] Students are a desirable group of future consumers whose attention and loyalty universities can help deliver to corporate providers. That the practice is taken for granted now indicates how cozy the bond has become between college and markets.

An old-fashioned way public higher education compensates for the loss of taxpayer support is to tighten budgets—slimming down academic programs, eliminating faculty posts, cutting course offerings, enlarging class sizes, relying more and more on contingent labor, and undertaking other such austerities. Not so traditional is the outsourcing of tasks formerly done in-house: feeding students; housing them; providing them with books and supplies; cleaning, heating, and maintaining buildings; sometimes building whole dormitory complexes and running them like for-profit apartments. In recent years, universities have also tried contracting out work that faculty members, librarians, counselors, and other full-time professional employees used to do, for example, streamlining large courses and taking instruction online. Arrangements like these can be a sensible delegation of processes that specialists can do more efficiently than university administrators and departments and that may have little to do with teaching and learning. But they belong in this summary because they participate in the reimagining of colleges and universities as businesses, in privatization, with quasi-corporate chains of command, a sharp divide between administrators and faculty members, performance standards that can be quantified, and the market as the final court of appeals. Through bottom-line management and through outsourcing and kindred strategies, the university erases the boundary between public good and private enterprise. Its decisions may be inconsistent with or bad for learning, but they are guided by the invisible hand of neoliberalism, for which, as Margaret Thatcher put it, "there is no alternative."

Business thinking has long since colonized the shoptalk of university administrators and trustees, and of legislators on the interface between higher education and the public. Nearly 30 years ago, I collected these examples from a book called *Measuring Institutional Performance in Higher Education*: "stakeholders," "client feedback," "make or buy options," "client," "use synergy," "benchmarking," "best practices," "TQM" (total quality management), and "BPR" (business practice reengineering);[41] and these from speakers at a 1999 conference on "Market-Driven Higher Education," sponsored by University Business: "product" (i.e., certified learning), "markets" (including students), "brand" (a university's name and reputation), "value added" (to students' employability?), "resource base" (chiefly, the faculty), "marginal cost," "customization," "just-in-time learning," "assessment models," "policy convergence."[42] A keyword in this lexical cluster is "accountability," which suddenly burst into educational talk around 1970, partly in reaction to sixties rebellions and partly as a punctual harbinger (it turns out) of the "conservative restoration," both in and outside schooling.[43] Twenty years ago, managerial jargon expressed both the wish to make universities more efficient and the belief that businesses knew how to do that.

Today, businesses and universities seem closely enmeshed in a network of market relations. That idea is not hidden away in the insider business talk of college administrators but is out in public, taken for granted, commonsense. Thus, when in 2015 the Obama administration announced its "college scorecard" (https://collegescorecard.ed.gov/), a website where anyone would "be able to see how much each school's graduates earn, how much debt they graduate with, and what percentage of a school's students can pay back their loan" (as well as the school's average annual costs and what percentage of its students graduate), it billed this project as providing "consumer information" to prospective students and their parents.[44] What does it mean to "consume" the product of a college or university? Parse the information offered in the scorecard, and it's evident that Obama and his secretary of education, Arne Duncan, had in mind a calculus of investment and return: weigh college costs and the debts incurred to cover them against the student's eventual earnings. Those earnings are the one "outcome" of a college education that is accorded a place in the calculus. The percentage of students who graduate is important to consumers because an associate's degree "leads to" a higher payoff than study ended without the degree, and because a bachelor's degree has a much higher payoff than unfinished work toward one.

Plainly, President Obama and Secretary of Education Duncan grounded their consumer guide on extensive studies of the return on investment in college education. Interestingly, the scorecard project was for them a step forward (or retreat from?) an earlier proposal to rank all 7,000 American universities and colleges, thus shaming the lowest-ranking ones into improving their payoff. University leaders all but unanimously condemned that idea, as did some conservative politicians, because it looked like a flagrant intrusion of the federal government into the affairs of universities (especially for-profit ones). The scorecard project, in forswearing regulation, liberated the market and cast the student as pure consumer, searching rationally for the best investment: *Homo economicus* in search of utility. An instructive example, this, of how political imperatives blend with economic orthodoxies.

A tidy one, too: students as customers who seek the best product. The product is an investment in high future income. The sellers are universities, competing with one another in a market. Their aim is . . . just what? Here the model becomes messier, except as applied to the for-profits. The nonprofits have a number of aims: prestige, public service, alumni loy-alty, meeting the needs of regional employers, the advance-ment of knowledge—a motley assortment, to most of which the market model applies awkwardly at best.

Nor is conceptualizing the student as a consumer all that simple. Colleges and universities do compete to sell their product to students. If they want to call their admissions staff "marketers" or rename their top admissions job "director of marketing and student recruitment," some may see a loss of dignity in the change, but it is semantically defensible.[45] Not so, however, at colleges and universities that turn away large numbers of "customers," often far more than half of all appli-cants. These places are called "selective," and in fact their pri-mary activity is choosing customers, not doing most of the tasks that make up the broad activity of marketing. Even Whole Foods, Nieman Marcus, and the like do not turn away most of the would-be customers who come to their doors. Then there are the pricing policies of colleges. True, each pas-senger on the plane may have paid a different price for their ticket, but there's nothing comparable to the certainty at some ivied universities that the family of one arriving student will pay close to $300,000 in tuition and fees over four years, while their roommate pays nothing. Financial aid policies, special deals for baseball or basketball players, lower admissions stan-dards for "legacies," and so on can be fitted into a marketing model only through procrustean efforts. The conceptual and practical gains don't seem worth the trouble.

Neither does the intellectual work it would take to sort out overlapping, contradictory, vague, and changing applications of the market idea. Colleges market their product to possible applicants for admission, while applicants market themselves to admissions offices. In the "job market," employers tout the pay, perks, job satisfaction, and future careers they offer to graduating seniors, while the seniors offer for sale to employers their "marketable skills"—now often digitally gussied up in "experience transcripts."[46] Mixed metaphors abound in talk of this sort. The transcript is a "signal" to the "market" that "vouches for" skills acquired in college, a "bidirectional signal" that is "part of a conversation across the job market between supply and demand," said the CEO of a "labor market analytics firm."[47] Market lingo is a kind of seasoning in the talk of university managers, demonstrating their respectability and usefulness in the economic system that is the home of higher education.

Conceptual power and clarity cannot be the main point. Ideology is, I suggest. The intellectually slack way university leaders and mid-level officers use the lexicon of markets announces an effort to identify higher education with corporate goals, to rationalize it through the logic of accountability. In that logic, the idea of return on investment has a privileged role, along with its satellite the idea of the college wage premium. This is a relatively recent way to think about higher education and the socializing of young people in our society. Its meaning for those young people and its broad import for US politics and culture are main themes of this book.

Chapter 2

Does Going to College Raise Lifetime Earnings?

The idea I skeptically examine in this chapter is that of the college wage premium or, more formally, the return on investment in college. Take that phrase literally: think of a college student as having *invested* tuition payments, living expenses, travel costs, book purchases, and wages forgone while studying for a bachelor's degree. The payoff of the investment in college education will be how much more money the graduate will earn by some future date than will their equally qualified contemporaries who went straight to work after high school.

I mean to challenge this predominant way of thinking about higher education. But I take its premises as my starting point. I look at the data and reasoning that give it support and at the kind of advice it implies for people making college-or-not decisions. The hypothesis of a college premium appears simple but opens out into many difficulties that economists and other scholars have addressed, and some that they have not addressed. The college path to a career that will pay off also seems natural now, and beyond challenge. But it evolved gradually and has only in the past 40 or so years assumed the solidity of common sense. So, I spend a while examining the sorts of evidence and interpretation that went into its formation, along with the practical, historical, and political consequences that result from the major part it plays in family decisions, in debate about government policy, and in the actual shaping of higher education.

Formulations of the idea vary. For convenience, I begin with the bold phrasing of a report from the Georgetown University Center for Education and the Workforce, one of the most prolific and influential think tanks, issued in 2011 and reconfirmed in 2021: "The data are clear: a college degree is the key to economic opportunity, conferring substantially higher earnings on those with credentials than those without. A 2002 Census Bureau Study estimated that in 1999, the average lifetime earnings of a Bachelor's degree holder was $2.7 million (2009 dollars), 75 percent more than that earned by high school graduates in 1999."[1]

To determine how much the average student of that cohort invested in the bachelor's degree, add up all fees and collateral expenses the student incurred by going to college, plus the amount he or she could have earned by going straight into the job market after high school. Then subtract that figure from the student's $2.7 million in lifetime earnings to get the college premium—in this example, a little more than $1 million in expenses, yielding about $1.7 million over costs. That would be the student's return on investment. Over 40 years of work, it amounts to about $40,000 annually, though as you would imagine, the return is lower in the early years of work and higher as time passes, and it also varies depending on major and occupation, gender and race, as I will elaborate.

Look at the premium from another angle: in only about ten years after graduation, the average BA or BS will have earned as much money as a classmate who began employment right after high school and avoided paying for further education. You've probably heard other numbers, reached at different times and by different computations, but I think my simplification represents the basic claim pretty well. Since that claim is about averages, it is not invalidated by facts such as the growing number of young people who have been incurring college *penalties*, dropping further and further behind their contemporaries who went straight from high school to work, in part because of the rapid rise of college tuition and, consequently, of student debt, in recent years.

College as Cause

Even if we level out good and bad financial outcomes into bland averages, something strange and interesting abides in the idea of the college premium as its advocates present it. I refer to the claim that credits undergraduate education with, in the Georgetown Center's words, "conferring substantially higher earnings" on those who achieve it. To decode: it explains their prosperity. Without it, person X would be earning the same as his or her averaged-out contemporaries who skipped college. In still plainer words: finishing college *causes* those with the bachelor's degree to earn more than those with no more than a high school diploma.

This feature of the proposal (in combination with its treatment of college as an investment) is what makes it compelling. If college does not *cause* higher earnings, a correlation between them is a fact of little interest; it yields no practical guidance about whether college is a reliable path to prosperity for a young person trying to make a rational, self-interested decision—or about whether making college education as nearly universal as possible will greatly advance national prosperity (a related proposition that I examine in chapter 3). Important individual choices and social decisions about educational policy thus depend on the hypothesis of the college premium. That's why I devote this chapter to unpacking the causal claim and what it would take to establish its validity. Close examination of the causal claim involves more than a casual reading of data and more than a comforting encounter with loose talk that conflates causation and correlation, so pardon the tight focus on the data.

To begin with, no one suggests that *only* a college degree enhances lifetime earnings. Anyone can think of other characteristics that might affect lifetime earnings, both for those with bachelor's degrees and for those without—including such dispositions as competitiveness, ambition, laziness, greed or indifference to wealth, industriousness, persistence, a clear way of speaking, and so on. Then there are physical attributes such as height, weight, gender, skin color, and conventional attractiveness. Further complicating the chain of causes are characteristics that might explain both earning a degree and earning a good living: intelligence, the quality of a person's K-12 schooling, the wealth of his or her family of origin, and so on. Defining the college premium as a causal relation sets a high standard for its advocates to meet, but not the (impossibly) high standard of showing college to be the sole cause of monetary success. If it is one of several or many causes, an advocate must show that the other causes do not by themselves account for the higher earnings of college graduates.

Admitting multiple causes, however, does not get around a logical problem for the advocate who infers cause from a correlation between a specific, measurable attainment, completing college, and the average difference in earnings between those who did so and those who left formal education after high school. Carnevale's claim that a college degree "confers" higher earnings on "those with credentials than on those without" bumps into that problem when tied to the situation of an individual 17-year-old deciding whether to go on to college. For that student, the practical implication of Carnevale's formulation is, "If I earn a bachelor's degree, I will earn more during my working life than if I don't" (by over $1 million,

according to the Georgetown Center). That could easily decide the matter for a high school student not otherwise drawn
to higher education.

But that argument for college is invalid, because it commits
the *fallacy of division*: that what is true of a group is true of
each individual in it (e.g., the average IQ of Minnesotans is
higher than that of New Yorkers, so my brother in Duluth
must be smarter than I am in Albany). Perhaps high schoolers
themselves would wonder if the general case were a guarantee
to their particular case.

Economists certainly do spot this difficulty. Carnevale and
his colleagues, having posited "a general earnings boost conferred by a degree," go on to note that "earnings vary greatly"
(2) with individual characteristics and, specifically, that some
people without bachelor's degrees earn more than others who
did graduate from college. Yet such "overlap," as the authors
call it, does not stop them from advancing many specific prop-
ositions like this one: "All graduate degree holders can expect
lifetime earnings at least double that of those with only a high
school diploma" (4). Apparently Carnevale et al. see no contradiction. This reversal of the college premium, wherein high-
wage jobs are offered to candidates without college degrees,
has been a contrary feature of the US labor market, notable in
the booming information tech and home construction sectors, both short on labor. In some urban sites, like New York
City, where information technology continued expanding
through the pandemic, many IT employees earn above-average
salaries without college degrees or after short-term certificate
training.[2]

Serious scholars often talk or write loosely about the monetary results of education. Cecilia Rouse, a professor of economics at Princeton and dean of the Woodrow Wilson School
of Public and International Affairs, said in an interview for the

alumni magazine of the Harvard Graduate School of Arts and Sciences, "The biggest cost of dropping out is to the individual, as over a lifetime a typical high school graduate will earn 50 to 100 percent more than a nongraduate."[3] In deducing an "individual" outcome from an average outcome ("typical high school graduate"), Rouse commits the fallacy of division to support a causal claim: that not finishing high school cost the hypothetical dropout one-third to one-half of what she would have earned by graduating first and then going to work. From the fact that the average income of nongraduates is lower than that of graduates, it does not follow that dropping out causes any particular student's lifetime earnings to fall below that line.

One more example: Claudia Goldin and Lawrence F. Katz, professors of economics at Harvard and authors of a prize-winning book on the economic value of education to individuals and whole societies, propose in their last chapter to "demonstrate . . . that education is still a very good investment" and that an "individual . . . who does not graduate high school, who does not continue to college, and who does not complete college is leaving large amounts of money lying on the street."[4] From a fact about averages—the correlation between educational attainment and lifetime earnings—Goldin and Katz conclude that an "individual" who leaves the educational system in or after high school or during college thereby *causes* the reduction of their lifetime earnings by "large amounts of money." Needless to say, in this time of high costs and student loans, a number of actually existing individuals who chose college have financially ruined themselves by doing so. The fallacy of division, again.

Experts slide in and out of causation talk with words such as "confer," "may expect," "typical," and "individual." Does the slippage matter? Might we accept formulations like those I have quoted as relaxed ways to say that reaching a particular level of education causes a big loss in lifetime earnings for some and not for others, just as one might informally say that the "bite" of a deer tick sometimes causes Lyme disease? I think not. The cause of Lyme disease is the colonizing of tissue by a bacterium. The tick that bites you may or may not be carrying the bacterium, and if it does, quick removal will prevent infection. The practical difference between these two similar ways of explaining Lyme disease is great: if tick bites cause it, you should do whatever it takes to prevent bites—for instance, stay indoors all summer. If the cause is a bacterial invasion, remove the tick in time or, failing that, take suitable antibiotics.

Similarly, if going to and completing college will cause a student to earn an extra million dollars, the economically rational choice is plain: do whatever you must, short of bank robbery or cheating, to earn the degree. But if earning it may cause impoverishment in your later life, making a rational economic choice at age 17 becomes trickier. And it's trickier still if pursuing the college premium causes impoverishment in a student's *current* life.[5]

There's no need to take up, here, the theoretical puzzles of cause and effect that philosophers have wrestled with since long before Hume, who took seriously the skeptical view that to say one thing is caused by another is to say no more than to say that it always follows the other. John Stuart Mill added that to prove that x is the cause of y, one needs to rule out all other possible explanations.[6] Both Hume's and Mill's requirements far exceed what I think is needed to show that "college" is a cause of the wage premium, or just to facilitate clear thought and sensible policy in this area. The action of one billiard ball on another (an example Hume took up) is transparently simple compared to the interaction of an educational system and a labor market.

In actual chains of individual and group action, outcomes of action, outcomes of the outcomes, and so on, I doubt that any one act can be established as the necessary and sufficient cause of one particular outcome. Be that as it may, social scientists tend to work with a less demanding requirement than the one Mill proposed. They seek not to rule out every possible cause of y other than x, but to show that although many causes may be entangled, x is the primary one. Sometimes the requirement is still less demanding: to show just that x is a significant cause of y. This is a long way short of necessary and sufficient (i.e., y if and only if x). Yet, in assessing a hypothesis such as that of the college wage premium, it is also a lot more than nothing—for a 17-year-old deciding whether to apply for admission to college, or for legislators deciding whether to broaden access. Even though singular conditions often have complex causes, we are still able to evaluate "significant causation" by asking: What would it take to prove the hypothesis that a college education significantly increases lifetime earnings?[7]

Consider a thought experiment that would satisfy even Mill's third condition. Take a large number of people who have completed college and then worked until age 65. Make them once again exactly as they were at 18. Send them into the job market (also exactly as it was back then) with only high school diplomas. Then compare each one's earnings at 65 with what that person earned the first time. Only "college" could explain the difference in lifetime earnings. But since in the real world it is not possible to rewind and rerun history, the question arises: How might a research design most approximate this perfect comparison?

Planned Experiments, Random Assignment

The best answer so far is to assemble two equivalent groups of subjects from the same population—let's say, kindergartners in a public school system—and put each group through one of the two experiences whose educational results you want to compare. The experiences are called "treatments," on a medical analogy. You'd like these groups to match up perfectly in every attribute that might affect the result of the treatment, other than the treatment itself. For example, and to pick up on the medical analogy: if you want to know whether a new drug prevents heart attacks, some of the obvious characteristics on which to match the groups would be age, gender, body fat, blood pressure, previous medical history, and parents' medical histories. If you want to know whether small class sizes cause children to improve faster in reading and math, from kindergarten through third grade, than do classes of the usual size, you might match your two groups in IQ, medical histories, time in preschool or lack thereof, diets and food insecurity, parents' incomes and levels of educational attainment, amounts of reading material in the children's homes, and so on. Control for enough possible causes (variables) and maybe you could satisfy Mill's third condition.

But it is impossible to control for everything; "enough" could be a very large number; the variables could be as ill assorted as those in my short list of examples; and they could be a mix of independent and interdependent. (Large numbers of related and unrelated variables spoil linear regressions, too.) A better way around the difficulty when studying complex social processes is to assign subjects randomly to the groups that will have the educational experiences to be compared. The larger those groups are, and the larger the pool of kindergartners from which they are drawn, the closer random assignment will come to yielding groups well matched in gender, race, the amount of time parents spend reading to toddlers, and so on—well matched, too, in characteristics not under study, such as having been born on odd- or even-numbered days of the month. In fact, assigning five-year-olds born on odd-numbered days to small classes and the others to classes of the traditional size would be a suitable way to achieve random assignment, precisely because an odd or even birth date is not conceivably a cause of fast progress in math or reading. In addition, random assignment prevents contamination of the study by any bias the researcher might have.

The study of children in K–3 to which I'm referring is not hypothetical; it is Project STAR (Student-Teacher Achievement Ratio), perhaps the best-known experiment of its kind.[8] About 40 years ago, the Tennessee state legislature authorized and funded a longitudinal study to find out whether children learned math and reading better in smaller classes (13–17 pupils) than in those of the usual size (22–25). Well more than 10,000 students participated, as did 1,300 teachers (also randomly assigned). The study took factors other than class size into account, as well, but class size drew the most attention then. And since the completion of Project STAR some 30 years ago, educators and politicians have continued to cite the significantly higher test scores of Tennessee students in smaller classes, to argue for smaller classes in widely differing contexts, across the United States and beyond.

A number of problems—some of which had to do precisely with random assignment—have called that result into question. For example, kindergartners at each participating elementary school in Tennessee had indeed been distributed randomly into small- or regular-size classes. But the study was not a secret. No surprise, then, that some parents wanted their children shifted to small sections and got what they wanted after a year or two. Parents often advocate for their own children's advantages in school, some with remarkable persistence; and regarding small classes, they intuit this as a desirable measure for gaining more teacherly attention to students (after all, small classes, a luxury of affluence sometimes available in charter schools funded by sponsors, is a key marketing item, especially for expensive private schools).[9] Because some parents succeeded in shifting their children to the smaller classes in the STAR program, this spoiled the effect of random assignment and muddied the causal question that researchers had sought to clarify. Very likely, some of the difference between the two groups in test results at the end of third grade owed to differences in the ambition, determination, rhetorical skill, persistence, and influence of parents, not just to differences in class size.[10]

So one reason it's hard to establish causality by means of random-assignment experiments in this area is that, unlike bacteria, which don't care and have nothing to say about whether their host is treated with a new antibiotic or with a placebo, parents, teachers, and other "actors in the educational system typically care a lot about which experimental [groups] . . . are assigned to particular educational treatments, and they take actions to try to influence these assignments."[11] Specifically, parents are likely to care more about whether their six-year-olds receive the best treatment than they care about advancing scientific knowledge.

Similarly, teachers might reasonably identify their self-interest with how the experiment goes. For instance, should the experiment convince legislators that smaller is better, workloads might become lighter. That expectation would give those teaching small classes an extra incentive to take pains preparing students to score well on the standardized tests that would measure the causality of class size. Again, administrators and school boards of the schools that volunteered to take part in the STAR study might have differed from officials in schools that did not, in commitment to improving schools, in leadership capabilities, and so on. In short, as Murnane and Willett note, all the participants in an experiment of this kind have stakes in its outcome and have power to shape how education proceeds in a school. To the extent that their actions make student learning better or worse, the experiment will prove less about the effect of class size.[12]

There are still other reasons it's hard to debug randomized experiments, the gold standard in educational research. To refer to Project STAR once more: in a study that follows participants for a period as long as four years will have significant attrition. As Murnane and Willett reported, "Half of the students who were present in the Project STAR kindergarten classes were missing from at least one class over the next three years of the experiment" (71). Quite possibly the ones who left differed from the ones who stayed in causal ways. A randomized experiment tracing participants over more than 40 years to see how college affected lifetime earnings would face a monumental problem of attrition—were it otherwise possible.

In short, for several reasons, designed, randomized studies—the gold standard for research on social causes and effects—are not feasible as a means of testing the idea of the college premium in its strict form.

Quasi-experiments

What about other methods that social scientists have developed to study causes, without interfering, godlike, in the life chances of subjects; without letting investigators' biases or the self-interested manipulation of participants muddy the waters; and without stumbling over such obstacles to random assignment as those that troubled Project STAR. One common strategy is to examine what happens to people placed in groups not by researchers wanting to study the effects of various treatments, but (for example) by officials who need two (or more) groups for some administrative purpose. The purpose could be as mild as setting a maximum size for elementary school classes, or as dire as picking soldiers to fight a war. The point *for researchers* is to learn with confidence that, over some stretch of time, x caused y to happen to a group that was treated one way, while y did not happen to a group identical in all attributes except in having been x'ed. The two groups may have been created through random assignment but not by an investigator whose aim is to find out whether x caused y. To put it more broadly, scholars using this approach are trying to derive reliable causal knowledge from experiment-like comparisons designed not by investigators seeking that knowledge but by officials solving practice problems. Such repurposing of a social project like building a school system or raising an army is a "quasi-experiment."[13]

Murnane and Willett describe an example that bears on the causality of class size in students' learning. After 1969, the Israeli Ministry of Education used Maimonides's twelfth-century rule that class size should be limited to 40 to decide how many teachers to assign to each grade in each school. The ministry was not conducting an experiment, but whenever it divided a large age group into two or more groups of fewer than 40 students each, it created small and large classes by random assignment. That is, neither parents, teachers, nor school officials decided which children would be in classes of, say 21 to 23 and which in classes of 41 to 46. The number 40 made that decision. Since the ministry kept track of reading scores, later analysts have been able to compare the progress of groups, with class size as almost the sole possible cause of different outcomes.[14]

Another social project that could measure how different experiences at an early age might cause different outcomes later on (including differences in income) was establishment of the Vietnam-era draft lottery. It made millions of 19- and

20-year-old men eligible (or not) for the draft through a lottery that figuratively put 365 slips of paper in a hat, each bearing a date of birth, and then chose dates blindly until reaching an estimated quota of draftees. This random process—adopted because it was fair—put some of the young men on a path that led to early deaths or to spoiled lives, outcomes a good deal more consequential than the differences in lifetime earnings that eventually came under academic analysis. But to stick with earnings: even though not all the draft eligible went on to do military service, and though a fair number of the ineligible did serve, the mere treatment—*being put at risk* of the draft—was causal. Specifically, men who were unlucky in the draw earned less, fourteen years later, than those whom the lottery exempted.[15]

The author of this study (and coauthor of the one on class size in Israel), Joshua D. Angrist, later went on to consider whether draft eligibility made a difference in educational attainment—a question more directly linked to the hypothesis of a college premium. The answer was yes. Why? Angrist noted that a larger portion of the draft eligible than of the other group that went into the military received a substantial incentive (a subsidy from the Vietnam-era GI Bill) to do college work. Considering their healthy return on investment in college, why didn't this cohort earn more than its counterpart? Because veterans also incurred a wage penalty, owing in part to having lost time and experience in the civilian workforce. The penalty more than offset the premium.[16] This example suggests the ability economists have, through analysis of quasi-experiments, to trace the causality of a "treatment" across many years.

But it also flags a serious problem that I approach by noting an anomaly in Angrist's findings: the offset of wage penalty by wage premium held for white veterans but not for Black veterans. More specifically, in spite of the GI Bill's incentive,

Black veterans did not reach a higher level of educational attainment than Black nonveterans; and even without the premium, Black men who served earned more (by the year 2000) than those who did not serve.[17] Possible explanations abound: job discrimination may have meant that the experience in the workforce lost by young Black veterans—think unskilled, dead-end jobs—was less valuable than what white veterans lost. Or young white men were in better positions than Black men, on average, to use the GI Bill subsidy for college education. Or a larger proportion of Black youth than of whites chose to volunteer for service (and stayed for a career), because racial barriers to advancement and dignity were lower in the military than in civilian life. Or, while both white and Black veterans often use their military service as a positive credential when seeking civilian employment, white veterans not attending college are preferentially situated in the labor market over Black veterans not attending college because of racism in hiring.

Whatever value such conjectures might have, one generalization seems obvious: racial difference in the United States was (and is) directly and indirectly causal. African Americans faced a different array of choices and obstacles in 1970 than did whites. To be sure, random assignment via the Vietnam-era lottery meant that the draft eligible and draft ineligible groups included Blacks and whites in the same proportions; that the two white groups included men with closely matched backgrounds, as their pathways in life sharply diverged; and that Black eligibles closely matched ineligibles in the ways they had experienced white supremacy. Yet, on the day when both white and Black youth learned whether the lottery had made them draftable, the news altered their circumstances differently. Yes, whites and Blacks who were draft eligible had in theory the same menu of choices: enlist in one of the military services and hope for a better assignment than you would get as a draftee in the army; let yourself be conscripted; try for a deferment; apply for recognition as a conscientious objector; honestly or dishonestly seek medical exemption; refuse induction in civil disobedience; leave the country; and so on. Yet, in reality, white privilege enhanced the menu choices of draft-eligible whites while diminishing those of draft-eligible nonwhites.

Analyzing how race worked for young men in 1970 is beyond the scope of this book; rather, my aim is just to suggest that the asymmetry of outcomes for the two races might offer lessons for those with a more general interest in social causality. In particular, the complex of causes and branching consequences that lead from "college" to later earnings may be as dense, though not so historically intense, as those linking Vietnam-era draft eligibility and earnings.

Complex Causes

As a college teacher working to support draft resisters in 1966 and after, I knew many students who dealt individually and politically with choices put before them by the draft. I read movement newsletters, tracts, and academic analyses. I went to strategic meetings, protest rallies, induction refusals, and the like. I was in touch with networks that helped resisters get to Canada or Sweden. Both where I worked and elsewhere in the United States, I saw that this kind of resistance was chiefly a white response to draft eligibility and to the facts of the war. Why? Let's take a closer look.

Resisters and exiles did not passively accept the draft lottery as a project of social sorting and did not believe that random assignment made the draft fair or separated it morally from the war. Their thinking followed a shifting network of pathways across a troubled and confusing historical landscape.

A few numbers will indicate that landscape's complexity: About 2.2 million men were drafted during the Vietnam era. Meanwhile, perhaps half a million refused induction, and 170,000 became legal conscientious objectors. An unknowable but large number who faced induction presented (or faked) physical or emotional conditions that would disqualify them for military service. Many more—estimates scatter widely to either side of 1 million—quietly opted out of the lottery by never registering for the draft at all. An estimated half of them were African American.[18] If that figure is accurate, a most interesting (and to my knowledge unexamined) additional cause of different outcomes for Blacks and whites is that the lottery pool itself had been formed by nonrandom, self-interested, and deeply cultural processes. Could the higher proportion of white youth than of African Americans who were in the pool help explain why the wage premium and wage penalty do not balance out the same way for the two groups?

To arrange the figures this way is to see that becoming subject to the draft put 18-year-old men in a situation defined by extreme choices with sharply contrasting outcomes. Entering the Selective Service institution was not a routine next step for them, in the way that beginning the fall semester was routine for kindergartners assigned to small or large classes in the STAR project. Rather, being (randomly) assigned a low lottery number pushed men along toward other choices: most starkly, whether to go on living lawfully, to cut legal corners, or to act criminally. Possible consequences of disobedience included arrest, prosecution, incarceration, and the remainder of life as an "ex-con." The 2 million who were drafted risked permanent injury or death in battle, or disabilities of many kinds back in civilian life.[19] Moreover, even the lawful path led many draftees to consider another felonious choice later on: to leave the military without being discharged. Hundreds of thousands of men (and some women) deserted from 1966 to 1973; many of them became exiles, along with an equally large number who had already gone to Canada or Sweden to put themselves beyond reach of the draft board. When random assignment puts one group into a labyrinth of such hard choices leading to dire outcomes, the causal effect of the group's original placement on modest differences in income years later seems a will-o'-the-wisp—unless one defines cause in a way only distantly related to how we conceptualize it in daily life, or to what we might want to understand about how history happens.

A further obstacle to figuring out what caused what in the wake of the lottery is the fact that a far larger group than those tallied above (almost 9 million) *enlisted* in some branch of military service during the time of the Vietnam draft. Some had high lottery numbers, some had low, some enlisted before the drawing for their cohort took place. The institutional fact of the lottery presumably influenced the existential choices of these three subgroups in different ways. For instance, those who enlisted before receiving lottery numbers were not necessarily expressing patriotic fervor, or accepting a civic obligation, or seeking low risk of death in combat (for instance, in the navy). De facto and probably in conscious intent, they were making career choices. They could have been drawn to the honorable commitment signaled by enlistment, to the possibilities it offered for learning a marketable specialty within the military or for impressively winning promotion there, or to the educational opportunities it might open after discharge. (Presumably these potential benefits appealed differently to Blacks versus whites.) The same hypothesis applies, more weakly, to enlisters who had drawn low lottery numbers. They were making the best of a dangerous predicament, but perhaps also with a thought for enhancing their (racially unequal) economic choices in postmilitary life.

Most likely, then, the very existence of the draft and establishment of the lottery had organized 18-year-olds into groups whose members already shared certain attitudes toward risk, success, continuing education, adult working lives, and (yes) future income, before the first birth date capsule was randomly picked. If so, the process of men's "assignment" to such groups did not achieve the kind of randomness sought by designers of planned experiments—specifically, did not neutralize self-interest as a difference between treatment group and control group. Nor, to look at the matter from another angle, was this method of selection likely to have evenly matched the two groups in patriotism, in family wealth, in educational goals, or in race, among other potentially important causes.

Finally, another 9 million of the 27 million men who reached draft age during this period neither enlisted, nor were drafted, nor refused or evaded induction. Some were classified as ineligible for medical or other reasons. Most simply took advantage of good luck in the lottery and went on with youthful lives free from the constraints on choice that bad luck in the lottery imposed. Putting it like that makes the treatment in this quasi-experiment seem profoundly consequential: the drawing instantly tracked one group into a web of stark choices, with outcomes including exile, carrying out treasonous conduct, killing civilians, being gravely disabled, dying young, whereas the other group went back into the same matrix of quotidian choices it had faced the day before, including those related to future economic well-being. For the draft eligible, considerations of future income and educational pathways likely to increase it had been abruptly devalued. Look at the matter this way, and you might wonder that the two groups differed so *little* in their earnings fourteen years later.

To come back to the college premium: I am trying to spot difficulties that may arise when, in order to address questions that for ethical or technical reasons are not open to direct study, social science research reorganizes and interprets information originally gathered for other purposes, in lieu of designing experiments. I and (presumably) readers of this book would very much like social science to answer two questions of this kind that are embedded in the hypothesis of the college premium: How does education contribute to the prosperity of those who receive varying amounts and kinds of it? And, what are the causes of economic success and failure? It is not permissible to assign 17-year-olds (even randomly) to college or the job market in order to learn what difference college makes in lifetime earnings. Nor would it be permissible to assign 18-year-old men randomly to draft eligibility or draft exemption in order to find out what effects such an assignment has on later income. The basic principle is that no investigator should, for the sake of science, put subjects through a treatment likely to ruin the lives of some or deny to some a strongly beneficial treatment.[20]

Alternative Strategies

All the studies of a return on investment in college that have in recent years accompanied and strengthened the belief in a college premium have been based on quasi-experiments or (more commonly) on existing data banks. These observational studies organize information into possible causes and outcomes. *The College Payoff*, for instance, uses data from the Census Bureau's American Community Survey to establish causal links between the completion of a bachelor's degree and higher lifetime earnings for those who attained it than for the main control group, those who ended their education with high school diplomas. Other variables taken into account are race, gender, and occupation. I return to *The College Payoff* after reflecting on how quasi-experimental and observational studies deal with such intricate webs of causality as those in which the Vietnam lottery was embedded or those responsible for making some people more prosperous than others over a long stretch of living.

A basic risk of such strategies is losing the focus of the questions about education and earnings that prompted the inquiry, or even the very point of asking those questions. In adapting the method to a particular batch of data, it may even be impossible to achieve the desired random assignment. For example, the Vietnam lottery left out very many men who enlisted before dates were drawn for their cohort or who had not registered for the draft in the first place. That meant that along lines of race, patriotic and civic values, social class, and other likely causes, both draft-eligible and draft-ineligible groups were unrepresentative of the whole population whose later attainments we set out to explain. The method's skewing of random assignment is bound to violate Mill's third condition.

Likewise, the *treatment* provided by the draft lottery differs in important ways from what researchers usually attempt in planned experiments such as STAR, in which the two groups were put on parallel tracks to learn reading and math from Kindergarten through third grade. Supposedly, the curriculum and goals were the same for both groups; only class size differed. By contrast, draft eligibility was a treatment that, in an instant, radically changed the circumstances of men with low numbers. Each one now faced an array of possible choices with uncertain consequences, and each decision he made could abruptly change his options again, immediately and over his lifetime. Nothing like that happened to five-year-olds randomly assigned to small classes in STAR. School experiences next week, next semester, next year were to be the same for them as for the other kids, except as influenced by class size. Nor did assignment to a small or large class confront the kindergartner with a host of new possibilities for choosing life pathways, as did draft eligibility in 1970.

The draft lottery was of course not designed to explore the causes and effects of education, or the determinants of high and low earnings. But data derived from this quasi-experiment, like the findings of planned experiments, have often been adapted to the study of "labor market outcomes." It has also been used to study why individuals decide to continue their educations, a choice that may in turn affect their incomes later on. So this account of problems should be helpful when I return, shortly, to evidence for the college premium.

To summarize: First, unlike a planned experiment, a quasi-experiment does not begin with a clearly formulated question that will guide the research toward causal knowledge specified in advance by the investigators. The designers of the Vietnam draft lottery in 1969 (Congress and President Richard Nixon) did not set out to discover whether draft eligibility would bring higher educational attainment or higher incomes to individual men, years later, than would draft ineligibility. They were in fact guided by no research question at all, but by a military need and political concerns. To draw causal conclusions by pairing lottery outcomes with bodies of data assembled years later for various purposes is at best a daunting task. Or, to look at the matter another way, analysts focused on labor market outcomes might have wanted to ask something like, How does military service affect the later employment and pay of individuals? Since they cannot plan an experiment to address that question, they must come at it obliquely. So, too, with the college premium.

Second, designers of experiments must specifically identify what population is under study. That might seem easy to achieve in a quasi-experiment. For instance, draft lottery studies were ostensibly about all-male American citizens aged 19 to 26. But their population actually included only those who had registered for the draft. As noted earlier, estimates suggest that nonregistrants were disproportionately African American. So a potentially significant cause of later education and earnings was blurred in advance, elided from consideration in guiding the research—as was a relaxed disregard for the law, or some such quality that might have caused later outcomes among men of all races and ethnicities.

Third, experimenters must divide the population into two or more groups that are *representative*. Random assignment by birth date took care of that requirement in Vietnam lottery studies, but I propose that at the height of the war in Vietnam the cohort of draft-age men had already self-selected, driven by reasons and qualities that might well have led to more or less income later on.

To be sure, an analyst can be more exact about the population under study. Not "men who were 19 years old in 1969," for instance, but "19-year-old men who had registered for the draft, who had not enlisted in the military, who were not (legally) conscientious objectors, who were not classified 4-F," and so on. To improve accuracy in this way is to move the inquiry further and further away from questions that might have driven inquiry in the first place. Bear in mind that a broad ethical principle had precluded designing research to find out what effects military service has on later income: you mustn't randomly put people at high risk of death and injury for the purpose of learning more about labor market outcomes, though it's acceptable to do that for purposes of war. So, if you detoxify the question by changing "military service" to "eligibility for military service" and turn to the draft lottery for a quasi-experiment, you find yourself forced to exclude from the population under study men who had already solved their risk problems in various ways. In this way, too, ethics and the requirements of valid causal research have in effect changed the subject.

Fourth, as for treatment, how is it affected when barriers to planned experimentation lead analysts to adapt already-existing data to their purposes? A clearly specified treatment, limited in scope and easily distinguished from other possible causes, is essential for anyone wanting to know what educational approaches work best or what causes different incomes, especially across long stretches of time. Becoming draftable meets the criterion of clear specification nicely, but it is hardly "limited in scope" or "easily distinguished from other causes." Unlike children in Project STAR, whose treatment was three years of reading and math instruction in smaller-than-usual classes, the young men who received low draft numbers in 1970 did not then pass through an experience that was otherwise pretty much the same for treatment and control groups. For young men with bad lottery numbers, life abruptly changed—and kept changing—along many dimensions, as did the likely results of choices they made regarding college, jobs, family, and so forth.

Fifth, for all of us, each act, each pathway chosen leads to a new array of future choices. For Vietnam draft eligibles, a decision (enlistment, exile, etc.) could more seriously transform one's situation and prospects than decisions children are likely to make while learning to read in regulated first-grade classes. Causes compound. Clearly, in raising or lowering future earnings, some causes cancel out others. I don't propose that draft status heavily determined income; clearly it did not. Rather, I suggest that in chains of individual action set moving by a piece of bad or good wartime luck and measured in an item of data such as earnings a decade or several decades later, causality blurs. It's hard to believe that such a quasi-experiment can rule out all causes of greater or less affluence except one and, in that way, satisfy Mill's third condition.[21]

In brief, designing an experiment to find out whether x causes y is a complicated business. Random assignment ensures that, if scrupulously carried out, it will yield dependable knowledge. But a commonsense ethical rule forbids studying many questions in this way, especially over long stretches of subjects' lives. An alternative way to study causation in such cases is to take advantage of a quasi-experiment. But such a study cannot proceed from the research question the investigator would like to ask, because the "experiment" has already been initiated for some other reason. Then there's the tangle of interwoven causes and the swirl of forces and conduct that is social life. Draft eligibility, service in Vietnam, and many other things that happened to young men because of the lottery numbers they received could have influenced their college attendance and completion and directly or indirectly affected later earnings. How to untangle those forces and reckon their relative causal power and their interaction?

I've explored these difficulties with reference to the Vietnam-era draft because consequences of different acts or "treatments" were often sudden, stark, and influenced by strong, interwoven and overlapping historical forces. Pathways from education through the complexities of the labor market and other social institutions are similarly complex, so I would expect similar problems to arise in mining quasi-experiments to find out how going to college affects later economic welfare.

Observational Studies

Most studies of the college premium, especially those that address the hypothesis in its most general form, and those intended to gain public notice and influence policy makers, are based not on quasi-experiments but on batches of data gathered and organized as a resource for lawmakers, government agencies, lobbyists, nonprofit organizations of every sort, businesses, independent scholars, and others. The spectrum of databases runs from small private archives to massive, continuing, official collections like those of the Census Bureau—which may in time be dwarfed by the wild catches of such large nets as Google and the National Security Agency. There's a plenitude of data out there. Studies that use it are called "observational," a term meant to contrast them both with designed experiments, which generate new data to test specific hypotheses, and with quasi-experiments, which put "found" random pairings to work.

Some collections of data are built by following individual subjects over an extended period of time in order to support research in a particular field. One of the best-known examples is in medicine: the Framingham Heart Study. From 1948 to 1968 it conducted biennial testing, medical exams, and interviews of several thousand people from the namesake Massachusetts town, tracking their blood pressure, body mass indices, cholesterol levels, smoking habits, exercise routines, and so on. Hundreds of investigators have used the data from that and two follow-up projects to develop much of the knowledge we now have about the causes of heart health and disease. There are comparable (though less comprehensive) databases that track people through and after schooling—for example, the US Department of Education's "High School and Beyond." But research on what education accomplishes has relied chiefly on multipurpose collections like those of the Census Bureau.

Working with data of either sort, analysts try to move from correlations (people who go to college earn more, on average, than those who just went through high school) to causality (a college degree pays off). In medicine, correlations can have practical value—for instance, as "risk factors," a phrase, incidentally, that came from the Framingham study. Risk factors for ischemic stroke include age, gender, race, heredity, having had a previous stroke, atrial fibrillation, diabetes, a high level of bad cholesterol, smoking, and heavy drinking. A person can't do anything about the first five of these but can take steps to eliminate or moderate the latter five. Knowledge of these correlations can substantially help prevent strokes and thus reduce deaths and damaged brains.

Interestingly, promoters of the college premium do not make the same move from correlation to risk factor: they do not say, for example, "Leaving school after grade 12 is a risk factor for earning less than $1 million in the next forty years." One rhetorical reason those who see college as an investment avoid putting the case this way is that the formulation implies the existence of other risk factors, such as being female, Black, or poor, some of which might correlate more strongly with low lifetime earnings than ending one's education with high school.[22] Investors in bonds and equities do not assume risks like these that are socially constructed and thus involuntary. Also, "investing" makes a good outcome sound more likely than does "reducing risks." ("Conferring" higher income sounds like a sure thing.) I offer more along this sardonic line of thought later.

There is a basic conceptual problem with sifting correlations for causes. The number of facts that could in principle be correlated with lifetime earnings above a certain amount is infinite; there's no chance of finding a few needles of causality by aimlessly searching through such a haystack. Even the number of correlations that could be created by pairing items from existing databases would defeat a mechanistic search for causality. An observational study needs guidelines, set by a theory or at least by an intuition as to likely causes of more or less prosperity. Without guidance, there's no reason to focus on such factors as educational attainment, gender, and intelligence, rather than, say, frequently eating Grape Nuts or having had an appendectomy.

Faced with that choice, intuition grounded in common knowledge is a good enough guide. For instance, it's common knowledge that being male or female correlates with large differences in pay. Recall that people with college degrees made on average (in 2002) 75 percent more than those who left off formal education after finishing high school. For the past twenty years at least, we've known that men with a bachelor's degree had lifetime earnings 25 percent larger than women with the same level of attainment. Carnevale and his fellow investigators do not conclude, in *The College Payoff*, that there is a gender premium, but anyone familiar with the history of the United States and its hierarchies will find it plausible that the gender correlations reflect causes: being male still pays off, as does being white, in spite of political efforts over many decades to end discrimination on the basis of characteristics that do not in themselves contribute to productivity at work and that individuals have neither earned nor chosen. No theory is needed to guide an investigator toward including gender and race and ignoring routine surgeries and breakfast preferences among causes of high lifetime earnings.[23]

Speaking of political reasons behind interest in the college premium: clearly, there are other qualities than being male or white that give the possessor an edge in competing for good pay, qualities that they have neither earned nor chosen, but that seem not to have risen above the threshold of perceived unfairness or to have stirred the concern of legislators. Height in men is one such characteristic; blondness in women is another. Further blurring the intuitive line between earned and unearned are such qualities as slimness in women or conventional attractiveness (worth more than $300,000 and more than $200,000 in lifetime earnings, respectively). These advantages are morally problematic, both because the attribution of "beauty" to a woman is grounded in coercive, historically created gender and racial imperatives, and because, to at least some degree, choice is also at work in meeting or flouting those imperatives. (A woman can put much effort into conventional good looks or, for that matter, into violating such conventions.) Yet the largest wage premium for an individual attribute is unchosen and supposedly unearned: the one conferred by IQ. I have not heard that premium (as high as three-quarters of a million dollars, depending on cutoff lines) criticized as unjust. Intelligence seems to rank right up with industriousness as a quality that *should* be rewarded. Or, to put it the other way around, nobody is proposing affirmative action for lazy people or equal pay for those with low IQs.[24]

I have added this cultural dimension in order to propose that the hypothesis of a wage premium for college graduates is surrounded on all sides by debates about whether our social and economic system is fair, about how to remedy injustice, and about deeper points of ideology such as that individuals are or are not, should or should not be, responsible for how their economic efforts turn out. In a common way of thinking, if there is a dependable return on investment in college, and your child does not take advantage of it, then you and your child are responsible for their failure to thrive economically.

Those who do seize the advantage deserve the monetary reward. The system is fair.

Or, to put a liberal spin on the issue, if birth or circumstance keeps millions of youths from undertaking and completing a college education, "we" must remove the barriers, widen access, create the equality of opportunity that makes a wide range of outcomes just. Without carrying this line of thought on into the rhetorical mist of the American Dream, where it often leads, I hope to have suggested that a heavy freight of ideology accompanies and presses in upon talk of the college premium. Ideology's presence is even weightier when discussion moves from the return on education for individuals and families to the return for US society as a whole, as it does in later chapters of this book.

Human Capital

Back to the main theme: although intuition and common knowledge can help distinguish likely and important causes from improbable or minor ones, inquiry into the payoff of education almost always proceeds with the guidance of theory, too. For the past fifty years, human capital theory has usually assumed this role. The mass of scholarship that goes by that name in economics may not be explicitly referenced in papers from policy centers like the one at Georgetown that published *The College Payoff*, and it is scarcely mentioned in journalistic stories on whether the college premium is fading or is glossier than ever. But it was the work of economists during and after the 1950s that picked up an argument of Adam Smith's about different pay for different kinds of work, focused it on the costs of learning to do particular jobs, and theorized the whole issue as one of a return on investment—by employers in the human capital that they put to work in and on their physical capital (e.g., their factories and machines) and by future workers in preparing to compete in the labor market.

"Human capital" refers very broadly to knowledge, skills, character traits, learning abilities, punctuality, obedience—whatever abilities and habits an employer can turn into profit. It is easy to understand why midcentury economists working in the United States, where primary and secondary schooling were free and heading toward universal, would narrow their inquiry to the knowledge and habits produced by formal education and thus focus on the choices young people make whether to continue and when to end schooling.

Also, mountains of data were available to people studying how particular levels of educational attainment affect later life. Does some college cause more satisfaction, greater civic virtue, or greater earnings than no college? Does finishing with a bachelor's degree bring still more? It's easy to see how answers to such questions put causality in play, and also how greater precision and insight might be achieved about earnings than about satisfaction or civic virtue. A specific historical reason economists have looked more closely at pay than at other outcomes is that earnings are at the center of Adam Smith's hypotheses about choices workers make as they prepare for employment. And, of course, the wealth of nations and of individuals has long been a main emphasis of the intellectual project that evolved into the modern profession of economics. On top of all that, the methods of neoclassical economics were well adapted to studying correlations between educational attainment and pay.

So it's natural that knowledge and debate about the topic of this book have evolved mainly under the leadership and within the conceptual world of economics. That genealogy has made for analytic precision and sophistication far beyond what was possible from the immediate postwar period through the 1960s, when the United States was building the educational institutions and methods that served its productive system so well. To be sure, there were the usual simplifying premises that enabled theoretical and empirical progress: frictionless markets; choices made therein by buyers and sellers acting on ample knowledge; economic interest as their chief (or only) motivation; level playing fields for borrowers and lenders, for workers and employers, and for participants in contracts generally; economic life sufficiently independent from politics and culture to warrant isolating it as an arena of choice—for instance, the choice between college education and a job right after high school.

I side with the generally leftist outlook of this critique in my more specific discussion of how human capital theory directs the study of education's effects over time.[25] In particular, I question the narrowing of the theory's scope from everything that does or might make workers valuable to employers, to investment in the *learning* of useful knowledge, habits, and skills; from there to the *formal education and training* workers bring with them into the labor market; thence to the *fact of their having attained a particular point in formal education*, that is, finished high school, some college, a college degree, or what have you; and on to the *fact of their having registered for study* toward some credential—or even to the fact of their having been offered a voucher or lost out in a lottery that might influence educational choices they would later make.

Such narrowing enables economists to use the data they have rather than the data they might wish for, and to make an impressive array of valid inferences from it. But it simplifies the idea of education in ways that might have troubled Adam Smith and that certainly diverge from what most educators and, until recently, most college students have thought they were doing. Furthermore, narrowing the focus on investment and its outcomes as economists have done stretches and squeezes the common idea of cause. I have dwelt on this point at some length and will be brief about two additional problems I see.

The first has to do with how random assignment permits the identification of causes, not just correlations. In combination with a large sample population, random assignment guarantees that the treated group and the control group are "identical in expectation prior to the intervention," so that any difference in outcome between the groups "must be a causal consequence" of the treatment.[26] For example, in a well-designed experiment to see if children learn to read faster when taught in small classes, a significant difference in posttreatment scores will not owe to other causes. Yes, it's possible that high IQ, or lots of books at home, or being the oldest sibling, or being female, or any combination of such factors accelerates the learning process. But random assignment assures that the group taught in large classes includes about as many smart kids, girls, oldest siblings, and students with lots of books at home as does the group taught in small classes. So the effects of these and other causes are the same for children in both groups, and the experiment has proven that small classes do matter.

Because quasi-experiments divide "subjects" into groups without the possible bias of an investigator or of group members who sought their own advantage by joining up, they offer the analytic certainties that designers of experiments achieve through random assignment. But they do this for purposes other than those of scientific study, and a scholar wanting to use data from quasi-experiments for their own purposes must follow a circuitous route. No educational economist in the late 1960s studying military service, education, and later earnings would have begun by randomly tagging young men with good or bad numbers in the draft lottery, had that been possible. The pathways from draft eligibility or ineligibility in 1970 to higher or lower salaries 15 or 30 years later would have looked labyrinthine, and the lines of causality impossibly various. Simpler designs would have prevailed. When all the data were in, analysts would have been able to see which of their well-chosen possible causes had explanatory value and which hypotheses could be discarded.

In any case, few quasi-experiments bear directly on the hypothesis of the college premium, and most of those that do bear on it obliquely, throwing only small shafts of light on the main question, while raising difficulties comparable to (though less historically complex) than those I noted in discussing the Vietnam draft lottery.[27] Since planned experiments with random assignments are ruled out by ethical and practical barriers, scholars have, perforce, relied on observational studies to carry the burden of argument.

The demographic groups used in such studies are of course statistical artifacts, assembled from census data and the like entirely without benefit of random assignment. *The College Payoff*, for instance, divides all Americans born in a year around 1945 into one group whose members never finished high school; another whose members went to work right after high school; a third that completed some college but not enough to earn a degree; and so on, up the educational and income ladder to those born in the same year who earned degrees in law, medicine, and the other professions—a total of eight groups. The analyst can then use 2009 income data for each of these in order to find that the median life earnings of those who left formal education before the end of high school were a little under a million dollars; of those with just high school diplomas about $1.3 million; of those with bachelor's degrees $2.27 million; and on up to $3.65 million for those with professional degrees.[28]

This representation of the data makes educational attainment the independent variable and lifetime earnings the dependent one. The relationship of the two could arguably be causal if the people in each educational group had been randomly placed there, rather than having chosen when to leave school or to end their collegiate or postgraduate studies in order to advance what they saw as their best interests. The fact of their having so chosen leaves open the possibility that any number of experiences, traits, advantages, and so on *other* than education may be responsible for where they landed in the life income rankings.

Furthermore, no investigator made a theoretically guided, historically plausible winnowing of possible causes and built a few of the most likely ones into the design of the inquiry. There was no design. What the authors of *The College Payoff* do, forty years later, is pick a small number of such factors (gender, race, and occupational category), correlate life earnings of subgroups with educational attainment, and compare them to one another. Intuitively, it seems certain that gender, race, and choice of occupation do affect earnings, but why just these three likely causes out of many? Perhaps because gender and race are politically urgent, because occupation is plainly causal, and because including a lot more candidates would clutter up the analysis— not to mention the arena of public policy, where legislators may put the think tank's findings to use.

In the three or four decades since social scientists with easy computer access sought to track down causes by including more and more independent variables ("control for everything"), economists in particular have developed sophisticated ways to put aside that part of observed data on a possible cause that may be contaminated by bias or self-interest and use only the part that is not. This is how Murnane and Willett describe the technique called instrumental-variables estimation

(IVE). They carefully explain its prospects and challenges and those of other strategies—including use of multilevel random intercepts models, stratification of the sample population, and propensity scores analysis—for bringing potential causes (covariates) into focus and separating out unknown conditions that could be predictive, for example, whether one or more of a person's ancestors arrived in the North American colonies before 1650—to invent a silly-sounding yet plausible candidate for causality.

Economists have taken the quest for causality to high levels of sophistication in the past few decades, just as the hypothesis of the college premium was gaining at least plausibility and at most the standing of received truth, in policy circles, among politicians, in the media, and by the last-named route to a broader public, including prospective college students and their worried parents. In this process of diffusion, reputable think tanks that serially put out reports about investment in college education, such as Georgetown's Center on Education and the Workforce, are influential. Yet *The College Payoff*, published by that center in 2011, though it deploys a rhetoric of causation, includes no argument linking its implied claim of causality to the data. Nor does it make discernible use of the techniques economists have developed to demonstrate causality and estimate the effects of educational causes. If I am right in this, Carnevale, Rose, and Cheah flat out fail to justify language such as "a general earnings boost conferred by a degree" and "the obvious returns to more education" (2).

To repeat: what they do is show that more education correlates with higher life earnings, across levels of attainment running from high school dropout to holder of a professional degree. A bit later they allow that some people at each level earn less than some with less education, and some earn more than higher educational achievers. As I note earlier, the authors call this phenomenon "overlap." For example, "about 28 percent of workers with Associate's degrees earn more than the median earnings of workers with Bachelor's degrees." The ubiquity of overlap in these findings would imply that even if more education does cause more income, there must be additional causes. But at this point the authors do not speak of causality; they speak of covariation: "Earnings vary not only by educational attainment, but by occupation" and "also by gender and race/ethnicity" (3). So, even though Carnevale et al. go on (inconsistently) talking cause—"Obtaining a high school diploma adds 33 percent more to lifetime earnings"—they make no case for doing so. It would be unreasonable to fault them for overlooking other possible causes, because they did not structure the analysis as a search for causes in the first place. In effect, they organized their data as an array of covariates, but they write as if they had identified causes.

How much does it matter? Maybe we should welcome reports like this as modest aids to prudent choices on the part of anyone deciding whether to continue their education—for instance, by going to college. Whatever its gaps, *The College Payoff* does show that college graduates earned more on average by age 65 than did workers who ended their schooling after grade 12. And it shows that the point holds for many subgroups. Female workers who went to college earned more than women who did not. Supervisors of retail sales workers earned 50 percent more on average if they had college degrees than retail supervisors with just high school diplomas. Latino college grads earned more than Latinos with diplomas but no college study. And so on, with great consistency, across gender, race, and occupational group. Does that pattern not make college strongly advisable for all young people trying to make rational economic choices?

No. The data analysis presented in *The College Payoff* does not show that college "confers" high earnings, or that it "adds" a "large increase in lifetime earnings," or that on average "a Bachelor's degree is worth \$2.8 million"—does not in fact show that the "college payoff" of their report's title exists. In the more formal terminology the authors sometimes take from economists, there is *no* proven "return" on investment in college to an individual student. That's not because the authors are speaking of "average" (= median) returns, so that there's a good chance that 18-year-olds choosing college will find themselves earning *less* than counterparts who chose to get jobs straight out of high school—though that possibility is not easily shrugged off in a time when college costs as much as it does now. Rather, it's because the authors have not engaged with causality, much less established it. This omission is common in public discussion of the college premium. It invalidates many inferences drawn there, both about individual choices and about social policy.

To add two more points about which I am skeptical: First, the problem of relations among causes that came up in my look at Vietnam-era draft eligibility and later earnings. Possible causes are many; they overlap and blur into one another. Economists are good at sorting them out, disentangling the causal from the possibly-causal-but-contaminated-by-bias, and ruling out "third paths." To take a made-up example: family wealth could be a predictor of going to college, and college a predictor of high earnings, but since family wealth directly predicts high earnings, we can forget about college. I am skeptical that the interactions and overlaps of cause can be sorted out by IVE or other methods into a collection of discrete causes, some more and some less responsible for an outcome, without seriously misrepresenting what we commonly mean by cause. That doubt extends to the implicit idea that small, as yet undiscovered causes must explain the rest. A potential infinity of causes seems like a statistical convenience, not social process as we live it. Social process (everyday life) embeds ideologies that underly the making of difference and inequity in society. Ideologies thus lie behind the unequal distribution of wealth and power that creates unequal access to the schools and colleges launching each generation into the labor market.

Second, although, with Murnane and Willett, I take Mill's bare-bones definition of cause as a handy point of departure, many people (including laboratory scientists) rely on richer concepts. In medicine, "mechanistic evidence" of causality, as discovered through planned experiments on animal or human populations, rates above epidemiological evidence based on statistical analysis of observations. Knowledge about physiological processes that are initiated when a patient swallows a medication and that lead to fever reduction complement studies showing that lower temperatures reliably follow taking of the pill and can't be explained by other known events. A process appears in an otherwise-empty explanatory space.

Something similar happens when analysts look inside the space between random assignment of children to classes of different sizes and the emergence three years later of better readers from the smaller classes. The treatment caused the outcome, but by what specific mechanism? Maybe pathways form more quickly in the brain when the classroom is less socially and visually complex? Or (a less exotic mechanism that has actually been proposed) maybe teachers can limit disruptions better with fewer students in the room, and thereby give more time to instruction. The explanatory need for a more robust idea of causality is still more evident when the subject is the college premium. What happens inside the black box called "college" that makes a difference in the job market and on through the following four decades?

These two reservations do not put into dispute the work economists have done since the 1980s to lay a foundation for causal research. The burden of my critique in this chapter is, rather, that the knowledge coming out of that ingenious work reshapes the (admittedly unsophisticated) notion of cause that inspired the research to begin with. An empirical tightening of that notion is an intellectual gain. What may be lost alongside the gain is the complexity that makes deciding how to advance one's interest so tricky, and that makes even trickier deciding what educational arrangements would benefit a society.

That politically influential studies such as *The College Payoff* have backslid from economists' conceptual advances makes things worse.

Chapter 3

What Makes People "Well-Off"—or Not?

Suppose that instead of beginning with this question, How much does a college education pay off?, investigators had taken another as their starting point: What makes a person "well-off" or not at retirement age? Investigators would undoubtably have scrutinized not just individual actions such as earning a college degree but other social determinants as well. For certain, the material circumstances into which people were born is an obvious one. Likewise, how families seek to preserve and pass on what advantages they have; how adults raise kids through infancy and early childhood; what kinds of formal schooling parents have arranged for them; what boosts (if any) the young receive from family networks when they became adults; and whatever other social helps and hindrances come their way could well make a difference in a person's lifetime earnings and wealth.

Observation and common sense would also have suggested to scholars that abilities and traits people inherit or gain in early upbringing lead to prosperity or the lack of it. Intelligence would seem to be an important asset, as well as a tempting candidate for study because it has been relentlessly tested and measured for more than a hundred years. Ambition, industriousness, acquisitiveness, persistence, creativity, cooperativeness, respect for authority, and the like, though less amenable to standardized testing, seem obvious subjects for research. Investigators would have considered that, on average, men earn more over the course of a working life than do women, and white workers more than nonwhite workers: gender and race, though of course not easily interchangeable, could be worth studying as possible causes of high pay. Other inherited job market advantages such as height in men and slimness or blondness in women might have seemed too trivial to warrant the attention of scholars, though they also factor into the equation.

As noted in the previous chapter, because people have infinitely many attributes that could conceivably help make them affluent, deciding which ones to study requires guidance from intuition or theory or a blend of both. The political interests and values of the investigators will also guide inquiry—unavoidably and, in my view, properly. Thinking inequality a social ill and hoping to learn its causes and possible remedies would entail a different approach than the way you'd organize your research if individual prosperity and economic growth across economic systems were your main values.

Historically, research on the college payoff flourished in the latter of these frameworks. Appropriately, it took theoretical guidance from human capital theory, whose proponents in the 1950s sought to understand what worker qualities and skills were most fruitful in the production of economic value.[1] Economists thus took employers' need to make profits and to keep as much as possible for themselves as a given, not as a historically variable condition or ethical dilemma to be interrogated. This perspective was political only in acknowledging that capitalism was in fact the set of arrangements that produced economic value in most parts of the world, not in favoring those arrangements—much as Margaret Fuller's "I accept the universe" was an acknowledgment of reality, not a Panglossian cheer for the best of all possible worlds. Human capital theory also assumed that before entering the labor force,

young people would make rational choices (given the information and advice they had) about how to prepare for economic success, how to become the kinds of human beings
most valued by employers.[2] Economists in the field would
want, among other things, to help young people to be smart
in that way.

The politics of framing education this way are oblique, but
distinctly conservative insofar as the status quo is taken as a
given. More explicitly political is the way some economists
join with policy makers in wanting to expand the economy
and looking to education as a process that can turn out workers who increase profits. Youth hoping for good jobs will ad-
just their educational plans accordingly, with urging from
families and counselors. Through such a bundle of needs and
interests, research on the return on investment in college quietly aligns itself with neoliberal goals—even though most
economists are not neoliberals or traditional conservatives
but are traditional liberals and registered Democrats.[3]

To return to the thought experiment: if tasked instead to
find out "what makes people well-off," liberal economists
would no doubt include college education somewhere on
their preliminary list of possible causes. But, more likely, the
form of the question would turn their thoughts to old puzzles
such as why some prosper and some do not, why more don't
than do, why the ratio differs from one country to another,
how unusual it is for a person to start poor and become "well-
off," if not outrightly rich, and so on. From there it's a short
step to familiar issues of equality, fairness, justice, power, sub-
jection, liberty, and democracy. Values and politics bristle
from the question. So does history: how is inequality now
like and unlike inequality fifty or a hundred years ago? How
have groups (including political parties) acted to increase or
reduce it?

To zoom closer in: how do individuals and families secure or improve their economic conditions? This train of analysis puts college education in a very different frame. It invites attention to the fact that some rich people did not *become* rich; they were rich from the start. Families pass wealth on to the next generation, and though income from trust funds and portfolios does not count as "earnings," having a lot of it makes daily life comfortable and the future secure, just as a million-dollar salary does. This points to "family of origin" as a key factor for "being well-off" in post-collegiate adulthood.

Most parents want their kids to prosper and will spend money to help. Wealthy families can, without sacrificing or borrowing, spend large sums to place their three-year-olds in Montessori preschools or the equivalent, then enroll them in private elementary and secondary schools where high tuition pays for smaller classes and an enriched school culture (respectful, plush, and pleasant while demanding and stimulating) that is distinctly high-end college prep, thus rehearsing their imaginaries of life paths through open doors of prestigious colleges or universities. Other strategies are of course available: moneyed families can buy costly homes in wealthy suburbs, pay high property and school taxes, pay for private academic and art lessons, provide a library at home of books and magazine, send their children on trips to distant places, and aim their children toward upper-level colleges for "free" (via tracking in schools that selectively restrict access to the top-rank classes).[4] On the other hand, because students from these upper-level families do not need to treat college as an *investment* (they already have stocks and bonds and high-value connections), they can give low priority to learning marketable skills and developing social ties that will ease the climb into high-paying careers. More likely than undergraduates from middle-class and working-class homes, upper-class students can skip accounting, nursing, education, and the STEM fields to major in art history, philosophy, or filmmaking. They can forgo social club membership and join instead groups that organize against racism or in favor of confiscatory taxes on inherited wealth.

Well, except for that last, fanciful bit, everyone is familiar with the itineraries just sketched out. Everyone understands that "college" figures differently in the life stories of wealthy, middling, and poor people. Everyone knows that for children growing up on the high end, the issue is not college or no college, but which selective university or college; that for middle-class youth, too, college is scripted into the story but more fraught with financial worries and urgencies; and that for poor children it may be a remote ideal or a future not even imaginable. Such differences are highly pertinent to the line of analysis set in train by asking what makes some people "well-to-do" and for whom the college premium is more functional or less. By contrast to this social portrait of college outcomes, simply asking what the payoff is on an investment in college tends to flatten out economic differences, by positioning rich, middle-income and poor alike as consumers facing an economic decision and showing them how to make it rationally. Fatefully, the economics underlying a child's choice of college is laden at birth by the social status of the family.

A stripped-down procedure for choosing rationally, for instance, is to tote up the price of four years' tuition, fees, room and board, supplies, transportation, and other costs (less financial aid) at the college or university you want to attend; add the total cost of loans you will need, including interest; and add the amount you would earn in the next four to six years if you took a full-time job now instead of going to college and working part-time or not at all if family financed. That total sum equals the "opportunity cost" of attending college immediately after high school instead of entering the workforce and earning wages. Subtract that total opportunity cost from your expected earnings during the 40 years after graduation, compare the resulting figure to the expected earnings across those same decades for a person with just a high school education; and discover whether going to college or going to work full-time will put you in better financial shape when you're 65.

This plan for rationality begs fewer questions than I posed in the previous chapter about deciding yes or no to college on the promise of the wage premium it brings. But even the more nuanced plan just outlined omits other, nonmonetary goals, interests, risks, and family circumstances, which could add questions to the calculus, such as: How much do I *care* about earning an extra million dollars, given that I expect to inherit more than that from my grandparents, and that I prefer a working life in museum curatorship to one in commercial banking? Or, how can I forgo the potential extra million dollars given that my parents will expect me to subsidize their retirement and medical bills in the coming years?

What Economic Rationality Leaves Out: Two Guides to Choosing a College

In practice, one does not choose college education in the abstract; one chooses an institution of some particular type—research university, community college, art school, or whatever—and, in the end, a specific college or university. Let's look at two aids that are on offer to help with that choice and see what they take to be economic rationality.

First, "Payback," an interactive simulation game or, as the designers put it, "an immersive online experience that educates students to make wise decisions on how they'll pay for college."[5] It assumes that players have applied to a number of schools; have been admitted to four institutions of varying types, from a community college to a private university that costs about $60,000 a year; and want to "understand the real cost of college and the far-reaching financial implications of decisions they're making at the age of 18." Even though, in the real world, high school seniors are unlikely to apply to and be accepted by both an elite private university and the local community college, "Payback" is fairly specific about the maze of choices and outcomes they face. They must decide not only what kind of institution they will attend but also what field they will study (based in part on the average starting salaries of majors in that area); how intense or relaxed they'd like their academic efforts to be; what level of comfort or elegance they want in their food and living quarters; what kinds of computers and furnishings they'll buy; whether they'll join Greek societies; how they will travel (or commute) between school and home; and so on. As they click on each choice, they view a running total of what the tab will be. They also note how much they can shave off that total when deciding how many hours (if any) they will work at paying jobs while at school and whether they will take summer jobs. At the end, Payback tells each player how much debt he or she will have assumed.

It does not ask them how much of that amount their real-life parents would pay. In fact, it asks them nothing at all about themselves except their grade point average in high school, the strength of their "extracurriculars," what state they live in, and how highly they value "academic focus," network building, and happiness. In short, it virtually eliminates social coordinates from the calculus and thus from this virtual experience of a critical moment in becoming an adult and a worker. The game's silence about wealth and inequality will, Ron Lieber says, avoid discomfort in high school classes that use the game. Exactly. Avoiding such discomfort is an unstated rule of Payback and of most aids for students and families considering postsecondary education.

The best known of these aids is the "College Scorecard" (collegescorecard.ed.gov), developed by the US Department of Education during the Obama administration (see chapter 1). It organizes information about cost, graduation rate, median salary of alums after ten years, and much else, for almost 4,000 real colleges and universities. Although far more detailed than Payback, the Scorecard also encourages its users to think of themselves as discrete, classless, rational consumers entering a market. In fact, its headline message blurs economic differences by burying them in a (dubious) average: "On average, college graduates earn $1 million more over their lifetimes than high school graduates."

The College Scorecard has been consistent, then, in heartily recommending college as a good economic choice—by implication, for *everyone*. Through 2017–18, its home page further obscured the facts of inequality by announcing, "You could be eligible for up to $5,920 for free in Pell grants to help pay for college. **No repayment needed!**"—with no mention of what might make the homogenized "you" eligible or ineligible for a Pell Grant. This federally sponsored "aid" undermines itself by failing (as in the Payback model) to note how few high school seniors apply to either community colleges, Ivy League schools, or faraway residential colleges. Family income powerfully limits choice when it comes to kids attending college, as it does when nonwealthy families consider any big-ticket item, like a new home, a new car, taking a vacation, putting on a wedding, or even going to a restaurant.

The third and last claim on the home page came in the form of a question: "Did you know almost 40% of undergraduates are 25-years-old or older?" The subtext here: if you failed to make the economically sensible decision when you finished high school, it's not too late to correct your mistake. The page accented the meaning of rational choice by putting "$1 million more" and "$5,920" in by far the largest type size on the page—and in greenback green.

The information in the College Scorecard's financial aid section was helpfully specific, and also (not so helpfully) reassuring: "most people" can get loans, regardless of age, race, or field of study; lenders will want to know your income, but it won't disqualify you; the loans are "affordable." To be sure, that depends on many factors that the Scorecard slides past, from how much spare wealth your family can mobilize for your education and how much you will actually earn upon graduation and through the rest of your working life (which of course remains unknown), to how "average" earnings for chemistry majors differ from those for film or accounting or education majors, to the lower accessibility and earnings of some tech careers to women. You might also wonder, when you sort the 3,983 colleges according to the percentage by which their alums' salaries after ten years exceed those of high school graduates, why everyone didn't chose MIT or Harvard or one of the other schools whose graduates earn over $90,000 or more ten years out; or why any savvy consumers at all would have chosen one of the hundreds of institutions near the bottom of the list, whose bachelors' degrees pay off with starting salaries of between $15,000 and $25,000. That a fair number of those institutions are rabbinical or evangelical colleges hints that some applicants choose colleges for reasons other than payback. A larger number of the low-payback colleges are on or near Native American reservations, or in Puerto Rico, which fact may suggest another kind of take on groups for whom college is and isn't "affordable."

Understandably, the Scorecard is silent on such differences. Inequality is a historically rooted condition, incurable societally by individual acts of achievement or consumption. Payback and the College Scorecard do not proffer political guidance. The College Scorecard would be excoriated or removed from the internet if it did. Of course, privileging the market is itself a political act, laden with ideology. From another side, if guides like these did discuss the limits on what a buyer can achieve through a purchase, that might even help students make *economically* sensible choices (like not applying to for-profit universities).

Just as different phrasings of a pollster's question yield different results, small changes in the question, What is the return on investment in college? can strongly affect not only what specific studies are undertaken but also their scope and their political valence. That question leads into a tangle of issues about causation, and to address them in a way that would approximate scientific experiments, researchers have had to define the "treatment" precisely. The receipt of an earned bachelor's degree provided one definition, unambiguously differentiating a pool of high school graduates who received the treatment "college" from a pool who did not. But at a cost: Proceeding in this way made college a black box. What goes on inside it (courses taken, fields studied, instructors' abilities, students' academic efforts, sports played, clubs joined, internships undertaken, love's labor lost or requited, and so on) obviously could foster knowledge, skills, work habits, emotional growth, and the like, all of which, on one hypothesis of human capital theory, compose what makes some graduates worth more than others to future employers—a million dollars more. Also, a very general definition of "treatment" obscures the possible effect on earnings of going to one or another type of institution (small or big, public or private, selective or open in its admission policy, religious or secular, vocational or general). Investigators are of course interested in that, too. In many hundreds of studies, they have peered into the black box, looking for more specific causes of high earnings than "college." (More about that in the following section.)

But even as that inquiry went forward, centers like the one at Georgetown were circulating the vague and misleading idea of the *college* premium, as opposed to (say) the *economics major* premium or the *school of pharmacy* premium. Policy makers like Obama's secretary of education, Arne Duncan, their voices amplified by the president of the United States, were advocating "college" for everyone as the bringer of high individual earnings and of growth in national productivity. And crowds of young students were committing family funds or borrowing tens of thousands of dollars in expectation of big returns on their investments—with very mixed outcomes at a time when economic inequality approached a historic high and college completion set a new record.[6]

This mainstream way of framing the college premium tends to leave out another likely cause of economic success or the lack of it. Almost nobody denies that events and conditions shaping young people's lives before the college-or-no-college fork in the road may affect their lifetime earnings. Indeed, some events that happened or some conditions that obtained even before they were born are good predictors of their eventual wealth and incomes. For example, were their grandfathers princes or paupers? Tycoons or convicts? Black or white? Investigators have been less diligent in framing hypotheses and analyzing data to test commonsense responses to questions of that sort. Had they begun with the question "What makes some people more prosperous than others?" as their guide, factors other than "college" would naturally have figured more centrally in their inquiry.

But setting the agenda for research and theory in a way that lifts college education out of its social context and isolates "college" as a *generic or undifferentiated investment*—a factor in an equation—does not eradicate social and historical factors and forces. It leads analysis back toward their inclusion, albeit less directly. Next is an example of how that happens.

What Kind of College?

Trouble begins straight off with melding all US colleges and universities into just plain "college." That move satisfies the methodological requirement that a "treatment" be clearly specified; doing so allows use of some large databases. But it also results in adopting several unrealistic assumptions. The pertinent one here is that choosing to enroll at college X and complete a bachelor's degree there is equivalent to an investment in studying at college Y. Such misrepresentation is a form of ideological or political manipulation in that it invents a false aggregate called "college" to support the claim of a universal college premium, which only some graduates of some institutions may claim. The postsecondary field is an enormous terrain stratified by type of institution as well as by class, gender, and race. Unequal access, learning experiences, facilities, curricular offerings, and outcomes are the actual features of the stratified "college system" built and functioning (think community college versus Ivy League, residential college versus commuter campus, historically Black college and university versus predominantly white university, small liberal arts school or women's college versus state flagship, proprietary and religious college versus secular). Researching this actual hierarchy would complicate simplistic and misleading claims for a generic college premium available to all while also foregrounding the social inequalities that institutions represent and reproduce.[7]

As noted in chapter 2, for the past twenty years, it has been a commonplace that going to college paid off with a million dollars more in lifetime earnings than did just finishing high school. Some universities advertised the education they offered as if the payoff were a guarantee; a few insurance companies marketed student loans on the same premise; lobbyists and politicians based their policy recommendations on the received wisdom of the million-dollar premium, which was widely circulated by the College Board. To be sure, controversy already surrounded it, especially when cited as an argument for policies that would enable everyone to get a college degree.[8] And skepticism was warranted by the simplistic analysis on which public discussion often rested: most critically, measurement of the payoff compared average earnings of all college graduates with earnings of their contemporaries who went straight to work from high school. But colleges and universities differ, and lumping them together as undifferentiated providers of a uniform commodity—college education—is not a move that promises clarity or promotes equity.

Yes, "college" can serve as a uniform "treatment" for purposes of economic analysis, but as things are in United States, college manifests itself as a few thousand institutions that provide a wide variety of offerings, experiences, and outcomes. A bachelor's degree from the for-profit University of Phoenix (with its online programs and its hundred or so campuses and centers) counts as "college" for purposes of measuring the college wage premium. So does a BA from Alverno College, a Catholic institution in Milwaukee with 1,400 undergraduates. So does a BA from Brooklyn College, awarded for two years of courses at Borough of Manhattan

Community College followed by two upper-level years at Brooklyn, over a total of nine elapsed years from start to finish at these City University of New York campuses. What confusion results from leveling out differences across such a medley of institutions, and thus implying that what takes place inside the black box doesn't really matter? What if a college degree leads to job market distinction only if its academic address is from a top-100 college or research university? From a different lens on culture and the college premium, perhaps just the fact of having gotten through all the obstacles, requirements, deadlines, and tests on the long road to a degree signifies that a graduate has the work discipline so prized by employers in general? Further, given that white students enter and graduate college at higher rates than do students of color, what if achieving the degree sustains white privilege by filtering dark-skinned applicants from the premium job market?

These are some of the obvious problems circulating in the black box of college in society; scholars of education and human capital have of course addressed them. Perhaps the simplest or most direct way of doing so would be to determine whether alums of universities that educate well earn more than graduates of universities that educate less well. But how to build an experimental framework around that contrast? Not only is it too vague, but there are also deep disagreements about what constitutes good education. In addition, the project of measuring the wage premium carries with it the tacit assumption that a good education earns its recipient a lot of money. So it yields a circular argument: check out the earnings of graduates, and you will know which schools offer good educations. Scholars have tried to escape the circle by finding an independent measure of quality. Although ranking and bunching colleges and universities in tiers has become a predominant activity since *U.S. News and World Report* began doing it in 1983, the proliferation of rankings and of disagree-ments among the journalists and experts who produce them disqualify them as predictors.

How about comparing tiers defined by something more concrete than reputation? For instance, California's public universities that award the four-year degree are divided into two unequal systems. Ten campuses, including Berkeley and UCLA, make up the University of California (UC—tier one), whereas California State University (CSU—tier two) comprises 23 campuses and several centers. The systems have separate ad-ministrations and budgets and missions. UC has the edge in material ways that are likely to affect its reputation and its ap-peal to applicants. It spends more per student and its students have smaller classes on average, a lower dropout rate, fewer years to graduation (and thus to whatever wage premium awaits graduates), fewer years paying tuition, fewer hours working for pay while in college, less student loan debt. It also has higher admission standards than CSU, and it admits a smaller percentage of those who apply. All these measurable attributes of the top tier might well make a UC education, in spite of its higher tuition costs, a better financial investment than a CSU education. To look at it from another angle, em-ployers could be measurably more willing to hire, pay well, and promote graduates of a first-tier university. Economists Alan Benson, Raimundo Esteva, and Frank S. Levy have shown that a UC degree in fact *was* a better investment for 18-year-olds beginning college in 1980, 1990, 2000, and 2005–10. The differ-ence was a few percentage points a year, enough that young people would have been significantly mistaken to think they would achieve the same large return on their investments in "college" at a second-tier as at a first-tier university.[9]

Disaggregating "college," as many studies have done, puts in doubt the value of guidance to young people and their families about the payback of getting a bachelor's through a single dollar amount. Presumably, most people get that the high number is an average, not a guaranteed result, as are figures showing that graduates of top schools earn more than those with less illustrious degrees. But a high school senior may not grasp more specific, practical implications, such as that if they go to a second-tier university, they may take on a greater risk of financial distress (in particular, crushing debt and bankruptcy) than they would by choosing a top-tier school. Nor are they likely to know that the actual return is well beneath the glitzier numbers in wide circulation.

Benson, Esteva, and Levy show those glitzy numbers to be best-case estimates that depend on unrealistic assumptions. For example, (1) "risk neutrality": most studies do not take into account the risk of financial distress, or families' differing abilities to survive hard times, or differences in their aversion to risk. On the other hand, studies do generally assume (2) that students who begin college go on to finish their degrees and (3) that they do so in four years. But in fact, only a few highly selective institutions come anywhere near the 100 percent completion rate for first-year enrollees.[10] And fewer than half of all American college students earn bachelors' degrees in four years. Another common assumption disputed by Benson and colleagues is that higher earnings for graduates result solely from what they learned in college, or from employers' biases in favor of college grads (the "sheepskin effect") or from both. But obviously, college grads entering the job market do bring with them marketable knowledge, skills, and capabilities that they acquired before college or apart from formal schooling.

Such as intelligence. Most university admissions offices seek and favor smart applicants. To the extent that they succeed in enrolling such people, their alumni will differ from others in the same age cohort who went to work straight from high school, not only in having college educations but also in having high IQs, SAT scores, and the like—and probably in being more academically curious, more ambitious, more mannerly, more skilled in studenthood.[11] It follows that the high earnings of those graduates ten or forty years later cannot be an economic return just to "college." This problem is thunderously obvious. College premium enthusiasts tend to overlook or minimize it.

Could "college quality," at least if based on rating or tier, be the wrong concept to use in explaining why some groups of colleges have higher economic payoffs than others? Attempts to explain earnings differences in this way have not in fact come up with strong and consistent results.[12]

A narrower and more easily measurable feature of colleges—selectivity in admissions—turns out to be a better predictor of lifetime earnings. For example, in 2003, people who went to "very selective" schools were earning, ten years after graduating, about 11 percent less than their counterparts with degrees from "most selective" and "highly selective" colleges; those from "selective" colleges, more than 13 percent less; and those from "less selective" or "non-selective" colleges, 21 percent less, according to Dirk Witteveen and Paul Attewell in "The Earnings Payoff from Attending a Selective College."[13] Given the intensely competitive scramble for admission to top colleges, it's perhaps not surprising that the winners of that contest keep on succeeding in other competitions. But, in the context of an inquiry into how study at one or another class of college predicts earnings, the finding is odd.

Fixing on selectivity as a predictor reduces "college quality" to a single feature, omitting many others (e.g., up-to-date facilities, distinguished faculty, the social capital gained from networks of graduates and peers) that would seem likely to result in a good education and a career advantage. To be sure, theorists of return on investment must define the "treatments" they study with precision. Selectivity meets that criterion nicely, by relying on hard numbers: the percentage of applicants a college accepts, for instance; or the median high school grade point average of its first-year students; or their ranking among high school classmates; or their average SAT scores; or a mix of all these (as in *Barron's Profile of American Colleges*). The precision ensures that treatment groups are objectively similar, not skewed by the prejudices of investigators or expert raters. There can be no dispute about which 25 (or 50 or 100) American colleges are most highly selective if selectivity is defined by such numbers.[14]

What's peculiar is that the gain in precision effectively changes the subject. "Quality," so measured, no longer refers to the resources, practices, and traditions that universities deploy in educating their students, or to what and how much students will have learned by the time they receive their sheepskins, but to a fact about brand-new students before they attend any classes or have their first meetings with faculty advisors—that is, before they begin their studies. How could that be so, if the underlying premise is that "college" teaches something that gives graduates an edge in competing for high earnings? The colleges most likely to yield a return on investment, then, are the colleges that select the most successful students for admission.

My aim is not to figure out what kind of college provides the best return to investment; rather, it is to propose that merely formulating the issue that way means entering a maze of theoretical and methodological detail while losing track of urgent concerns about education and well-being that propelled the inquiry in the first place.

The question, What makes some people better-off than others? points a way out of the maze. Think about selectivity from the perspective of a high school student and family. Imagine they are planning their college admission campaign, are hoping for a good return on investment, have read and taken seriously "The Earnings Payoff," and have learned there that a degree from an institution in the most selective or highly selective group is worth 11 percent more than a degree from the next group (very selective), while the difference between its payoff and that of the third group (selective) is only 2 percent. Having already written off the fourth and least-selective group of colleges below investment quality, the family may see the second and third group as roughly equal, mediocre bets. The obvious conclusion: bend every effort toward acceptance by highly selective colleges.

That advice seems even more compelling in light of a slightly different analysis of the data that estimates the lifetime payoff for graduating from one of the very most selective colleges to be $2.1 million, compared to $1.2 million for getting a bachelor's degree from one of the almost-as-selective colleges in the next group.[15] Careful qualification is in order, but there is plenty in academic studies as well as in practical guides like the College Scorecard to fuel the conviction that although "college" is an economically rational choice, going to one of the most highly selective colleges is a far better investment, whether or not it results in an education that is good by some nonmonetary standard. Moreover, simply to have been admitted to one of the fifty or so colleges (some outside the United States) that reject more than 80 percent of those who apply puts a gold star on the successful applicant's résumé—an early signal of more success to come and a boost to the young person's confidence.

The perceived awards of acceptance by an Ivy League university or one of its compeers also help explain why selectivity is a lodestar for those high school students and their families who have the wealth to consider this option, or who intend to go into debt to secure this option, or who are pushed in this direction despite modest or low income because the child's teachers and counselors identify the daughter or son as academically advanced. This moment is a landmark on the long march toward college and explains why so many families willingly pay a high price to improve their offspring's chances of joining the chosen few. Good strategies can cost a lot: more than $40,000 a year for tuition at New York City private high schools considered gateways to a top-fifty college; $50,000 and up to live and study at one of the prep schools that have sent generations of students to the Ivies, the Seven Sisters, and such. New York families that can afford schooling of this sort have probably begun investing in it much earlier. A private elementary school is nearly as expensive as a private high school; a Montessori toddler school charges around $25,000.

Then there are the parents with similar ambitions but less money. They can hope to get their child into Stuyvesant, Bronx Science, or another of the city's highly selective, public "exam" schools. Living in a catchment district with good elementary schools is a start, though housing in such a neighborhood will be pricy. Easier on the family's bank account, but costly in time and effort, is a decision to opt your child out of a neighborhood school deemed to be mediocre and into a more distant elementary school, usually with fewer poor students and higher test scores—for example, from Harlem to the Upper West Side. Forty percent of New York City kindergartners begin their public schooling with such commutes.[16] Private tutoring (online or in person) for the citywide exam is a common additional investment—as is private tutoring during high school to prep for the Scholastic Aptitude Test. Kaplan offers such a program for $2,500. And a student following any of these routes may, if his or her parents can afford it, buy professional admissions counseling for around $5,000.

A third strategy for New Yorkers eager to get a son or daughter into one of the most selective colleges: move to a suburb with a high school ranked in the top 25 nationally, whose graduates enter the most selective colleges in about the same proportion as do graduates of the best NYC private schools and the exam schools. Figure on paying a million dollars for an ordinary house in Rye, New York, or Montclair, New Jersey (about as much as for a modest apartment in many NYC neighborhoods); property taxes for the suburban house will be around $25,000—more than for the similarly priced city apartment.[17]

Along the way, parents will have considered many other purchases that could help get their child into Dartmouth, Cal Poly Pomona, Stanford, Princeton, or Georgetown: the help of nannies and au pairs; shelves full of good books; an iPad or other e-reader; an array of other digital devices that foster curiosity and critical intelligence while also delivering immediate pleasure; dance, ceramics, painting, drama, or filmmaking lessons; tennis, soccer, lacrosse, or gymnastics; hockey or baseball travel leagues; summers hiking or biking in Europe to promote cultural and linguistic fluency; computer camp. What part of such costs should a family figure into its return-on-investment calculations if it's aiming for one of the colleges that rejects 90 percent or more of those who apply?

Clearly the real-world economics of planning for college diverge greatly from the decision as modeled in academic studies. The studies posit a fairly straightforward decision, made a year or two before the student finishes high school, on chiefly economic grounds, to purchase four years of education at a particular kind of college for a definite price.[18] In real life, families may cobble their plan together in fits and starts and may pay many of its costs over the first 18 years of the prospective college student's life—or even before that life begins if, for instance, they buy a house in a particular suburb or neighborhood, partly for the educational advantage it will confer on a child growing up there, or set up a tax-deferred college savings account for their newborn.

Would it be reasonable to locate college planning of this sort even further back in a family's past? Probably not. But to imagine grandparents and still-earlier generations having pondered the cross-generational transfer of wealth as a *down payment* on their descendants' *eventual* investments in high lifetime earnings seems a stretch. More likely, such forebears hope to underwrite the general security, comfort, and culture of the unborn, not script in detail the unborn's use of old money to sustain the prosperity and reputability of their forebears. All in all, then, multigenerational wealth building is a largely unaccounted factor in the scaffolding that lifts any child into privileged candidacy for a highly selective college. Here, social class certainly figures into the ability of any parents to construct such scaffolding, but race matters far more because white families have about eight times the median household wealth of Black families.[19]

"Reputability": education is usually a keystone in the edifice of a family's social standing; it acts as a stamp of cultivation, gentility, friends of the right sort, practical knowledge, moral leadership, deserved prominence. In the early years of the republic, when colleges were few, small, and widely scattered,[20] they played that role chiefly for local or regional elites. The connection of the Boston upper class to Harvard is the most familiar example. In general, early colleges prepared young men for the ministry, for law, for public life, or for the genteel pastimes of the already rich, rather than for the hard work of *earning* riches on which to build a gentleman's life and found a distinguished family.[21] Pre-Jacksonian colleges were "conceived and operated as pillars of the locally established church, political order, and social conventions,"[22] not chiefly as pathways to well-paid employment.

Beginning in the last quarter of the nineteenth century, those sleepy colleges finally grew and coalesced into the national system of higher education that reached maturity after World War II: the universities at the top with their broad and stable array of departmental disciplines, first-year composition ("freshman English") as the sole universally required course, undergraduate curricula of introductory courses followed by upper-division major classes, the four-year degree, masters and doctoral programs, extensive facilities for and support of research, scholarly requirements for faculty members, bureaucratic layers of administration, and all the rest. Some of the old colleges became such universities; some stuck with undergraduate education, preparing students for postgraduate and professional degrees or for other paths to the professional-managerial class. This system emerged to serve predominantly white, male students from privileged homes, becoming in its evolution an aid to good earnings and (often) satisfying labor. (The undergraduate student body would not be 50-50 male-female until 1980 and is still overwhelmingly white; community colleges did not become a national tier of mass higher education until about 1970, after a decade of nationwide two-year campus construction.)[23] The multitiered postsecondary system provided the organized knowledge, expertise, and managerial know-how that corporate capital required.

Education at an old college retained some of its traditional connotations, too: walking across the quad and up worn stone steps to lectures in ivied halls, membership in social clubs and networks, a glow of connection to history, the satisfaction even years later of telling people where you went to college, the familiarity of its name on your résumé to the job interviewer at any firm where you might seek a job, the message its brutal rejection rate sends to such an employer about your distinction.

Attractions such as these ambiguously conjoin social with economic advantage. For instance, most of the Rockefellers were and are rich; many of them have gone to Harvard. But the durability of such links tells more about the family's social habits and desires than about its plan to give later younger generations an edge in competing for highly paid jobs. Harvard and wealthy families like the Rockefellers mutually empower each other's distinction. The power elite display distinctive markers of several kinds that signal status and authority. Distinctive academic addresses are purveyors of high-value knowledge (cultural capital), while their names on diplomas confer highly regarded status symbols (social capital) that graduates and families can deploy to secure advantages. Advantaged graduates, in turn, enhance their alma mater's endowment (economic capital), while their prestigious names on buildings they finance further enhance the institution's reputation (social capital).

This is one way hegemony works in higher education, but it also says something about Harvard's admissions practices. Although no group of applicants can count on breezing into Harvard, an applicant with at least one parent who went there is three times as likely to be admitted as one without. In recent years, around 30 percent of Harvard undergraduates have been legacies.[24] And a great, great, great-grandchild of (say) John D. Rockefeller would no doubt have an advantage in applying there, even without benefit of a Harvard parent.

Such hypotheticals do not imply a conspiracy of the rich, but rather suggest how power and wealth work to reproduce themselves, embedding affinities of feeling and desire that saturate institutions and endure across generations. Like that generalization, many ideas sketched out in the past few pages rest on observation and conjecture, not economic research. Admittedly, it would be difficult or impossible to test some of them, using the strategies and methods developed by social scientists to study the outcomes of education. In any case, a thousand separate but related investigations of the return on investment in tuition at a Montessori toddler school, in a private tutor, in a home in Rye or Greenwich would require an army of economists. Furthermore, I suggest that family strategies for education are not assemblies of discrete or random moves. Nor are they easily parsed as portfolios of investments. They are integrated into whole ways of living, guided by a variety of wishes and principles, *including* economic gain but *also* respectability, taste, social connections, good citizenship, enviable display of wealth, political and cultural leadership, power over others, and much else. Such systems of custom and action may be messy, troubled by contradiction, often unconsciously chosen. They can stretch across generations, both in fact and in imaginative reconstruction—as in much do-it-yourself genealogy. They modulate with broad historical changes. They may wither or dissolve.

To sum up: the argument of this section began with the question: What makes some colleges better economic investments than others? The answer of social scientists rests on two plausible hypotheses: (1) a good education teaches knowledge and skills that employers will reward; and (2) a good college or university is more likely than a mediocre one to provide a good education to its students. Selectivity in admissions is better as a predictor of earnings, especially if we draw a sharp line between the few *most* highly selective US colleges and all the others.

But this is a puzzle: if the effectiveness of colleges is best predicted by qualities that students have before they begin undergraduate studies, how can their extra earnings be a return on investment in college? Another question deepens the perplexity: given the difficulty of gaining admission to the Ivies and their ilk, and the intense competition to do so, how much do parents invest in that project even before they make the first down payment on college tuition?

A lot. But parents who have the money to advance their children's chances in this way are plainly paying not just (or even primarily) to invest in high postcollege earnings for those children. They are paying for many things that add up to a family lifestyle and position, a network of wealthy or professional and managerial elites, a way of life freighted with social meaning. And that outlay can reach back not just to the future student's birth but to earlier generations. The term "investment" seems less and less apt as we widen the historical and social lens in this way. College education begins to look more social and political. The question, What kind of college is the best investment? seem less central than the question I pose as a thought experiment at the outset of this chapter: what makes some people *well-off* and others not?

Social scientists may reasonably counter that they abstract from complex reality a quantitative model in order to learn deeply about it. A reasonable reply to that reply is to ask what is gained and what is lost in the modeling, and how well the understanding that emerges from the process of abstraction serves individuals planning their educations, or policy makers seeking the greatest good for the greatest number of their compatriots. More specifically, how useful is the knowledge yielded by studies of the college wage premium in guiding young people as they decide whether to head for college, come September, or to head directly for the job market? And how useful is it as a guide to legislatures, government agencies, and foundations in deciding whether to spend more money or less on broadening access to college education?

My critique is skeptical about big claims for the practical use of most research on this subject—not, however, skeptical about the idea that useful knowledge as to the economic results of higher education is in principle closed off to the kinds of inquiry economists conduct. I've drawn on several mainstream studies, and I end the chapter by citing another, which models the relation of college education to earnings without downplaying social complexity: a fairly recent working paper subtitled "The Relation between Family Income Background and the Returns to Education." Human capital economists have not generally found family income to be a significant cause of high lifetime earnings and have detached it from the focus of their interest, college education. In other words, they have made college the *treatment* and have taken *lifetime earnings* as the *outcome variable*, and *controlled for* family income, along with many other factors. The authors of this paper take *family income* as the treatment and *return on education* as the outcome. Complicating the equation in this way brings it a little closer to modeling the multiple and interacting causes that pervade social life and produces the findings that the authors call "startling."

Specifically, Timothy J. Bartik and Brad J. Hershbein of the W. E. Upjohn Institute for Employment Research compared the college wage premium of individuals whose families' earnings had been low enough to qualify them for the National School Lunch Program when the children were of high school age, to the college premium of those whose family earnings had been above that threshold. Not only did children from relatively prosperous families gain more dollars by having gone to college than the poorer kids; the richer kids' lifetime earnings were above what they would have earned without college by a higher *percentage* (136 percent) than what kids from poorer homes gained by going to college (71 percent). If that conclusion survives critical examination and is confirmed as a cause-and-effect relation by later research, it will mean that as post-secondary education continues to become more widespread, it "can actually increase earnings inequality."[25]

Also, on some plausible assumptions about the economic future—for example, that most new jobs will be relatively unskilled and low paid, that there will be less work for people and more for robots, and that Congress will not create welfare measures to make such an economic system tolerable—the college premium could turn into a college penalty, as it already has for many young grads with high debt. Put another way, going to college would then be an economically *irrational* choice for working-class youth, made worse by the politically irrational choice of delegating control of our collective future to billionaires.

Social scientists would do well to follow up on Bartik and Hershbein's central finding, and on some of the authors' explanatory conjectures. It's no surprise if teenagers growing up in working-class or poor families experience family practices, "neighborhood . . . and peer influences, [and] school quality" that limit their hard and soft skills, their social networks, and thus their chances of landing good jobs later on, independently of whether they earned bachelor's degrees or just high school diplomas. But it would be big news in scholarship on this subject if "childhood poverty . . . affects the return to [college] education . . . over the whole career" for those who do make it through college. That would mean that the painstaking search for earnings-generating elements in the black box of "college" has been seriously misdirected. It could turn attention to how individuals, families, and social classes seek prosperity.

That is not Bartik and Hershbein's aim in this paper. But many of their more detailed findings point that way: for example, that almost all of those whose returns on investment were in the top 1 percent grew up in the richest sliver of rich families; that people from richer-than-average families turned their educations into high earnings was attributable to their previous financial advantage; that the "college premium" was largely a return on investment for completing degrees beyond the bachelor's, which of course is required for admission into professional and business programs; that whites and men had more robust college premiums than African Americans and women; and that those children from the very poorest families who managed to get college educations had very high college premiums compared to the rest of those who came from other families with below-average incomes.

The authors left the testing of hypotheses that could explain such matters to future research, some of which they planned to undertake themselves. They do briefly mention a number of causal possibilities, such as the edge that children from wealthy families have in competing for admission to highly selective colleges, along with other advantages I've labeled "social." These precollege advantages should of course be considered investments if one is following that line of thought. In the analytic framework I recommend, they look more like cultural capital, social capital, and class privilege.

Chapter 4

Education for Jobs and Careers

In discussing what makes "college" a good economic invest-ment for young people, I have barely touched on what they actually *learn* as college students that might help them land highly paid jobs, win promotions, and succeed financially over their working lives. Nor do most of the many studies I've discussed examine with much care the education that hap-pens in college. Why might that be so?

My main interest thus far is in the different, though related, question of how the social backgrounds of students and work-ing people influence their eventual prosperity. For example, in the previous chapter I draw attention to what students, their families, and others had done before the young aspirants regis-tered for their first college class: how their parent(s) raised them; the thirteen or more years of pre-, primary, and second-ary schooling that led up to college; the unequal resources that families could put toward improving their children's chances of success; and what earlier generations had done to seek wealth, social standing, and culture and to pass along those advantages. That emphasis on precollege investments follows from the hypothesis that families and groups with at least moderate wealth, social standing, and cultural resources are at an advan-tage over others with less in securing and improving the lot of their inheritors, and that "college" is more a strategy they can use in that project than a stage their son or daughter must pass through to learn things that will pay off in eventual earnings.

Few social scientists who have debated whether a bachelor's degree causes prosperity in later life or merely correlates with high earnings have framed the inquiry in the way I just did, or launched it from the question of what makes some people well-off and others not. Starting from questions about human capital and ways an individual or a society might invest in it, they don't explore the payoff of a family's wealth, social standing, culture, history, or other characteristics that might conveniently be bundled together under the heading of "class."[1] That's because human capital theory is about making choices in free markets to maximize one's well-being, not about finding ways to take advantage of unfree markets and in the process normalize them. However, an unexamined contradiction is that greater economic choices for labor in the job market risk lessening management's control of employees. When the demand for labor is high and the choices for employment expand, as for some during the COVID pandemic, workers can more easily walk off lower-paying, unsatisfying, or oppressive jobs in an optimistic search for better ones; when working hours and conditions are abusive, employees in a burgeoning job market not only can quit more securely but can stay put and go on strike for more flexible and hospitable terms of work.[2] Thus, human capital theory, which assumes that more educated and skilled workforces generate more revenue for owners and more prosperity for the nation, also equips employees with assets enabling them to sell their labor elsewhere on better terms, when conditions permit. Human capital theory, then, situates the college degree and the college premium in an aspirational myth that there is a free market system in which everyone has a fair chance of winning.

Dressed in this aspirational myth, human capital theory asserts positive potentials for management and labor as well as society from developing skilled and educated workforces.

The questions foregrounded by the theory also steer research toward the study of specific decisions and acts, such as completing high school or going on to law school after college. With some methodological straining, such choices can be represented as investments, from which enhanced lifetime earnings are a return. Needless to say, it would be ironically revealing to formulate class privilege as parental capacity to invest accumulated assets (wealth, culture, connections) in the next generation's status.

One advantage of human capital theory is that relating college costs to benefits is conceptually straightforward. That helps in explaining the appeal of the theory as the foundation of an inquiry enlisting hundreds of investigators and stretching across several decades. Another methodological appeal of this strategy is that "college" can be precisely defined (usually as attainment of a bachelor's degree), and earnings precisely quantified, enabling scholars to develop rigorous mathematical techniques and put them to work on enormous databases, the census chief among them.

To be sure, in addition to these practical advantages, there were also, in the Cold War university, clear political and professional *costs* for social scientists who might have wanted to study education as an arena of class formation and conflict. Thus, reasons of very different kinds joined to favor the study of "college" as a monetary investment for the consuming individual—and, for the state, as a commitment that would foster economic growth and thus improve the lives of rich and poor alike. This liberal view of schooling as universally beneficial to all classes in society (originally asserted by Horace Mann) was challenged by the campus movements of the 1960s and after, when millions of young people disrupted the status quo, which had opened higher education to them, by protesting the Vietnam War and militarism, racism, women's inequality, authoritarian schooling, and homophobia, among other causes. "College," apparently, may not only be an instrument for advancing human capital societally and a wage premium individually for some graduates, but also a site of critical social thought questioning the status quo and generating mass opposition. These ideological outcomes do not easily appear in the quantitative metrics of researching a "college premium."

With "college" as the focus of scholarly attention, and earnings as a routinely measured outcome, more complex influences on prosperity tend to show up in the analysis as either (a) competing possible causes, for which the investigator must control; (b) selection biases that threaten to contaminate random assignment; or (c) choices made before, after, or apart from college. The most prominent examples of (a), competing causes, are race and gender. Everyone knows that people of color earn less than white people, and women less than men. What part of the college premium, if any, should be counted as a reward for being white or male, rather than for getting a bachelor's degree? Other examples of (a) include age, place in the birth order of siblings, parental education, distance of home from college, ambition, industriousness, and extroversion, before even getting to such factors as height, slimness, conventional attractiveness, most of which social science properly declines to take up.

Ability is at the heart of (b), selection biases contaminating random assignment. If the group that went to college had unobserved abilities that would have won them good jobs and salaries even if they had ended their education with high school, "ability bias" (as it's called) would then have nullified the strategic benefits of random assignment.[3] Among abilities, intelligence (as measured by IQ, SAT, or other tests) is clearly linked both to college going and to job performance and, probably for that reason, has been studied a lot. Qualities such as ambition, industriousness, inventiveness, coopera-tiveness, and respect for authority could appeal to employers but are harder to define and measure.

An important example of (c), choices made apart from going to or preparing for college, is the choice to study for an advanced degree after finishing college. The MA, LLB, MD, PhD, or JD each has its own wage premium—a perplexing matter because graduate and professional programs by and large admit only applicants with bachelors' degrees, so that some part of the college premium can be attributed to the eventual award of an MA, MD, PhD, or the like. Obviously, earning an advanced degree is not something that happens in college. Neither do other factors that may correlate with life-time earnings, such as one's eventual professional occupation, one's region of employment, or the trajectory (up, down, flat) of the GDP, or gross domestic product, at the time of one's graduation and labor market entry (which are social-historical factors influencing occupational wage levels).

In short, then, besides these complicating factors, it seems peculiar that scholars asking whether college leads to high earnings have devoted so much thought, time, and effort to factors *other* than college education itself, or to what learning on campus takes place to enable future success. That owes in part to the pursuit of methodological convenience and look-ing for causality in social action without experimenting (un-ethically) on human beings, and instead using data collected for other purposes. And in general it reflects human capital theory's commitment to framing people's actions as choices in a free market, and those choices as investments. But I think it only sometimes helpful to see routine choices as efforts to maximize utility (i.e., as investments), and I see the idea that "college" leads to high earnings as only one factor in a complex bundle of causes, most of which are not features of a college education. From this standpoint, the time and intellectual effort scholars have dedicated to separating "college" from the other factors might have been better spent on figuring out how the whole bundle works—or, to drop that metaphor, what part education plays in reproducing and modifying the social order.

In effect, the research urges individual students and their families to invest large sums in a bachelor's degree but provides few clues about which educational packages and which practices of learning activate the mystery element(s) that will bring prosperity. For those who make public policy, the moral of college premium studies is even cloudier: sure, fund more access to college, but should we do so without knowing which ways of doing it are most likely to increase economic growth? Without knowing what combination of mystery elements, lodged in the minds of more college graduates, will reconfigure the whole American workforce to make a future economy more productive? Policy makers untroubled by this puzzle can express the high-minded faith in education voiced by the recent American presidents cited at the beginning of this book, and (understandably) welcomed by university officials: faith that college enriches individuals and the nation.

Of course, some politicians and journalists disagree; the Tea Party movement resisted paying for education along with most other public services and entitlements. But faith in the economic benefits of college persists even among many who don't want governments to pay for it. Therefore, strategies abound for shifting its costs elsewhere: Raise tuition. Help students borrow money. Or—driven less by desperation and more by ideology—turn higher education over to private businesses. Universities run for profit multiplied early in the twenty-first century. Widespread corruption and predatory business plans led to stricter regulation of them during the Obama presidency, put many into bankruptcy, and sharply reduced their share of the college market. The Trump administration unsuccessfully tried to revive failing proprietary colleges.[4] The Biden administration returned to Obama's emphasis on public higher education, bundling college outlays into the omnibus "Build Back Better" proposal, which abandoned ("college for all") free tuition at community colleges.[5] However, Build Back Better, even in its final, greatly reduced form after a year of constant negotiation, could not win majority support in Congress, thanks to resistance by two conservative Democrat holdouts, Senators Joe Manchin and Kyrsten Sinema.

In addition to these practical and political difficulties, uncertainty about just what makes college pay off is intellectually embarrassing. Consider the two leading hypotheses about why college alumni earn more in the long run than do high school graduates. First, an important hypothesis for human capital theory has been that college-educated workers are more productive than others (hence worth more pay) because they are better able to understand new information and put it to use, and that the central benefits of undergraduate study are not specialized bodies of skill and knowledge but skills of literacy and numeracy, and the abilities to think critically and creatively, to reason analytically, to solve problems, and to communicate well, especially in writing. Students in many different programs of study at institutions of different kinds develop generalized capabilities such as these, along with dispositions such as cooperativeness and perseverance and habits such as efficient time management and quick learning from instruction, that make them effective on the job. Colleges do not directly teach these kinds of knowledge, but students acquire them, internalize them as an unarticulated curriculum of practice, put them to good use at work, and thus satisfy bosses, who reward the college grads with pay raises and promotions. The part of their education that boosts their earnings is a mystery only because it is distributed across many academic subjects, not flagged in most course descriptions, and not held out as a reason for going to college in the first place.

That sounds plausible to many corporate leaders, advocates for higher education, and political influentials. But some scholars have called it into question recently in the most fundamental way, arguing with a good deal of evidence that colleges do a bad job of conveying the tacit curriculum to students, and most students do a bad job of learning it. For instance, in *Academically Adrift*, sociologists Richard Arum and Josipa Roksa offer a wide-ranging critique. Its central claims bear directly on the first hypothesis above, that bachelors' graduates are paid higher salaries than those with only high school diplomas because college instills literacy and problem-solving skills that enable more advanced work. Disputing that, Arum and Roksa claim that the first "three semesters of college education . . . have a barely noticeable impact on students' skills in critical thought, complex reasoning, and writing"; and that 45 percent of the more than 2,300 students in the study made "no statistically significant gains" during their first two years of college in "critical thinking, complex reasoning, and writing skills."[6] If undergraduate study endows students with so little of what employers value in a hire, then paying for college is like tossing a coin into the fountain and wishing for the best; or, at best, it is a very wasteful and oblique way to acquire skills that could be purchased cheaply by getting one or more certificates—in water purification, say, or cardiac sonography, or some other directly marketable skill.

A second difficulty in fitting human capital theory to the college premium has to do with the labor of learning. Invest $50,000 in a diversified portfolio of equities, bonds, and real estate, and you can pay no attention to it (other than risk adjustment) for 40 years without penalty. Invest in college tuition, and you must study a lot or a little for the first four years or more. Where, in the formula for return on investment, do economists fit the doing (or shirking, or counterfeiting) of that work? It can't be part of the gainful labor forgone in order to do college. It does not seem analogous to buying tickets for entertaining experiences like concerts, cruises, or sports events. Undoubtedly, some undergraduates would do for satisfaction and pleasure alone the academic work needed to put college on their résumés, but by and large, students seem to regard it as obligatory, onerous, to be discharged with as little pain as possible.

Arum and Roksa report many student comments like this one: "I hate classes with a lot of reading that is tested on. . . . I rarely actually do reading assignments or stuff like that, which is a mistake I'm sure, but it saves me a lot of time."[7] Such candor may be unusual, but the behavior it describes is less and less rare. In 1961, for instance, 67 percent of full-time undergraduates reported studying more than 25 hours a week; in 1981, the figure was 44 percent; today, it's 20 percent.[8] Various changes may combine to explain this one. I'll mention only that through the 50 years spanned by those figures, grade point averages have stayed about the same, so that, as one author puts it, students have refined the "art of college management" to new levels, "controlling college by shaping schedules, taming professors, and limiting workload."[9]

Arum and Roksa endorse the hypothesis, dubious to me, that since the payoff for a college credential "is the same no matter how it was acquired, . . . it is rational behavior to try to strike a good bargain," getting the credential as one would buy a big-screen TV on Black Friday at a good discount.[10] Without adopting that cynicism, I do infer from the ethnographies Arum and Roksa cite (and from innumerable anecdotes from colleagues) that many students consider the academic labor they do to earn a college degree as, precisely, labor. Why not do as little of it as possible? Bryan Caplan takes this version of rationality (and the cynicism) a good deal further, especially in his proposals for getting through Princeton.[11] He is an advocate of my second hypothesis: the college degree is what Joel Spring called "a sorting machine," enabling the college premium though "screening/signaling."[12] Hypothesis 2 asserts that there are other ways and places to acquire employer-desired skills, knowledge, dispositions, and habits. These include elementary and high school, as well as family upbringing, children's books, summer camp, church, friends, the internet. Hypothesis 2 proposes that *before* college, some children learn a lot more of the tacit curriculum than others. Those in this academic fraction are also likely to apply for admission to college, along with a million or so of their less prepared peers. So college admissions offices screen a vast differentiated body of young people, culling those who lack qualities essential to being both good students and good employees. If the students make good on that prediction, they will have a bachelor's degree on their résumés. Employers understand (consciously or not) that colleges have already performed some of the hiring task, namely, the initial screening of candidates followed by four or more years of requirements for which the degree and transcript certify successful completion. More efficiently still, employers can *require* that applicants obtain and submit proof of a BA or BS before applying.

Signaling is a variant on this hypothesis: the bachelor's degree on your résumé shows that you had what it took (perseverance, powers of intense concentration, analytic quickness, etc.) to pass thirty-some courses, most with no direct connection to the job you're applying for, and that you can probably handle it well. In this vein, the bachelor's degree can be thought of as confirming a job applicant's capacity to put up with demands on their time and attention often not academically related to work, among them a corollary of persistence—patience with tedious demands and a compliant tolerance for authority and its routines. Thus, the wage premium is not the result of a hard-to-identify understructure of learned capabilities; rather, "academic success is a strong signal of worker productivity," as Caplan puts it. He notes that, on this view, the labor market "doesn't pay you for the useless subjects you master; it pays you for the preexisting traits you signal by mastering them" (3). This is of course a tendentious formulation. Nobody ever thought the job market, aside from a few niche occupations, paid wage premium for what applicants just out of college had learned about Greek philosophy, music history, number theory, Irish literature, Melanesian kinship systems, or African history. Even for undergraduate study of "useful" subjects such as economics, physics, and computer science, the premiums are relatively small. Those hoping for employment directly related to these subjects should probably get PhDs and hope for academic jobs, scarce as those are.

Vocational programs are a different matter. But then, a major in accounting, pharmacy, nursing, or physical therapy is a kind of *credential*, an entry pass into a narrow range of careers. Good wages over time for accountants, pharmacists, nurses, and physical therapists are not a reward for simply finishing college. The leading explanations of the return on investment have to do not with the immediate usefulness of academic courses but with the bundle of skills.

Erase particular academic subjects from the picture, and clearly hypotheses 1 and 2 are compatible. The wage premium for completing a bachelor's degree could owe *both* to having learned ways of analysis and reasoning that employers value *and* to what the degree signals, to wit: college admissions officers recognized in this applicant qualities that would make them a good student, and the student has confirmed that recognition by graduating.[13] No contradiction there.

The embarrassment lies in overlooking the fact that, with hypothesis 2, after the young person and family have invested a lot of money in a college education and degree, the monetary return on that investment derives basically from getting into college, not from anything that happens there beyond amassing the required credit hours and completing a major—that is to say, not from education. In short, the two hypotheses are at odds on a deeper level of understanding. On hypothesis 1, high earnings are a payoff for things you learned in the interstices of the curriculum while working hard on courses. On hypothesis 2, the earnings constitute a delayed payoff for where you came from, whom you grew up with, and who you became before you went to college.

Please accept that flashy simplification, in place of a reprise of chapter 3. My claim there as well as here is that retracing the moves economists and others in the human capital tradition made as they theorized and studied the return on investment in college education reveals serious gaps and contradictions. How can we know that there is a big return on "college" but not know why? How can it be that colleges of different types with a wide variety of aims all transmit some of the mysterious, fungible knowledge? Bear in mind that if policy makers and academic leaders who favor the economic rationale for higher education did know the answer to that question, they would surely have pressed for a core curriculum to separate precious secrets from academic froth and teach the secrets more efficiently.

Looking at hypothesis 2 from the investor's side opens up an even more surreal vista—plus an irresistible temptation to irony: if being screened by and admitted to Stanford or its equivalent is the signal employers are looking for, the applicant who passes that test might wish to enjoy a *Wanderjahr* or two (or four) instead of actually going to college. Their parents, too, might take a year off for mind-broadening travel, pay for it out of the quarter-million dollars they'd put aside for their daughter's (redundant) college studies, and still have a bundle left for an early graduation present—say, a year's rent on the one-bedroom apartment she will need in San Francisco when she begins working for the six-figure salary Wells Fargo or Google offered her, based on the signal from Stanford.

This system might be formalized by adapting an ancient rite of Oxford and Cambridge. Both universities grant a "complimentary" MA to anyone who earns a BA with honors, waits a few years, and pays a small fee. No further studies or exams are required. The Oxbridge MA apparently works pretty well as a signal: a survey a few years ago found that only 62 percent of employers realized its award did not call for any additional studies or exams. Supporters of a bill to end the practice said the complimentary MAs gave Oxbridge grads an unfair advantage in the job market.[14] But Parliament preserved an ancient tradition (and demonstrated its faith in the signaling hypothesis) by letting the bill die without a vote.

Were American universities to adapt this plan, they could reasonably charge an administrative fee of, say, $1,000, for each complimentary bachelor's degree and mail out sheepskins after a decorous interval. That small investment would save the admitted student's family up to a quarter of a million dollars and spare the student four years of laborious coursework. Eliminating most college costs in this way would of course greatly increase the size of the college wage premium, with results too complex to consider here.

Universities, too, would benefit mightily from such a plan. True, they would lose more in tuition than they would gain from the small administrative fee. But that loss in revenue would be trifling by comparison to the reduction in costs. Administrations could eliminate all adjunct faculty positions; end new awards of tenure; assign tenured professors to the instruction of graduate students or to research that would bring in additional corporate dollars; eliminate unprofitable professorships on the historically accepted rationale that permits abolition of programs with no students; and convert dormitories into condos and lavish athletic centers into luxury spas. Finally, the plan would with one stroke achieve many conservative goals, chief among them, deeper tax cuts; less spending on public goods; shrinkage of the administrative state; virtual elimination of a large, self-organized profession; outsourcing to for-profit companies the university's role in preparing the young for corporate employment; and shutdown of an arena for dissident learning (i.e., "political correctness") among young people.

I've spun this modest proposal out of the signaling hypothesis. Caplan takes it seriously as a reductio ad absurdum of the mainstream doctrine that college enriches the individual and the society. That's why the subtitle of his book *The Case against Education* is no joke: *Why the Education System Is a Waste of Time and Money*. He guesses that something like 80 percent of the college premium owes to signaling. If so, students who, once admitted, actually do the expected work to earn their degrees have been tricked by the system into wasting a lot of time and money. His dismissal of education without a dollar payoff as a "waste" situates him comfortably within the large majority of experts, politicians, and pundits who think the wage premium to be (a) firmly established and (b) the main rationale, along with increased GDP, for college education. This belief prevails across a wide spectrum of influential liberals, centrists, conservatives, and libertarians such as Caplan, who professes "a strong moral presumption against taxpayer support for *anything*."[15]

Although a conservative or libertarian can love it, the signaling hypothesis is close in some ways to the egalitarian, socialist critique I am trying to inject into the free market discourse of the college premium, by posing questions like: What makes some people *well-off* and others not? What does the income of one's family have to do with later earnings? Why is the selectivity of one's alma mater such a useful predictor? What do parents do to propel their offspring into Ivy League and other prestigious schools? Whose wealth, prestige, and power are sustained by these arrangements?

The idea of signaling may easily be broadened in response to such questions. For instance, a bachelor's degree from a prominent university on a job applicant's résumé may signal to employers that the university's admissions people had seen in the applicant not just cognitive abilities and polished work habits but a suitable blend of deference and independence, conformity overlaid on self-assurance, good manners, fluency in the "elaborated [speech] code" of the middle class,[16] ease in a context of privilege, liberal views on "social" issues, a network of similarly inclined friends, and maybe even a portfolio of shared tastes, aversions, vacation places, leisure activities, and the like. In short, "college" may signal attitudes and ways of interacting with people that have deep roots in social class and race and that resonate with employers who (consciously or not) want employees like themselves. Even shallow roots in the professional-managerial class signal ambition to rise and quickness in learning how.

Working-class youth, too, learn specific ways of talking, negotiating school, and interacting with teachers on the way to finding their place in the capitalist order. In a classic study, Paul Willis explored how the process worked in England, in the 1970s. Research continues in the United States, too, on how middle- and working-class families and networks teach children different moral rules and strategies for getting on, and how those play out in tracking American kids through school on divergent class pathways.[17] Learned ways of being a good person then figure in the screening of students for college and employment. I would speculate that relation of class to education and labor, combined with a sharp decline in the number of secure and decently paid jobs for high school graduates, may be adding fuel to the fires of populism that now burn in the United States.

Needless to say, an extension of hypothesis 2 into this territory of racial, gendered, and class-inflected socialization would not only strain the standard research methods but take debate on the college premium well outside the usual borders of mainstream economic thought.

Marketable Learning

I've questioned the historical assumptions and reasoning of reputable scholars in economics and sociology who agree that there is in the United States a reliable return on investment in college that has held up through economic cycles and, in the long run, increased.[18] Further, in this chapter I explore a persisting vagueness in the literature about *what* knowledge undergraduates gain that explains the dollar payoff of their degrees, and a nagging uncertainty about whether their prosperity does in fact owe very much to human capital accumulated in college.

Scholars have looked for the payoff either of abilities acquired before college or of marketable abilities acquired by most graduates from the *totality* of their studies and experiences in college. What about the payoff of studying particular subjects? Until recently, much less research took up that question. Of course, everyone knew, informally, that fresh engineering graduates in, say the 1970s, found higher-paying jobs at Boeing or Control Data than classmates with education majors found in the K–12 teaching job market. But what scholars sought, working as they did within the framework of human capital theory, was to calculate a student's return to investment in a certain level of educational attainment—high school diploma, associate's degree, bachelor's degree, and so forth—not in a package of skills that a TV network or a chemical company or a commercial bank could more or less directly count on to raise profits.

A conceptual and methodological obstacle stood in the way of adapting human capital theory to that inquiry: signing up to major in chemistry or philosophy was not an investment. Students at the point of choosing majors had already committed to an investment in college. They would pay no extra tuition and forgo no additional wages in choosing one major over another. So, to investigators in this line of research, differences between the lifetime earnings of engineers and dance majors or schoolteachers, if any, were merged in the conceptual melting pot of "college." College graduates earned more or less on their investments for many reasons that the method does not disaggregate. Choosing to measure the college premium via the median lifetime earnings of all students in all fields was a convenient and precise maneuver that, however, rendered many specific causes invisible.

In recent years, many public research universities (including, for instance, all of the flagship campuses of the Big Ten

Conference) have tried differential pricing for different majors. For some, the aim is to attract more students to subjects
that serve the state's economy or, in the case of community
colleges, the employment needs of local businesses. At least
one governor (Rick Scott in 2014 in Florida) proposed making tuition a bargain for STEM, business, and health majors in
order to channel students away from "economically wasteful"
liberal arts subjects or to make them pay extra for the "self-
indulgence" of studying, say, anthropology or philosophy. But
for most universities that have put different price tags on
different majors, the main purpose has been to increase support from tuition revenue for departments or schools such as
engineering, whose programs cost a lot to run, rather than
have students in humanities and social sciences subsidize
their classmates in STEM fields.[19]

How schemes of differential pricing survive remains to be
seen, but the impetus behind them is clear enough: generous state funding for public universities is erratic or gone for
good, and higher education has to find other means of support. Putting their "products" on sale in markets will be the
main strategy for many. As Dale A. Brill, the chair of Governor Scott's task force in Florida, put it, "The higher education
system needs to evolve with the economy. People pay taxes
expecting that the public good will be served to the greatest
degree possible. We call that a return on investment."[20] That
formulation indicates how the language of human capital theory has emerged from journals of economics and settled into
public thinking and debate about education.

Even though the marketing of undergraduate majors is still
a relatively new and irregular practice, correlations between
students' majors and their later earnings are so obvious, and
so obviously pertinent to the question of what marketable
knowledge comes with a bachelor's degree, that scholars have

examined a lot of data and drawn conclusions from it. While it would be even more complicated than examining the chain of causality of the college premium to speak of a *major* premium, the Georgetown Center on Education and the Workforce did a comprehensive survey focused on the "economic value of 171 specific majors," running from $29,000 for counseling psychology to $120,000 for petroleum engineering.[21] The list includes majors such as psychology and history that are on offer at most institutions, as well as rare ones like military technologies or cosmetology services, for which a student planning to major in one of those would have had to narrow his or her initial choice of colleges considerably. The most popular major, business management and administration, is far from universally available and accounts for 8 percent of all bachelor's degrees. At the other end of the spectrum, pharmacology, soil science, nuclear engineering, and a number of others on the list of 171 each account for fewer than one-tenth of 1 percent of graduates. Comparison of economic value across ill-assorted bundles of required and elective courses would seem to be of dubious use to scholars trying to figure out how knowledge acquired in college pays off in the labor market, or to students puzzling how to organize their college plans and working lives. For instance, a pharmacology major comes with a clear idea of what sort of work its possessor may now do and for roughly what pay. It is—along with state licensure exams—the ticket of entry into an occupation and the foundation of a career. But a major in business management and administration can lead to work of many kinds; to large and dependable or meager and precarious earnings; to a career or a series of disconnected jobs. The new grad might enter an elite executive training program at McKinsey and Company, say, with a high probability of being rich at age 50, or take a flyer (with borrowed capital) on starting up a marijuana business in a state that has just legalized the drug.

There's no core knowledge in a business major that might predict such a range of career choices and outcomes. Business is an eclectic field of undergraduate study *and* of employment. It looks still more eclectic if merged with the catchall "general business," second in popularity with 5 percent of all majors. Others from the list of 171 whose content overlaps with these two are business economics, international business, miscellaneous business and medical administration, and seven other less "miscellaneous" majors in the study's business group: accounting, actuarial science, hospitality management, human resources and personnel management, management information systems and statistics, marketing and marketing research, and operational logistics and e-commerce. Some of these put students through coherent and job-related curricula. But, taken as a whole, the business group is a mixed lot. The 25 percent of American undergraduates who major in business are acquiring widely disparate packages of knowledge. It's doubtful that most of those students based their pick on good information about what they'd be learning, about the kinds of employment business majors find, or about which combination of specific courses might take them to their desired careers and earnings. *What's It Worth?* gives only a modicum of guidance.

It does speak usefully to some related questions of pragmatic importance for students and families. For instance, what percentage of workers from a particular major "end up" in the corresponding occupation? At the high end, 82 percent of nursing majors are "health professionals." At the low end, only 7 percent of studio arts majors sculpt, paint, draw, animate, photograph, throw pots, or the like for a living. No surprises there. What might be more surprising to prospective college students and their parents is that few majors, even in STEM fields, land and settle as many as half of their graduates in the corresponding occupations. None of the 17 majors grouped together under "engineering" majors does so, in spite of the vocational results one might expect from programs called aerospace engineering, geological and geophysical engineering, and biological engineering, or from older specialties such as chemical, civil, electrical, mechanical, and mine engineering. Students who major in math, computer and information systems, computer programming and data processing, computer science, or information science do arrive and work in the corresponding occupational group, "Computer Services," but still at a rate of only about 50 percent.[22] To be sure, that's a lot higher than the 7 percent of would-be artists who turn their passion into an occupation or a career.

Most art majors know in advance that the odds against such a career trajectory are long. For that matter, not all engineering majors expect or even want to be engineers for their working lives. Some hope to become high-level managers—and do, as the most common undergraduate degree among Fortune 500 CEOs has long been engineering. Business is in second place, though, if size of the graduating cohort is taken into account, economics leads all majors as a prelude to running a big company.[23] The same holds in other fields: chemistry majors do not necessarily plan to be chemists, nor anthropology majors anthropologists; the latter are close to art majors in the poor odds of such an outcome. The occupation in which the highest percentage of humanities majors settle is management—presumably not upper management, since their median salary is $47,000. So a first- or second-year undergraduate whose chief goal in choosing a major is to qualify for immediate entry into a particular line of paid work might consider nursing, with its 82 percent safe landing rate, or elementary education (66 percent). I would conjecture that most students majoring in those fields began college knowing their occupational destination and its likely financial payoff (nursing, average; elementary education, low), while most other students, especially those in an arts and sciences field, know and accept that completing their majors does not give them a pass onto a particular career track.

Nor does majoring in most fields accurately predict earnings. The salary gap between the 75th and 25th percentile of petroleum engineering graduates in 2011 was $107,000; between the same percentiles for elementary education majors, $19,000; for nursing majors, $32,000. Business majors fan out into a wide range of incomes and of occupations; the gap between the 25th and 75th percentile for the whole business group was $50,000. This is another bit of practical knowledge the study offers to undergraduates about to declare majors. Business majors are taking on more uncertainty; elementary education majors, less. On the other hand, prospective business majors may not know the percentile implications of their choice, but they do know that a few of them will earn millions of dollars a year and that most will earn more than those who majored in education. People headed for K–12 classrooms can be sure they will not outearn business or tech majors.[24]

Another, closely related finding of the study also highlights risk and security: the employment rates of graduates. Of majors in geological and geophysical engineering, military technologies, pharmacology, and school student counseling, 100 percent were fully employed. Unemployment was and is lower on average for college alums as a whole than for high school graduates, but the difference between 0 or 1 percent for a number of fields and the highest rate—16 percent for social psychology—might dissuade some from majoring in it, or in one of the other subjects with unemployment rates

above 10 percent: nuclear engineering, educational administration and supervision, and biomedical engineering.

The fact that, in 2011, unemployment was high in those
two engineering fields points to a general dilemma for students who pick their majors with the aim of launching dependable careers in particular occupations: the job market
can change abruptly. A field that looks like a good bet when a
student enters college may be overcrowded four years later.
Consider that, from 2008 to 2018, the number of jobs in
biomedical engineering grew by 72 percent (from 16,000 to
27,600). That's far more rapid growth than the average for all
occupations—a compelling reason, presumably, to major in
that field. Yet in 2018 the University of California alone was on
track to produce 5,500 biomedical engineers in the coming
decade, nearly enough to fill half of all the jobs added across
the entire United States. A biomedical engineering newsletter
from the department at UC Davis made a sensible inference:
competition for the "new jobs will be fierce. We need to make
sure we continue to accept only the top students, and to provide them with the highest-quality training." Department officials did not add a cautionary note: that top students might
be wise to consider other fields.[25] Students flocked into the
major; programs overexpanded. One result was an 11 percent
unemployment rate for biomedical engineers.

For prospective nuclear engineers, the context of choice
was markedly different. Job growth from 2006 to 2016 was
close to the average for all occupations, 13 percent. The forecast for the following decade was only 4 percent, fewer than
700 new jobs. Nuclear engineering was a small field with a declining rate of growth.[26] The virtual halt of nuclear power
plant construction after the Three Mile Island disaster (1979)
and the gradual retirement of old plants were among the obvious causes. A rise in productivity may also have weakened the

job market. Students planning their major course of study and nuclear engineering departments eager to attract them lagged in responding to this downturn in the job market. In consequence, nuclear engineers also had an 11 percent unemployment rate.

A booming field, a stagnant field; an unwelcome surprise for graduating seniors in both. My explanations are conjectural— but the general point is not. Labor market conditions can change in four years; a student who picks his or her major as a safe path to steady employment in a particular field may find that the path has narrowed by commencement time. The same risk holds for a student whose main goal is high pay. Base your choice of major on recent information from the Bureau of Labor Statistics and from surveys like *What's It Worth?* and the next few years may show your research to have been wasted. Just the everyday working of supply and demand may radically change the job market by the time you enter it with your bachelor of science degree—especially in a small field like biomedical engineering.

A more extreme example is petroleum engineering, where employment has wildly fluctuated for 40-some years, causing even wilder swings in the number of undergraduate majors; it rose from nearly 2,000 in 1973 to 11,000 in 1983, dropped back to 2,000 by 1998, then rocketed up again to 11,000, in 2015.[27] The lagging supply of new graduates leading up to 1983 and 2015 lifted beginning salaries for new petroleum engineers and drew thousands more students into the field than—as it turned out—were needed to meet demand.

Supply and demand for specific kinds of labor are not autonomous forces. The ups and downs in enrollment correlated neatly with political and technological disruptions. In 1973, the increasingly militant Organization of the Petroleum Exporting Countries put a cap on extraction of oil from the enormous reserves of the Middle East, plus a few countries in Africa and Asia. The shortages of fuel and escalation of gas prices (with long lines at gas stations) that immediately ensued in industrialized societies, especially the United States, prompted a rush to find and extract more oil there. Hence the need for more petroleum engineers, and the flow of college students into that major. As usual, the companies chased profits until the profits vanished. Then came an (inevitable) oil glut in the mid-1980s, lower oil prices, cuts in production and employment, futile job searches for many new engineering graduates, and a steep decline in majors. After a decade and a half of level undergraduate enrollments in petroleum engineering, the cycle began again at the end of the 1990s, driven this time by the surge in development and use of fracking technologies. Then another boom, a recession, a collapse in oil prices, and a belated shortage of jobs just as the very large class of 2015 brought its fresh credentials to market. A year later, the Bureau of Labor Statistics (BLS) was predicting a jump of 15 percent in employment for petroleum engineers by 2026, among the highest increases for any occupation. By 2021, the BLS had reduced its predicted wage jump from 15 percent to 8 percent for petroleum engineers in the 2020s, cutting in half the optimistic prediction that may have guided some undergraduates to major in this field.[28]

Peter Cappelli describes a similar process in information technology, a broader area of study than the three engineering specialties just discussed, and not academically tied to a single major: "The recession in 1991 hit IT especially hard, and students in college switched to other fields. That smaller cohort graduated into the mid-1990s IT boom, helping push salaries way up. College students saw that and switched into IT, and many of that now much-larger cohort graduated right into the middle of the post-Y2K slump in IT starting in 2001.

As wages fell and also as IT work began being outsourced to India, college students moved into other fields," bringing about smaller IT cohorts and lower salaries in the late 2000s.[29]

Cappelli does not emphasize, as I do, how supply and demand may be abruptly activated or slowed by events and trends outside a particular job market or academic discipline. But he implies that idea by pinning the stages of his IT story to the Y2K frenzy (compare Three Mile Island), to economy-wide booms and busts such as the recession, and to decades-long historical projects of capital such as globalization, which propelled the outsourcing of specific labor to where it could be had at the lowest price and with the least organized resistance from workers—as with the export of IT jobs to India. The last-mentioned sort of profit-driven move often results in the lowering or elimination of academic qualifications for jobs. Cappelli notes, as I do above, that "most IT work is currently being done by people without IT degrees. . . . Having taken a course in the latest hot programming language may make you just as employable as someone with a run-of-the-mill IT major" (49–50).

Capital has repeatedly found new ways to deskill and degrade labor, both before and after 1974, the year of Harry Braverman's classic book on labor in the Fordist regime installed globally then and accelerated afterward by aggressive neoliberalism.[30] Since Braverman published *Labor and Monopoly Capital*, monopoly capitalism has morphed into the jumpy, high-risk, internationally integrated, digitally connected system we now inhabit: automated factories deploying robotics; assembly of cars from components sourced from around the world; anti-union warfare carried out by special union-breaking firms in court and by militarized police at the factories; plans for electric cars and trucks with no drivers; flexible work schedules in a gig economy. As in sending baristas home after the morning rush but keeping them on call during the slack hours, with no pay; or hiring part-time staff with no benefits and no guaranteed hours or shifts; or setting up call centers in Bangladesh to assist customers of local Wi-Fi providers in Portland, Oregon, or Portland, Maine, and most everywhere between and beyond. It's an ingenious, hydra-headed system of degradation and dispossession compared to scientifically managing unskilled labor or skilled workers on assembly lines, as manufacturing corporations relied on early in the previous century.

A small but important way of reorganizing and cheapening labor is implicit in the subject of this book. When companies in effect outsource the training of future employees to academic institutions, they are shifting much of its cost to students specifically and taxpayers generally; the corporate transfer of labor training costs to the public (tax levy budgets) and individuals (students paying tuition, and often their families as well) is smoothed by widespread acceptance of the idea that college is above all an investment for individuals and for the whole society and that raising the return on that investment is in everyone's best interest, thereby promoting the idea that everyone should pay. That idea, a given or common sense in American folkways, has in the past fifty years also driven a long shift in undergraduate studies away from liberal arts toward courses and majors that promise more directly to brighten the occupational outlooks of graduating seniors. Seen from this angle, the knowledge that enhances a student's future earnings loses some of its mystery. Vocational training builds human capital transparently while diminishing the critical social thought potential of the disfavored and defunded humanities.

Shifting labor-training costs in these ways also aided the anti-tax movements of recent decades, enabling legislatures to cut state and city support for both lower and higher education, and pressuring trustees and administrators to trim expenses. Since the largest constant expense in a school, college, or university budget is its payroll, administrators have naturally looked for ways to shrink it. Their main strategy in higher education has been to casualize the labor of postsecondary teaching—to the point that, now, 75 percent of faculty members are contingent. Imagine the *teacher* of that course on a "hot programming language": most likely a low-paid part-timer with few benefits, little job security, and no prospect of tenure. Then complete the picture: the students who take the hot course could also be part-timers, looking to earn a certificate or at most an associate degree, not a BS. The corporations that hire these students will save a lot on their salaries, compared to what they used to pay graduating IT majors. And they may be able to employ many of them as piece workers operating "from home." Note that this arrangement degrades both the IT jobs and the work of learning to do them. Such companies are also doing their bit, inadvertently perhaps, to lower the college premium. And universities have, since the postwar boom crested, helped illuminate the pathway to a post-Fordist, neoliberal workforce.

Casualization and contingency on the job; occupational and vocational tilting of curricula; part-time teaching and learning on campus. This transformation of schooling to fit the neoliberal economic and social order has come about through the efforts of many and diverse historical agents, not working on a common plan or under central direction but with an outcome that is nonetheless consistent and organic. The term "hegemony" comes to mind.[31] This particular hegemonic process, in revising the connection of higher education to employment, has both driven colleges to highlight the vocational uses of their major programs and made some of those programs less dependable as tracks to particular occupations.

This contradiction is only apparent: employers themselves know pretty well what kinds of workers they need to hire next year and the year after, but, for reasons just summarized, not so well what skills they will need five years out. There's a real contradiction at the top level of management and on boards of directors: CEOs and others who decide the futures of corporations want universities to provide a stream of graduates with the skills and habits needed in specific occupations, but they also want—the profit motive *makes* them want—to modify the structure of production so that it requires fewer workers with lower skill levels, so as to reduce the cost of labor in production.

In short, universities have added ever more vocationally oriented majors to their curricula (and made some of the old ones *look* more vocational). However, even those do not dependably land their graduates in career tracks that provide security and high pay, as claimed in talk of the college premium, though the confusion is less hurtful because picking a major doesn't usually require investing extra money beyond the already-billed tuition. When Carnevale and his coauthors say their research "finds that different majors have different value," unsavvy students may reasonably infer that majoring in X will procure them the earnings mentioned. Or they may reasonably take the authors' claim to have established "the economic value of 171 specific undergraduate majors" as a kind of price list. The blurring of cause and correlation is evident here: "The highest earning major earns 314 percent more at the median than the lowest earning major at the median." "Earns" is flatly causal: we're being told that majoring in X brings about the specified wage premium. "At the median" takes back the implication of cause. The comparison cannot show cause unless it holds across all percentiles—for example, it fails if (as is the case) petroleum engineers earn $189,000 at the 75th percentile, and counseling psychologists $42,000.[32]

Strict causality aside, a student who signs up for one of the specifically occupational majors has a better chance of landing and staying in the target field than one signing up for philosophy or fields like economics and art history that can be credentials for entry into a variety of occupations. That correlation suggests (but does not prove) that much of the learning behind the wage premium is specific to the more vocationally angled majors that are informally required for entry to some occupations, and is closely tied to necessary credentials in a few. For instance, a BA in accounting is a common requirement for prospective certified public accountants, in addition to passing the CPA exam; most registered nurses have majored in nursing at a four-year or two-year college and taken courses (e.g., anatomy) required for entry into the profession. Learning in such formats does not play well for human capital theorists as the general knowledge at the dark center of "college." But neither does it provide evidence for the signaling-screening hypothesis: a bachelor's degree on the résumé of an applicant for a job in petroleum engineering may send the right signal about intelligence, persistence, conformity, and so on, but that signal won't get them past the initial culling without the correct major.

Universities have in recent years added many more specifically vocational majors than before "to persuade applicants and their parents that they can provide a job at graduation," as Cappelli puts it. He mentions "the Bakery Science degree program at Kansas State, the Turf and Turfgrass program at Ohio State and Purdue University, Fire Protection Engineering at Oklahoma and other schools, and Economic Crime Investigation at Utica College."[33] A degree in turf management (the usual name for this field) qualifies one for groundskeeping jobs at golf courses, athletic fields, public parks, private clubs, and the like. But so does a certificate, or a high school diploma plus on-the-job training.[34] It would be interesting to know how much of an edge a graduate of the Ohio State or Purdue program has, over a high school graduate with experience, in applying to be head greenskeeper at a country club. Median salaries are around $30,000, so a sophomore looking for high lifetime earnings is unlikely to choose this major—or to get much of a wage premium for his or her initial investment in college.

Do economists need a causal hypothesis other than signaling or human capital to explain the outcomes of vocational majors such as turf management? There's a lot of conceptual slippage along the interface of education and occupation. The practice among some investigators of controlling for *occupation* in studies of how one's major affects earnings makes things worse. Obviously, many students decide what kind of work they would like to do for a living, then pick a major accordingly. If causality is at work between major and occupation, it runs in both directions.

That problem is less vexing if, instead of looking at 171 majors (or a much larger number if it includes turf management and the like), we aggregate them into conventional families; for example, (1) STEM, (2) business, (3) health, (4) humanities and social sciences, and (5) education. Each one connects to a number of occupations, with a good deal of crossover. A graduate from any of the five groups might become a manager, consultant, or teacher. But, pretty consistently, STEM graduates have the highest earnings, followed by business majors, and on through the other groups as sequenced above.[35] How might that affect the choice of a pragmatic first- or second-year student? It could certainly tip them toward a STEM field. But of course, at this point in their educations, many students lack the prerequisites for entry into math, chemistry, computer science, electrical engineering, or the like. And, famously, the trail to medical school has been unfriendly to females and students of color, or has been too steep in costs or too academically unappealing for many who set out to be doctors—especially when it passes through math in high school and biochemistry in college. Still another hypothetical: students hoping to be public school teachers may decide against that career when they imagine what it would be like to support a family on the median salary of an education major.

These facts and conjectures about undergraduate majors do not point to a simple conclusion about what, if anything, makes college pay off. In fact, the analysis weakens both of the two leading hypotheses: augmented human capital and signaling or screening. Let's grant for the sake of argument the Georgetown study's claim that some majors pay off handsomely, in fact more than enough to account for the whole college premium, whereas others lead to low-paid, precarious employment. In that case, it's plausible that the knowledge and skills that make college pay off are those that prepare some students for entry to lucrative occupations, thus making up for the failure of others to earn more than they would have by going to work straight from high school. And there's little or no need to posit a mysterious remnant of knowledge derived from the tacit curriculum that augments the human capital of all students.

As for screening: its importance diminishes if employers are tossing the résumés of job applicants who lack one of the qualifying majors into the reject pile without further consideration. A famous academic address on a degree is unlikely to seal a hire if an employer requires certified scientific or technical training. A distinctive college or family name reaches a limit of signaling when specific expertise is in play, unless competing candidates differ in race, gender, or network of references.

Still, adding a cause, perhaps called "vocational credentialing," to the list of contenders to explain or justify the college premium seems necessary, though the premiums and penalties for choices of major do not falsify either of the two main hypotheses or provide a unified theory to supplant or subsume them. Here are some hypotheses to help conceptualize the facts we have:

Theory 1. The soft, vocational credentialing acquired by completing *some* majors, as diverse as engineering, nursing, and education, gives access to a first job in one's chosen occupation, with a good chance of going on to a professional career.

Theory 2. (a) Having completed a bachelor's degree in *any* field signals to an employer that a job applicant has demonstrated the intelligence, capacity for hard work, cooperativeness, and so on required for a regular job. (b) Or the degree warrants that even before that, college admissions officers have already *screened* high school seniors for qualities such as task completion, communicative competence, academic predilection, and comfort with authority and work discipline, and that the ones admitted did not invalidate the initial judgment by failing out, quitting, or breaking too many rules. This variant of the college premium pushes its origins to a time before whatever education (or undergraduate "treatment") happens in college, to orientations learned from school, family, and social networks. I have proposed adding, to skills, knowledge, industriousness, and so on, a quality of "being like us" in looks, manners, speech, past experience, networks of kin and friendship—in short, being from the right social class, in some combination with gender and race. For those from the right social class, supplemented by a fraction from the lower classes and from families of color identified for upward mobility

("scholarship boys" *and girls*, in a rendition of Richard
Hoggart's class-climbing identity),[36] college continues
the social construction of already-complicated but
unfinished late adolescents seeking the wage premium.

Theory 3. The college premium is a payoff for the nimble
intelligence and deep general knowledge privileged by
human capital advocates because these abilities help
college graduates do well in first (or second, third, or
nth) jobs, leading to the promotions and raises that
make them high earners over the long run, even in
fields far removed from their undergraduate majors.[37]

Step back another pace, and the picture begins to look like
this: "college" as a whole correlates with high earnings, partly
because it lumps together students whose majors count as quasi-
credentials for entry into specific occupations (theory 1 above)
with students who majored in fields that lack such standing. So
some of the all-purpose human capital that "college" supposedly
teaches (as per theory 3) owes instead to the preferences of employers for new hires from vocationally oriented programs.
Employers also prefer candidates with the good-worker habits
(theory 2[a]) signaled by completion of a bachelor's degree. To
put it baldly: the economic advantages of going to college on
both the human capital hypothesis and the signaling hypothesis
can be traced back to the kind of labor employers think they
need in order to sustain or increase profitability.

That leaves unaccounted for theory 2(b) above, screening—a hypothesis that does not credit college education at all
for the wage premium, but only *being admitted* to college, plus
the knowledge, skills, traits, parents, and social networks that
brought the newborn infant, the child, and then the adoles-
cent to that point. The value of this growing-up story at hiring
time is largely the assurance it conveys to an employer that

the applicant is of the right sort, is like us, will fit in, can be taught what they need to know to do the job well. Back in the day of the "organization man," that preference could be openly acknowledged. Now, among law-abiding employers, it probably operates from a lair deep in the class unconscious and the cave of white male denial.

My summary attributes the college wage premium chiefly to the necessities of capitalist accumulation, to the preferences and needs of employers, to systems of domination (e.g., class, race, gender, able-bodiedness), and to the dynamics of social reproduction—that is, the maintenance and adjustment of those processes systems. The politics of these priorities are evident. That, however, is not to politicize the question, What use is higher education? Mainstream treatments of that question are *already* political, though not readily perceived that way, because ideas such as the wisdom of the free market, the economic rationality behind human decisions, and the individual person as main unit of social action and of theorizing are deeply embedded in public discussion and academic inquiry. This ideology saturates talk about education and the economy, in the halls of Congress and the halls of ivy and the halls of cinderblock colleges and the halls of family homes where parents worry what's best for their kids. The college wage premium is an organic part of our neoliberal world system and has played a small part in establishing it. Regarding that global system, "there is no alternative," as Margaret Thatcher pronounced. One aim of this book is to contest that.

Chapter 5

The Payoff of College Education for the United States

The belief that investing in college is economically wise for an individual seems like common sense to most economists and laypeople. So too does the belief that public investment in higher education brings economic benefits to the whole society. The two claims are often conjoined as if to suggest that the national economic gain is the sum of the extra earnings of individual college graduates. In previous chapters, I question the first belief—of a generic college premium—at length and from various perspectives. In this chapter, I skeptically consider the second belief—that public tax outlays to higher education benefit the whole society, not only individual graduates. Along the skeptical way, I argue that national benefits do not follow so directly from individual benefits. Then, I move on to the college premium's relation to inequality.

That decisions by young people to earn bachelor's degrees cause the whole economy to grow is an empirical hypothesis but one that is hard to disentangle from ideology. It's politically comforting to believe that the financial success of individuals harmonizes with the health of the economy, especially since that harmony depends on and helps bring about the productivity that enlarges the profits of the companies employing college grads. The ideology assures its believers that no structural conflict pits workers against bosses; the two groups share benefits they have jointly achieved, with a little help from the invisible hand of the market economy and maybe some nudges from the government. Furthermore, in this way of thinking, college education for more and more people will eventually level the gross inequalities and conflicts that exist between capital and labor. That's a pie-in-the-sky outcome announced most famously by Horace Mann, applauded and questioned by many since, perhaps most soundly rejected by Herbert Gintis and Samuel Bowles's *Schooling in Capitalist America* (1976) and John Marsh's *Class Dismissed: How We Cannot Teach or Learn Our Way out of Inequality* (2011).[1]

Mann's Panglossian harmony was nicely sloganized in a once-famous claim by Charles E. Wilson, the CEO of General Motors whom President Dwight Eisenhower appointed secretary of defense in 1953, that "what's good for General Motors is good for the country." Wilson gave a corporate spin to the archetypal move of ideology wherein a dominant or hegemonic class equates its own interest with the interest of everyone.[2] But is more college in the interest of "General Motors"? Yes, in various ways. For one, as I note in chapter 4, it can boost profits for owners of businesses by outsourcing to universities some costs of preparing students to become employees.

Less obviously, expanding the university system's role in vocational training is in the interest of GM and of small-government conservatives, GM's political allies who would like to privatize many functions of the welfare state, shifting their tax costs to user-recipients reconceived as customers who buy services in markets. Mail, transport, health care, and other public services charge recipients for services rendered: why not higher education also? For-profit ("proprietary") universities became for a while a highly visible (and scandalous) example in the first decades of the twenty-first century, a brief boom that especially gamed students of color into programs which left them very deep in debt.[3] Nonprofit universities, too, have steadily added courses to their traditional arts and sciences curricula that might make a graduate more attractive and valuable to employers.

Other groups, too, have material interests in expanding American higher education. Professors and administrators obviously do. Not that their advocacy can be reduced to enhancement of their own salaries, perks, and careers; most of them (or at least some of us!) sincerely hold college education to be intellectually, socially, and emotionally valuable, apart from any wage premium it may bring about. In fact, a regular reader of the educational press and of opinion pieces in the *New York Times* might conclude that professors on average do not much care how well off their students become. Certainly, many of my colleagues at a small liberal arts university were, if anything, pleased to watch students who arrived with personal prosperity in mind rescript their life plans in the direction of art, education, or social justice—by no means taking vows of poverty but putting aside dreams of wealth and privilege. Teachers who take that kind of pleasure in their work can endorse the idea of "college for all who want it" but reject arguments for it based on expected monetary return to investment. On the other hand, for decades, millions of lower-middle-class and working-class students have enrolled in non-elite, underfunded campuses, hoping to finish with a degree that does pay off for all their time, sacrifice, debt, and tuition, which morally compels their teachers to take their students' vocational aspirations seriously.

More abstractly (and stripped of nuance), the rule of capital gains legitimacy if citizens believe that more and better schooling can repair the inequalities and divisions troubling our society (along lines of race and gender as well as class)—or, to put it as Lyndon Johnson did, that education is "the answer for all of our national problems, the answer for all the problems of the world."[4]

But the actions that might turn that "answer" into a social reality are not so obvious as the policies that General Motors and other corporations consider most beneficial for the country. The Trump administration had no trouble in understanding the most urgent wishes of GM and other capital giants—reduce taxes, shut down regulatory oversight over labor and environmental practices, generally remove encumbrances to the pursuit of profit (like filling the judiciary at all levels with pro-corporate justices)—or in granting those wishes via the tax reform law of 2017 and a barrage of executive orders canceling hundreds of regulations. The stock market chimed its approval. After Trump grudgingly left the White House in the wake of the failed insurrection of January 2021, President Biden proposed higher corporate taxes and levies on upper-bracket personal incomes so as to finance investments in education, the environment, and social services, but he withdrew the new levy proposals when corporate advocates in Congress refused to vote for his omnibus "Build Back Better" measure in 2021 or support these progressive items when put forward separately in 2022.[5]

Instead of viewing the country's needs through so focused a corporate lens, if Biden and "moderates" in Congress wanted a stronger discourse to advocate raising high-end taxes to fund investment in college education, perhaps they should have reasoned thus: the more workers who are college educated, the more productive the workforce will be, the higher aggregate lifetime earnings will be, the more goods and services workers will buy, and the faster GDP will grow. That sounds like the script for a robust return on investment—one based on the hypothesis that a nation's economic gains from having a college-educated population equal the sum of individual college premiums. However, that hypothesis is wrong. But let's trace its implications for a bit.

Proposals have been at hand for testing what a mass in-crease in college enrollments could do for individual expenses and for national income. For example, the "College for All Act," as Senator Bernie Sanders and Representative Pramila Jayapal called their 2017 bill (which morphed as it was folded into Biden's failed Build Back Better bill in 2021), originally proposed raising taxes on corporations and on the highest in-come earners, above $400,000, in order to use the resulting revenue to end tuition payments, subsidize other college costs, and compensate high school graduates for earnings forgone during their years of undergraduate study. Such a program could permit every high school graduate to enroll in college and, if able and willing, to finish college largely debt free. That distinction is worth emphasis: although the flow of high school grads into college substantially increased in the 1960s (driven in part by authoritative-sounding promises of a large college wage premium and relatively low tuition at public colleges), the growth plateaued in the 1970s, while the dropout rate remained high, college costs and debt rose dramatically, and achieving only "some college" paid off poorly in increased lifetime earnings compared to a bachelor's degree.

That's not to say that if a million more American high school seniors, acting on rational grounds provided by a "College for All Act" (which the Biden plan reduced to "community college for all" but later withdrew), were to choose college this fall than did last fall, the sum of their individual investments would be an economically fruitful investment for the United States—not to say, for example, that the $750 billion wage premium those students collectively pocket over the next 40 years would trans-late into a $750 billion boost in GDP. But one can't extrapolate directly from individual costs and benefits to their impact on the national economy. Two difficulties that arise when attempt-ing to do so will clarify what's at stake.

First, how much would this public investment cost, and who would pay? If "College for All" is to be a national program, the federal government must pay for tuition, whether through grants to individual students or through direct payments to universities and colleges. Either way, decisions must be made about which students will receive the benefit: All who go to college in the first year of the plan, even those who would have gone without the incentive of free tuition? Students who enroll in expensive private universities or for-profit colleges? Only those attending public colleges (as the Sanders-Jayapal bill first proposed)? Only those whose families' incomes are below some threshold? Or only those who attend community colleges (as Biden's plan later designated before it was withdrawn)? Any legislation will need to respond to these tactical questions in the process of determining what portion of college costs individuals will pay and what part will be taken from public moneys as an investment in economic growth for the good of all. The two are difficult or impossible to disentangle.

To highlight the point, here's a thought experiment: how might US colleges and universities respond to the sudden arrival of a million additional students, who would not have shown up there but for the new incentive? Rich, highly selective institutions like Stanford, Amherst, and Dartmouth would probably admit a few from that cohort and could easily accommodate them without modifying curriculum, building new dorms or labs, or hiring additional faculty members. They would actually save money on financial aid if, in the new, college-for-all regime, the government would now pay part of the tab for students from poor families, not only those attending public colleges.

But most of the million extra students would enroll, not at Princeton, Swarthmore, or the like, but at community colleges or, if allowed, at nonselective four-year institutions that accept most or all applicants with high school diplomas. Were those colleges simply to absorb the newcomers in existing programs and facilities, the aims of college-for-all would be defeated. Class size would balloon; instructors would have less time to teach and mentor the extant and additional students who need extra guidance; electronic resources would be stretched thin; labs and classrooms would overflow (dorms, too, at residential campuses). In short, "college" for the new students would be diluted or forced to be delivered online for lack of classroom space. Hence, in achieving college-for-all, weak public funding would make such higher education a worse investment than it had been for the new students' predecessors, who in previous decades had flooded into the new community colleges (which had opened at the rate of one every ten days through the 1960s).[6] Furthermore, its quality would continue declining through the following three years of college coursework as swollen entering classes replaced smaller graduating classes. And not only for the college-for-all cohort: their peers who did not need that incentive would also learn less of whatever it is in college education that makes for high earnings.

To maintain the quality of learning and the value of the college premium, universities would need to hire additional instructors and staff, build new academic buildings, add labs and technological systems of various sorts, and fund whatever else it would take for college to enrich the surge of newcomers as much as it had enriched earlier cohorts. In fact, the pre-Biden, Sanders-Prayapal "College for All" bill would have provided for such costs, but rather halfheartedly, saying that government funds left over after tuition subsidies may be used to increase "academic course offerings and . . . occupational skills training," the size of the "full-time instructional faculty," "professional development opportunities, office space," and "student support services such as academic advising, counseling, and tutoring." It also specified that these funds could be used to build a stadium or student center, support varsity athletics, pay "the salaries or benefits of . . . administrators," and so on.

If the federal government does not itself use tax revenues to pay for this new investment in human capital, college-for-all legislation could let each institution scramble to pay its higher bills through some combination of state aid, hikes in tuition, support from foundations, gifts from wealthy donors, loans, bond issues, or other sources—all very unequally distributed in the hierarchy of higher education. Whether federally managed, left to the decentralized, unequal positions of colleges, or a combination of both, college-for-all would not only motivate individual students to invest in their postsecondary studies but also demand further investment by universities and government(s) in the means of producing undergraduate education. These costs would be almost impossible to disentangle for purposes of deciding whether college pays off as a social investment.

The second difficulty in deriving the national return to investment in college directly from individual returns has to do with measuring payoff, not costs. Some of the benefits of college education usually listed as noneconomic in fact have monetary consequences, both for individual alumni and for the state. For example, people with bachelor's degrees are healthier on average than contemporaries who ended their formal educations before that point. Which is good news in itself, but it also sounds like good economic news: healthy grads save on medical care and insurance, and the government spends less on programs such as Medicaid. But another social return that is closely linked to health has an adverse financial outcome: students who go on to college after high school live longer than their classmates who do not. What are the economic consequences of longevity? Do centenarians, on average, keep building up their bank accounts, or do their medical and living expenses outrun their savings, leaving the government to pay nursing home costs? A complicated question, for sure. But beyond doubt, longevity raises the government's liability for Social Security payments and Medicare.

A further difficulty that muddies calculation of the social return to public investment in college is the possibility that not too many years from now a shrinking cohort of young, active workers will have to support an ever-larger army of the retired. It's awkward to read that outcome as either a win or a loss for the whole United States. Should it instead be registered as a pecuniary gain for old people and a loss for the young? What if the growing cohort of retirees cannot live adequately on fixed government incomes in an economy where prices keep rising and the cost of living is uncontrolled? What about the social costs of health care for especially vulnerable seniors should a pandemic strike, as COVID-19 did in 2020 and after, which claimed disproportionately more lives among the aged? Competing complications and interests such as these reverberate through the economic and social system. Maybe it would be more perspicuous to conceive the outcome of College for All as a redistribution of poverty and prosperity than as an undifferentiated return on investment. In an unequal society, an investment that benefits everyone may be a will o' the wisp, displacing college-for-all with "economic equality for all" as the premier policy remedy. That thought will not surprise readers of previous chapters.

Further, other modifications of the labor system could turn College for All into a dismal economic failure. Suppose the largest increases in job market demand over the next few years are not for highly qualified STEM graduates and the like, but for security guards, fast food workers, custodians, baristas, home health aides, and other occupations requiring little education beyond high school. In that case, College for All now would mean millions of graduates taking insecure jobs with low pay and not much of a career ladder a few years down the line. And if, as widely predicted, robots displace something like half of the human work force, College for All will have helped create tens of millions of unemployed or underemployed people with bachelor's degrees, as happened in the 1970s when waves of baby boom graduates overwhelmed the limited domestic market for college labor.[7] In the twenty-first century, a burgeoning gig economy and the continued outsourcing of jobs to low-wage parts of the world are moving in the same direction.

To be sure, glimmers of utopian possibility reside in these shifts: among them, perhaps, a twenty-hour work week for all; plenty of leisure time for the amateur pursuit of intellectual interests and creative talents developed in college. But since the transformation of work is driven by the needs of capital, not by the needs of labor, it will be unlikely to proceed toward such goals without an upheaval in economic relations that's beyond the purview of human capital theory, which takes markets for granted as the main arena of economic action—including the sale therein of one's labor power as a commodity. Only a radically different organization of human activities would reorganize production, as Marx wrote, enabling "me to do one thing today and another tomorrow, to hunt in the morning, fish in the afternoon, rear cattle in the evening, criticize after dinner, just as I have a mind, without ever becoming hunter, fisherman, herdsman or critic."[8] In that universe, society might decide that making college available to everyone who wanted it would benefit all without necessarily raising their lifetime earnings (in a time when all labor is socially secure and is paid living wages) and without their having committed, by age twenty, to fishing (or to petroleum engineering) as a field of study and a self-defining occupation that results in long-term personal debt and long-term uncertain employment.

But back to my less euphoric main point: given the forbidding analytic challenge of untangling what's good for the nation from what's good for some individuals and businesses (and bad for others), scholars need a way to test the payoff of investment, a method that (1) includes the whole economy, (2) plausibly is a result of education, and (3) is unequivocally positive. Other measures of "the good life" besides rising GDP do exist: productivity of workers, for instance, or per capita income. But neither escapes the charge of being good for some at the expense of others. And these alternatives are less comprehensive than GDP: per capita income is about consuming goods; productivity is about making them.

In part for such reasons, economists have generally used growth in GDP as the main measure of a collective return on investment in education. Doing so brings necessary uniformity to a tangle of data, metrics, and values. But not only does that convention leave in place other analytic puzzles, but the neat simplicity of "gross domestic product" also conveys a tacit endorsement of the ideological premise that what's good for businesses will be "good for the country," not to mention the more neutral-sounding but even more profoundly ideological premise that more is better: "Accumulate, accumulate; this is Moses and the prophets," to quote Marx again.[9] Left out entirely is the question of unequal distribution, which enwraps the question of fairness that troubles simplistic claims of: How is the GDP distributed? Who gets the lion's share of the social product generated by everyone's labor? Who claims more than they can consume? Who claims less than they need?

Presumably the advocates of universal free access to college—chiefly liberals, progressives, and socialists—don't mean to imply that a growing GDP reliably benefits all. Surely the spectacular rise of billionaires whose wealth grew handsomely during the COVID years and the resurgence of Gilded Age inequality during the past forty years of economic growth warrant concern on the point. Almost all researchers in the field are in fact concerned about inequality; for academics wanting to celebrate both higher education and democracy and hoping to see them as mutually enforcing, this is a most unwelcome return on national investment in college. Rather than economic differences leveling as higher education spread in the past fifty years, inequality has risen tectonically.

To review: any new investment in college by the nation must be more than the total of all sums spent by individuals and family members on college costs, plus wages forgone by students in their years of undergraduate study. Without new investment in financial aid, university buildings, faculty salaries, support staff, online resources, computers, and so on, "college" for the new students could yield a smaller wage premium for them and could lower the premium for more affluent, traditional students as well. The funds needed for adequate expansion of the university system must come from governments, universities, and philanthropic foundations as well as from students and their families. Given such multiple and overlapping sources of support, it's hard to know how to measure the nation's investment in College for All.

Neither is the nation's payoff on investment in college education the sum of all wage premiums harvested by individual graduates. That number could enter into the calculation, along with others such as the productivity of college-educated workers or the amount they, their employers, and the government save on medical costs because college graduates are healthier than their less educated peers. Even returns to college that look to be purely social have pecuniary consequences. For example, more stable marriages may lower the costs to government of Medicaid, welfare, even of incarceration; higher rates of civic participation by college graduates (voting, volunteering, etc.) may lower the tab for addressing social ills; smaller families of college graduates may lower housing and schooling costs. Every social return has pecuniary consequences; the lines that divide social from individual payoff and both from corporate return are blurry. Can any social return not have pecuniary consequences?

The obstacles to neatly deriving the national return on investment in college (or to all education) from the payoff to individual workers arise partly from an awkwardness in using the idea of human capital as a unified explanatory theory across a field of economic action on which individuals and groups pursue different and often-conflicting interests. Human capital theory built on a simple, basic idea: that employers use the knowledge and skills of workers, in combination with the buildings, machinery, materials, and the like that make up their physical capital, to produce economic value. They should be able to measure the success or failure of an investment in human capital just as they measure the payoff on adding to their physical capital; and they should be able to estimate in advance which kind of investment will yield a higher return. At this level of abstraction, the equivalence sounds trouble free.

How does it sound when concretely exemplified? Fine, so long as the examples are carefully chosen. A steel company could sensibly choose to spend a million dollars on a program to teach welders efficient, advanced techniques or the same amount to refit an old rolling mill so it would turn out sheet steel faster and with less variance in thickness. But the comparison works only if augmenting the skills and knowledge of the company's welders as needed is a straightforward purchase with an available million dollars, like signing a contract for the rolling mill upgrade.

Clearly it is not. There are several paths to the desired increase in human capital that the company might follow. It could reassign foremen to bring one-fourth of its welders up to the new standard each week for a month, replacing the learners with temporary hires. Or it could arrange for a squad of master welders to come into the mill and teach workers on the job. Or it could contract with a local technical college to bring the welders to its campus for instruction in the advanced techniques. Or let the old welders go by attrition and replace them one by one with more skilled people at higher salaries. As we bring more complex strategies into the equation, the possibility of usefully matching returns to a million-dollar investment in physical capital with returns to an investment of the same sum in human capital recedes. Recall, for instance, Volvo's decision to make cars in Ridgeville, South Carolina (chapter 1). The state agreed, among other things, to train new employees in its technical college system for specific Volvo jobs. Should the cost of this investment in human capital be assigned to the company or to South Carolina?

That's more than a bookkeeping puzzle: it's a challenge for economists wanting to press human capital theory into use to explain how education produces economic value. The apparently direct quantitative approach of human capital theory is not transparent in this case. The pitfalls are deep and camouflaged enough to vex inquiries into the monetary value to individuals of more or less education, as I hope to have shown so far in this book. Obviously, reframing the question for research into the economic productivity of education for whole societies brings on extraordinary conceptual challenges. In this section, I've glanced at just a few illustrative examples. Needless to say, the difficulties are apparent to economists and educational researchers who have in recent years reframed the question of whether more higher education for more people is good for US society into historical terms: whenever more American children and youth went to school and to college, pursuing their educations for more and more years of their lives, what did that change cost and how much prosperity did it yield? To address this apparently forthright but actually tangled question, I return to Claudia Goldin and Lawrence F. Katz.

American History: A Natural Experiment in Return to Educational Investment?

Goldin and Katz would probably not accept my characterizing their 2008 study, *The Race between Education and Technology*, as a natural experiment.[10] And to be sure, the building of the American republic and its educational system has been a chain of events radically different from, say, establishing the Vietnam War draft lottery which (abruptly and randomly) divided young men into a highly draftable group and a draft-exempt pool, with major impacts on their later college attendance (see chapter 2), or from Hurricane Katrina (a natural disaster that facilitated the extreme privatizing of the New Orleans public schools).[11] A project of nation building and capitalist development that evolves across two centuries is nothing like a discrete legislative act such as Congress's passage of a draft bill and the president's signing it into law, or like a few days of catastrophic urban flooding. The making of American school systems is a story replete with contending forces and historical agents. It has gone on for nearly 200 years, so far. No central authority took charge—no education czar or national board of education. There was no master plan for US investment in education. Its history involved no random assignment of subjects to treatment groups. But Goldin and Katz try to draw from that history an orderly lineup of evidence to prove or disprove a straightforward hypothesis: that "simple supply and demand specifications do a remarkable job of explaining the long-run evolution of the college wage premium."[12]

One might think about the evolution of US schooling in this way: Americans expressed individual, family, and community demands in capitalist markets; the largely unintended product of those demands led to a supply of high school and then of "college" graduates that rose and fell in lawlike ways to first lift and lower a high school premium and then lift the college premium—much as happens with pork, eggs, crude oil, surgical masks, toilet paper, or any other commodity.

To be sure, in the opening pages of their book, Goldin and Katz summarize their argument as a good deal more historically specific. In the twentieth century the United States became the most prosperous nation in the world. It also invested more in human capital, via its educational system, than any other country. This correlation was "no historical accident." Economic growth required technological development, and that in turn required "educated workers, managers, entrepreneurs, and citizens. . . . Because the American people were the most educated in the world, they were in the best position to invent, be entrepreneurial, and produce goods and services using advanced technologies. . . . A greater level of education results in higher labor productivity. Moreover, a greater level of education in the entire nation tends to foster a higher rate of aggregate growth."[13] Note the unembarrassed causal language: "no accident," "required," "because," "results in," "tends to foster."

Here's the central hypothesis of the book, simply put: "Invest in education, get higher levels of technology and productivity, and attain a rapid rate of economic growth and a higher standard of living" (2). If the general principle holds, then "rapid educational demand would also increase the demand for more educated workers at all levels. With increased demand for their services, the earnings of the more educated would rise relative to the less educated" (2). From here, it's quick work to bring the college premium into the paradigm of supply and demand: informed students chase the college premium until it becomes vanishingly small. As the costs of achieving the premium and the competition for it rise, the demand for education levels off. Then more and more choose the job market after high school, until the cycle repeats.

The domain within which Goldin and Katz apply this hypothesis is large but not all-inclusive. It holds for a particular phase of capitalist development—human capital theory is intrinsically historical. Nor does their hypothesis apply to all countries; poor ones cannot become rich just by pumping money into schools and colleges. There are preconditions— among them secure property rights, egalitarian institutions and premises, decentralized school administration and funding. Furthermore, they show that something went wrong with the nation's way of investing in human capital and with the triumph of the American Century toward its end. Economic growth slowed; inequality deepened; the movement of the college premium departed from its lawful track. These tendencies, from the 1970s onward, look like evidence against Goldin and Katz's hypothesis, and also against their hopeful expectation that policies grounded in human capital theory would bring about a more democratic and equal society, not just a richer one. Much of their book addresses these concerns.

I address them as well, after assessing the authors' representation of twentieth-century US history as a sort of collective natural experiment proving (with some glitches) the claim that education drives national prosperity through varying processes, including the college wage premium.[14] Their story begins long before the twentieth century—that is, before the time when rapid technological development became vital to economic growth. New England states prepared the legal and economic arrangements for public schools, particularly decentralized financial control and the use of taxes to fund local schools. Such arrangements "originated in pragmatic concerns of the day, and not from a recognized sense of the potential benefits" to education (118). The federal government pitched in through Jefferson's Land Ordinance of 1785, which specified a source of funding for schools in new states added to the United States and would support common schools throughout the Northwest Territory after 1803.

The movement for free schools was well under way through the early years of the Republic, with an assortment of funding arrangements. For instance, Massachusetts required towns with more than 50 families to support six months of public elementary schooling. Parents could pay extra to extend the school year for their own children. At various stages of most states' history, rate bills appeared—basically tuition payments levied on parents with children in school. Many towns had pauper schools, funded by philanthropists. The "common school revival" was a movement to eliminate rate bills and pauper schools. When it won, it reorganized the jumble of public and private that had characterized schooling in the early years into a rudimentary system in which towns paid the costs of schooling for all children other than slaves. As for postelementary schooling, early on, the wealthiest families could send their children to private academies; these were eventually superseded and folded into the new public secondary units built during the "high school movement" after 1900.

Goldin and Katz hold that "demand" was a causal force in the spread of schooling through this period, sometimes exerted by individual purchases in markets—for instance, by tuition payments from families to extend the school year for their kids beyond six months. But legislation by and funding from local, state, and federal governments seem to have been a more consequential expression of demand. Taken together, the irregular methods of funding early common schools that Goldin and Katz mention seem to me more like *public investments* than like *demand for a product as expressed by customers in a market*. Towns and the federal government paid the tab but did not buy educational services in an exchange in which prices rose and fell according to demand. Nor were towns the consumers of the educational services they funded. They bought those services for citizens and their children, presumably to advance some tacitly agreed-upon social goal. What might that have been?

Goldin and Katz advance their own answer by citing Horace Mann, leading voice of the "school men" in New England, as "ahead of his time" in arguing for free elementary education in Massachusetts on the ground that it "produced efficient workers who were productive on the job, adapted easily to new technologies and even added to them" (147). But Goldin and Katz grant that the claim was "probably more a tool of propaganda than of scientific inquiry," one "tactic" in Mann's "tireless" advocacy of "mass education." Clearly, they are comfortable in molding historical facts to fit the supply-demand paradigm. As I suggest in chapter 1, another, more characteristic rhetorical tactic of Mann was to speak prophetically of education's role in turning "a wilderness into cultivated fields, forests into ships, or quarries and clay-pits into villages and cities." This is the language of empire building, not of return on investment, either by businessmen, by the Commonwealth of Massachusetts, or by the federal government.

Aside from their brief mention of the school men, Goldin and Katz themselves treat demand for and investment in schooling by public entities in the antebellum period as growing out of a tacit agreement to foster republican values, not to prepare a labor force to make new technologies work or to provide firms with more productive workers and higher profits. Their project of reading American history as a narrative about turning unprecedented investment in education into unprecedented wealth for one nation leads them, when fitting human capital theory to the early decades of the Republic, to stretch the categories of economic analysis almost beyond recognition.

Take "investment." Colonists and their westward-expanding descendants understood that they were making financial investments. In some interior parts of New England, that was their primary or only goal. The individuals and groups that first bought land there sought to profit by taking it from its former inhabitants or, once the indigenous peoples were forced out by war or disease, buying it at bargain prices, farming it, marketing some of its yield, and perhaps selling it for a small gain when more fertile and less rocky land beyond the Appalachians became available.

For example, in 1762, the colonial government of Massachusetts sold "Plantation Number 7," the 30.9 square miles that later became the town of Hawley, to a speculator and a group of "proprietors." As these terms suggest, it was an openly commercial investment. The proprietors of 1762, none of whom became settlers, divided the plantation into 90-acre rectangles and sold them to other proprietors. After eight years of such trading, with little or no economic return, some of the proprietors took the agriculturally most promising lots for themselves and became settlers. They cleared land for pasture, plowed fields for crops, and built simple homes. Those proprietors sold the remaining arable lots on the real estate market, then drew straws for ownership of the tracts that were too steep, rocky, or swampy to farm. Noah Cooley, the builder of the house I bought, won 90 acres of such "worthless" land in the draw. It turned out fortuitously to include deposits of iron ore, which he mined and built a forge to smelt. The Cooleys became wealthy enough to add a substantial house to the original cramped, dark, center-chimney colonial in the late 1830s.

In short, the town of Hawley began its independent existence in 1762 as a speculative investment. Then for eight years, before anyone lived in Hawley or initiated economic activity there, it multiplied by a sort of financial meiosis into many smaller investments.[15] (So far as I know, the indigenous people had hunted there but wintered in more sheltered valleys.) When the first seven families of settlers arrived in 1771–72, they labored chiefly to feed, shelter, and clothe themselves and to turn wilderness into farms, until they had significant agricultural product to sell for cash income and perhaps modest wealth.

With ingenuity, perseverance, and luck, some did better— the Cooleys, for instance, with their unexpected iron ore and the skills they used to make a business out of it. A sizable minority of settlers followed that path toward a decent return on investment, managing businesses instead of or in addition to farming the land. Their ventures included gristmills, sawmills, a tannery; the manufacture of broomsticks, rakes, furniture parts, hoops, and other wood products; and a few stores and inns. This was hardly an industrial revolution; the businesses were small, technologically simple, driven by waterpower, and close in conception and use of material to farming itself.

But to say that is by no means to imply that work in Hawley and the other Hill Towns of western Massachusetts around 1800 was primitive—all execution and no conception. On the contrary, farming called for fingertip knowledge interacting in complex synchrony with reliable (if largely intuitive) conceptual knowledge—about seasons and weather, plant nutrition, animal care, fabrics, cooking and preserving food, and much else. This was the *human and cultural capital* of New England farmers (the skilled labor and know-how necessary to exploit available resources), vested chiefly in individual and family producers. Where did they acquire skills to work the land and the knowledge of how to work the land to extract its latent wealth? At work in the family home, barn, woods, and fields. Likewise, sawyers developed their knowledge as formal or informal apprentices at the sawmill, tanners at the tannery, and so on across the spectrum of the small business enterprises in Hawley. No large employers invested in, developed, or profited from this reservoir of human capital.

Nor did the work of farmers, sawyers, wood turners, millers, and the other entrepreneurs of small-town New England depend on school or book knowledge, beyond the arithmetic needed to record costs and sales in the ledger books, plus a little chemistry for those who mined and forged iron, made potash, or tanned skins. So how much explanatory power does Goldin and Katz's proposal have, that elementary *education* before and after 1800 served as a basic system for nurturing human capital, thus laying down the footings of nineteenth- and twentieth-century prosperity? Formal or state-sponsored schooling did not generate the skills needed for the primitive accumulation of wealth that served development. Primitive accumulation emerged here not from schooling or book knowledge but rather from farmers and local artisans using the tools and skills at hand to produce more than they needed for their own livelihoods and then marketing the surplus. (Obviously, the slave plantations in the South used forced, unpaid, labor-intensive means to grow cash crops like cotton, enabling that region's primitive accumulation to develop also outside the education-technology nexus.)

Still, Hawley in western Massachusetts did provide formal education for its children from the beginning. I do not know how it did so between its first settlement in 1771–72 and its organization as a town in 1792. In the latter year, it budgeted 30 pounds for schooling, presumably to hire a teacher or two. The next year it appropriated 210 pounds to build seven schoolhouses, at 30 pounds each, "fit to keep a winter school by the first of November next." This vote could evidence a strong *demand* for education, but for one well-known fact: Massachusetts had established mandatory public schooling 150 years earlier, in 1642, the first colony in North America to do so. The law required towns to provide and pay for schooling. A second law (1647) made the requirement and the penalty for violating it more specific. Can those laws be read as meeting a *demand* for schooling?

There are two serious difficulties with conceptualizing them in that way. First, the demand was articulated by people long dead when Hawley in the following century complied with their law. Second, those seventeenth-century Puritans were not by any stretch of the economic imagination legislating a demand for human capital development that would improve the productivity of workers and their profitability to employers. Their aim is vividly captured in the second law's title: the Old Deluder Satan Act. Its premise: Satan relentlessly seeks to deny children salvation by denying them the ability to read and interpret holy scripture. For English-speaking children, Satan was served by keeping them illiterate. The first law made every head of household in the Massachusetts Bay Colony responsible for teaching his children, apprentices, and servants how to read and write. The Puritan fathers, concerned that some of their neighbors were derelict in this duty, ruled in the 1647 law that each town with 50 families must provide a teacher, and that a town with more than 100 families must establish a grammar school. Hawley's population in 1790 was 539; by 1792 it may have had enough families (200) to call for two schools, surely not for the seven it built. Could its extravagance in school construction signal the kind of demand Goldin and Katz postulate?

Unlikely. A different analysis that they offer, of public demand for schooling, seems more plausible to me: that through the Revolutionary period and after, many Americans continued to value universal literacy and favor its public support, not on Puritan religious grounds but because of strong republican convictions and concerns. To put it concisely, democracy could not flourish without a citizenry educated enough to govern itself and fend off tyranny, and the historically new democracy was precarious. As Benjamin Franklin probably said when asked if the Constitutional Convention had created a monarchy or a republic, "A republic if you can keep it."[16] But I see no reason to believe that this republican commonplace fronted for a tacit conviction among citizens of the new nation that schooling would also produce efficient workers and national prosperity, or that those results were needed to keep tyranny at bay.

In terms of return on investment and its applicability to schooling and economic development in the early republic, though little data are available, we know how much the town spent on schooling early in its corporate life up to the time of the publication of the first town history: 60 pounds, roughly equivalent to $300, in 1795, rising to $900 in 1885. William Giles Atkins, the town's first historian, considered this a "uniform increase, with the onward march of progress."[17]

Despite the muddiness of the data, that sounds like a plausible claim, but rephrase the question in human capital language—What economic return on its investment had the "march of progress" brought the people of Hawley?—and the picture becomes virtually unintelligible.

Here are some pertinent considerations: The original investor in Plantation Number 7, which later became Hawley, paid 875 pounds for it in 1762; count that as $4,500 (though the US dollar would not exist until 1792). In 1886, the assessed value of Hawley's land and houses was $119,626. Inflation had been slow through the preceding period and therefore does not require much discounting of the apparent increase in value. Much more significant is the amount of that increase attributable to a century's human labor that turned forest into farmland and homes and built commercial properties. On the other side of the ledger should appear the estimated value of the shelter and sustenance that Hawley families achieved. Alongside that figure should be one for the value of marketed farm products; in 1880, hay, butter, eggs, potatoes, and corn brought local farmers just under $43,000, according to Atkins's history (37). There's obviously no way to squeeze from these conjectural numbers even a plausible reckoning of Hawley's economic return in a hundred years of ownership and labor that came from appreciation of the original investment(s) in land, how much from improvements made by its residents, how much if any from the education of its children, how much wealth left the town by way of inheritance and outmigration, and on and on.

Admittedly, human capital theory was not built to capture the causes of prosperity (or poverty) in small towns with porous borders, transient inhabitants, and labor organized in family units. Explaining the prosperity of individuals and the wealth of nations is already a lot to ask. But, in proposing that the ways Americans invested human capital during the early years of the nation's independence had a causal relation to American prosperity from the mid-nineteenth century to the beginning of the twenty-first, Goldin and Katz are assigning causality to educational and economic arrangements in a whole society, the northern part of which was full of Hawley-like towns of small farmer-producers, while the southern part of which built labor-intensive agrarian production based on slavery until 1865, followed by peonage sharecropping and convict-labor impressment of "free" Black men. Around Hawley, people worked chiefly in family units, under their own direction, sometimes supplemented by apprentices and hired hands; the family-based producers kept whatever surplus income they managed to acquire, rather than have it appropriated by a capitalist boss or feudal lord or slaveowner or state tax assessor. This "domestic mode of production," as it is sometimes called,[18] was organized for production and reproduction very differently from the entrepreneurial and then corporate capitalism that followed aggressively in the North, the forms of capitalism that are Goldin and Katz's main subject. Could their hypothesis, then, be historically or regionally specific?

For now, note that Plantation Number 7 grew in population from zero to 539 in its first 20 years of settlement. In the following 95 years, it rose to 545, a gain of six people. But it did not stay level; it doubled to 1,089 in 1820,[19] then fell steadily for 140 years. It is no coincidence that in the middle of its first decade of decline, the Erie Canal opened, making better land in upstate New York easily available and rendering crops bountifully grown there cheaply transportable to New England for sale at prices hard for Hawley farmers to match. In the 1830s, railroads went through to Buffalo, completing the Hawley farmers' marginalization—and, around 1850, to Illinois, where there was six feet of black topsoil and no rocks. History had negated the return on investment in Hawley land.[20]

In sum: the bold hypothesis of *The Race between Education and Technology* is "Invest in education, get higher levels of technology and productivity, and attain a rapid rate of economic growth and a higher standard of living." Goldin and Katz derive it chiefly from their analysis of the American twentieth century. Investment in physical capital (factories, machinery, railroads, etc.) had driven economic growth before 1900, they say, but after that, "the path to ongoing economic success for nations and individuals became investment in human capital."[21] That's plausible, but I argue in the foregoing analysis that their account of human capital in the first decades of the republic—the period *before* that of their primary concern, before the industrial revolution—squeezes the arrangements for investment and production into categories that don't correspond well to those of human capital theory, and have little explanatory power for the effects of schooling on prosperity 200 years ago. That failure might not disprove their hypothesis for the twentieth century, but it negates the more historically inclusive form of that hypothesis: most seriously, it would put in doubt its validity for the twenty-first century.

The case Goldin and Katz make for the explanatory power of their hypothesis from 1915 to 1980 seems to me stronger. Newer technologies like the electrification of factories and transportation put employers in need of workers educated beyond grammar school skills and capabilities. They expressed that need as a market demand by offering higher salaries to such workers. The high school movement and then the rapid transformation and growth of higher education met that need. The average level of educational attainment rose through most of the century, as did the high school and college wage premiums.[22] The elements of the equation match the historical process of enlarging and extending the educational system, not simply but revealingly. For instance, high school for the millions came about not in a single open market where students (and their families) expressed their demand directly as customers, but in towns and cities around the United States. Local governments recognized the broad public desire for ninth- through twelfth-grade schooling—a sentiment often expressed through political pressure and voting. They responded by appropriating funds for the construction and staffing of high schools. Parents' willingness to be taxed for this purpose, along with the certainty that other parents were eager to move to towns with high schools and thereby increase tax revenues from real estate, amounted to a complex of demands. With such town growth would presumably come commercial development. Intensifying these attractions and pressures was the force of skill-based technological change in production: employers already in town wanted workers with the abilities of the new high school's graduates. So did companies picking sites for new factories and offices. This interactive process went forward across the nation, remaking its economy and culture.

It's conceptually tricky but historically clarifying and faithful to the spirit of a supply-demand model to bundle so many diverse needs and pressures together as demand, in the economic sense. "Supply" in this model is unproblematic, though hard to measure. It refers to availability of the kind of learning employers want, through schooling, as indicated in their hiring practices (many job listings required that applicants have a high school diploma, for instance). "Investment" comfortably joins the taxes leveed by towns and paid by residents. And "return" easily covers the wage premium of individual graduates and increases in GDP—though as my readers know, I believe the causality implicit in these measurements falls apart on close analysis.

Chapter 6

At the End of the College Rainbow

Ira Shor

Collecting Your College Premium

Eminent scholar Richard Ohmann spent the final years of his long life questioning an alluring and controversial pillar of higher education: the college premium. Also known as the college payoff, the big payoff,[1] and more formally as the return on investment in college, the premium is understood as the higher earnings of college graduates compared to nongraduates, minus all college costs for the degree (tuition, fees, books, loans, etc.) and wages lost while in class instead of on full-time jobs after high school (opportunity costs). For more than a century, there's been a premium wage in the job market for graduates (first for the high school diploma, then for two-year, four-year, and postgraduate degrees).[2] While the college premium grew significantly since flattening in the 1980s, higher education has been the scene of rising tuition and soaring student debt (to about $1.7 *trillion* weighing down some 46 *million* graduates and dropouts in 2022).[3] Public colleges especially are being challenged currently by cheaper online "badge programs" that compete with the four-year degree as a traditional job requirement; higher education as we have known it for seven decades is facing new delivery systems and curricular paradigms that threaten restricted access to public higher education, less influence for liberal arts in postsecondary schooling, and greater hardening of economic inequality, the last mentioned of which I explore shortly. Baccalaureate and postgraduate degrees have been pricey tickets of admission to the highest pay and status, longest career ladders, and greatest job security. Yet, despite a white-hot labor market for *low-wage* workers during the pandemic and after,[4] the baccalaureate often fails to deliver entry-level college jobs, with employers slow to hire costlier graduates and complaining of a "skills gap" among new diplomates; for example, recent bachelor's degree recipients aged 20–29 have an aggregate unemployment rate of 13.1 percent.[5] A *degree-plus* (bachelor's or master's plus a skill certificate or work experience, or internships, or apprenticeships) is increasingly demanded by employers dubious that graduates are "job-ready." Postcollege underemployment especially affects working-class and lower-middle-class students who cannot afford to gain admission to elite colleges whose diplomas still have distinction and privilege in the job market.

Economic inequality in college access and outcomes reflects inequality in society at large. The top 5 percent of earners in the United States have enjoyed a 40-year spectacular boom, especially beneficial for the top 1 percent; the top 0.1 percent, and the top 0.01 percent. Vast fortunes have accumulated for some 750 billionaires, enough for some private rocket rides to weightless space.[6] Working people, who constitute the majority of Americans, have faced soaring inflation (9.1 percent in June 2022).[7] After decades of neoliberal austerity (flat wages, higher taxes, rising costs of living, lower budgets for public schools and colleges, rising tuition, and the like), the median family has to run faster and faster just to stay in place.[8] In these conditions, higher education and the college premium are still marketed as necessary lifelines but are sought by fewer low-income students (COVID produced five straight semesters of declining undergraduate enrollments, especially at community colleges).[9] Austerity, of course, lands hardest on the low-income, the nonwhite, and the recent immigrant.[10] Education scholar Paul Tough put it this way: "Over the last few decades, we've quietly changed our system from one that allowed people from working class backgrounds to get a reasonably priced education that would improve their opportunities, to a system with dramatically reduced public funding, that puts the financial burden on individual students and their families."[11] In addition, even though female graduates' unemployment rate was about one-third the rate of males in 2021 (7.0 percent versus 20.9 percent), women earned less because men dominate fields with the highest incomes while female students collect in majors with the lowest wage scales.[12]

Inequitable outcomes of the college premium especially preoccupy Ohmann in this book. Indeed, the causes and consequences of persistent inequality form the gravamen of his arguments. One of Ohmann's key economic sources, Claudia Goldin and Lawrence Katz's award-winning *The Race between Education and Technology* (2008), served as an oppositional muse. He praised how much the depth of their data and historical attention to successive school development revealed but pointed out the power relations and class inequality they overlooked. Following Ohmann's skepticism, I propose a contradictory overview of the premium: *College pays off for some but not for most, making the college premium both true and false, real and illusory, accessible and restricted at the same time, depending primarily on race, class, and gender.* The true-false contradiction fits a collegiate system that has promised more than it delivers, that selectively distributes advantages to some while denying them to many, that confirms existing inequities while presenting itself as an open ladder to be climbed, and that faces challenges from short-term postsecondary job preparation modules (badges) which do not address structural biases disfavoring the majority and which undermine the critical jewel in the crown of higher education, the liberal arts.

Unequal access to college and unequal distribution of the premium are political consequences of a postsecondary system built to fit prevailing hierarchies.[13] The premium privileges the already privileged, recapitulating historical inequities. Because collegiate outcomes track economic and social inequality, higher education fits into and helps sustain the status quo. For sure, millions have graduated, but millions of others have dropped out, or never enrolled, or were left with unbearable debt or underemployment, or both. After decades of mass graduations from higher education, inequality has only a stronger grip on the nation. As one education commentator observed: "The postsecondary system mimics and magnifies racial and ethnic inequality it inherits from the K–12 system and then projects this inequality into the labor market. . . . [T]he country also has the least inter-generational educational and income mobility among advanced nations."[14] Tressie Cottom, among others, has exposed the failure of the predatory for-profit postsecondary sector to advance mobility, especially from the bottom up.[15]

Million-Dollar Promises

The allure of the college premium has long been difficult to resist. As Doug Lederman puts it: "Go ahead—just try to find an instance in the last few years in which someone trying to make the case that going to college matters hasn't trotted out the statistic that the average college graduate earns $1 million more over the course of a lifetime than a high school graduate."[16] Politicians, foundations, companies, and colleges themselves promote this million-dollar promise. The source of this happy news was a US Census report which announced in 2002 that college graduates earn in their lifetimes about a million dollars more than do high school graduates.[17] Ohmann argues that this big number is misleading, but it is hard to ignore.[18] Moreover, as Ohmann asserts in chapter 4, those most likely to enroll in college, to graduate, and to claim such an earnings payoff are those whose parents are upper income and have graduated college before them, as well as those who attend *selective colleges*. Further, the majority of adults in the United States still do not have college degrees.[19]

The lure of the "big payoff" mystifies the wide range of returns delivered by degrees as well as who gets what at the end of the rainbow. Ohmann lingers on this simplistic promise, whose alluring brevity is manipulative. Memes like the "college premium" and the "big payoff" misrepresent how education in society works. As we both suggest, certain majors (business management, STEM, preprofessional) deliver far higher premiums than others.[20] Graduates who capture the highest payoffs typically major in subject areas favored by white males, which makes the college premium a pernicious and contradictory lure: it is true, real, and accessible for favored groups while being false, illusory, and restricted for others, an ongoing national shame that deserves attention.

In his rhetoric and cultural studies career, Ohmann exposed another manipulative meme, the "literacy crisis," whose ideology he challenged in the early days of the bitter culture wars, the 1970s. He declared in the *Chronicle of Higher Education* that "the Literacy Crisis is a fiction if not a hoax."[21] He argued that it is a false conservative claim, misrepresenting test score data in order to undermine the credibility of public education in the wake of the egalitarian advances of the 1960s.[22] Some literacy scores were stable; however, a persistent decline (eventually discredited) over 12 years in the SATs led to the literacy drama in 1975, when a 10-point drop on the verbal and an 8-point points loss on the math was announced by the College Board. National finger-pointing was followed by a provocative cover story in *Newsweek* titled "Why Johnny Can't Write."[23] Ohmann's critical side of the debate argued that the SAT declines resulted largely from an egalitarian demographic change in the cohort taking the famous exam. Larger numbers of non-elite lower-scoring high school seniors showed up for the test in those years after college access became a popular mass option and public subsidies for higher education kept tuition relatively affordable.[24] Previous SAT cohorts were not comparable to that of the newer cohorts, Ohmann cogently insisted, and therefore the crisis advocates were comparing apples to oranges. Further, back then, some scores were even rising when disaggregated by race because minority students were closing about a fifth of the test score gap between themselves and white children.[25]

Race is one variable producing unequal college access, graduation rates, and returns from the premium. Other variables Ohmann mentions include gender, major, and occupation entered, to which I can add years taken to graduation, extent of debt incurred, and the degree-granting institution's distinction (or lack thereof).[26] Upper-class selective colleges and universities have higher retention and four-year graduation rates than other campuses and are also more likely to place graduates in white-glove jobs. Furthermore, the higher the income of a student's family, the more likely the student is to be admitted to more selective colleges whose degree bearers earn the most. Some economists like Goldin and Katz, as well as Anthony Carnevale, acknowledged these unequal outcomes. They lamented them (especially Carnevale) and included data delineating them but did not draw out the ideologies and social structures driving them or emphasize that they were imported into the collegiate system from power relations outside.

Power Relations

Power relations produce "winners" in higher education who look much like the "winners" everywhere else. The systemic interface maintaining such inequality reflects a feedback loop. Affluent families, overwhelmingly white, overinvest in their children's development from birth through graduation from selective colleges, which leads to high-income jobs whose salaries enable these graduates to overinvest in their own children.[27] The childhood overinvestments include educational toys and games; large-format books; state-of-the-art computer hardware, software, screens, apps, and internet access; private tutors for subjects their children are weak in; SAT courses and coaches; nannies from childbirth on; after-school, weekend, and holiday trips; private lessons in music, drawing, painting, dancing, singing, acting, cooking, yoga, filmmaking, robotics, and gymnastics; uniformed sports teams with transportation to "away" games; playdates at museums, aquariums, and zoos; themed and catered birthday parties; private psychotherapy and costly dental work; fashionable clothes and shoes in good condition, and so on. Affluent families privately provide their children what Annette Lareau described as "concerted cultivation," which working-class families cannot afford.[28]

Busy, organized, well-funded, adult-supervised childhoods produce kids holding high expectations of selective college admission followed by good jobs. Their college applications present personal essays in Standard Written English relating their diverse experiences doing community service, taking advanced courses, traveling, doing unpaid internships, and all the rest. Selective college admissions committees read signals of privilege in these applications, Ohmann observed. They admit students most likely to succeed in a high-end campus culture and curriculum, simplifying teachers' pedagogical tasks in producing outstanding four-year graduation rates. These applicants and future graduates are chosen and rewarded for traits and skills they acquired and developed through a privileged upbringing *before* arriving on attractive campuses where they receive an overfunded transition from adolescence to adulthood and from school to work (or graduate school, med school, law school, or MBA program). In this linkage, the selective college, the premium, unpaid internships, and employment after graduation all piggyback on precollege privileges.[29] The token admission of some high-performing "scholarship boys and girls"[30] to any entering class does not minimize the social class and racial inequities in this process. Perhaps the most egregious bias includes "legacy admissions," favoring applicants whose parents are alumni, and applicants whose parents are large donors to the college endowment.[31] Beyond egregious—in fact, criminal—are wealthy parents who simply pay brokers, references, and admissions officers to falsify achievements, scores, and transcripts.[32] Payoffs are outrightly criminal, but legacy admissions and favoring children of large donors are legal, standard practices.[33] Private schools, special tutoring, and access to elite internships are of course legal also. This social construction of the privileged young is not accidental or meritocratic (despite handfuls of bright working-class youth sprinkled into the mix), but rather is an organized replenishment of the elite for and from whom the lesser-constructed majority left behind will eventually work and take orders.

Unequal Social Construction

Replenishing the ruling elite in the social construction of an unequal society relies on the unequal development of the young in family life and in formal education. Schooling is an especially long-term, intensely differentiated process. We misrepresent this process with singular designations such as "higher education" or "the American college system" or "the university"; instead, we should represent it as a balkanized geography of unequal territories that unevenly and unequally develop each cohort. The faux equality of singular usage is applied again in the phrase "the American school system" for K–12, which is also compromised by its unequal subsectors: public versus private, religious private versus nonsectarian private, urban versus rural versus suburban versus exurban, urban elite versus urban inner-city versus urban middle-class, elite private versus elite public versus nonselective public and private, public schools versus privatized charter schools draining public budgets, and so on. In the fiefdoms of education, social class differences were so obvious to Ted Sizer, the legendary education dean of Brown University, that he declared after touring high schools in the early 1980s: "Among schools there was one important difference, which followed from a single variable only: the social class of the student body. If the school principally served poor adolescents, its character, if not its structure, varied from sister schools for the more affluent. It got so I could say with some justification to school principals, Tell me about the income of your students' families and I'll describe to you your school."[34]

Sizer also observed that the *subject* of "class" was universally absent from the high school curriculum. Its absence in every syllabus can hardly be accidental when everything in this education sector is overmanaged; intense overregulation of curricula by state authorities makes social class a forbidden subject matter, what Michel Foucault called a "subjugated knowledge."[35]

To understand the ideological frames and restrictions through which schooling molds students into adult workers and citizens, critical learning is needed instead of the standard curriculum. Critical learning asks teachers to unearth subjugated knowledges, including social class, patriarchy, or white privilege—in short, the unauthorized themes in traditional education. Such buried subjects are also not knowledges named, sought, or rewarded by the job market. Employers want education to produce job-ready, skilled, communicative, and compliant workers who can hit the ground running.[36]

Accumulating Job-Worthy Skills, Cognitive and Noncognitive

In the recent resurgence of occupational education, job skills come first, marginalizing the liberal arts where critical learning about self-in-society and society-in-self most occur. Job skills are typically categorized as *cognitive* and *noncognitive*. "Cognitive" refers to what people know and can do, and "noncognitive" to commercially productive behaviors and social dispositions. The cognitive generally encompasses "hard skills": analytic thinking and problem-solving; writing legibly in Standard English; comprehending manuals, brochures, and online instructional modules; operating email, spreadsheets, and other software and apps; typing, doing basic math, drafting or writing code; controlling applicable bodies of knowledge; practical know-how in handling tools, materials, processes, assemblies, and repairs of all kinds; knowing which tools to use for a task; knowing how to research knowledge in order to solve a problem or perform a task; knowing when, how, and who to ask for help; and so on. Noncognitive virtues are often called "soft skills," "human skills," or (by educators and psychologists) "social-emotional Learning" (SEL).[37] They include self-control, reliability, promptness, sobriety, courtesy, hygiene, ease with authority, conformance to rules, on-task perseverance, teamwork, resisting distractions, accepting criticism, responding appropriately when addressed, active listening, following instructions, patience (including tolerance for boredom and repetition), empathy with coworkers, and socially compliant dress and grooming.

Employers see soft skills as dispositions that go along with hard skills in producing more work, though what counts most for hiring are technical skills for doing the job at hand. The model job candidate has sometimes been referred to as a "T-shaped worker" who has both hard technical and soft human skills, which are imaginatively crossed to form a T. There are two versions of the T: (1) vertical technical skills crossed with horizontal human skills; or (2) horizontal technical skills crossed vertically by liberal arts knowledge. Version 2 is less common in job training than version 1.[38]

To gain traction in the job market, applicants are advised to make explicit on their résumés the technical skills they possess that are most relevant for employment. This is called keyword density by Ryan Craig, a training entrepreneur and founder of University Venture who advocates supplanting two- and four-year degrees as job requirements with short-term job-specific training programs: "As enterprises have digitized, digital skills now outnumber all other skills in entry-level job descriptions, across nearly every industry. . . . And without the digital skills employers are increasingly listing in their entry-level job descriptions too many college graduates are invisible."[39] The stunning rise of the digital sector, with its high demand for labor, has provoked employer demands for short-term training without the liberal arts component typically included in college, which Craig dismissed as a waste of time and money in his book *A New U: Faster + Cheaper Alternatives to College* (2018).

Tech Badges as Subcollegiate Alternatives
to Liberal Arts and the College Degree

The faster, cheaper alternatives, offered as lower-tuition *badges* or *badge programs*, emerged robustly in the first two decades of this century as a postsecondary alternative to mass college attendance. Mass campuses emerged during the "College Movement" (1950–70), according to Goldin and Katz, which had followed the "High School Movement" (1910–40). Mass colleges promised new avenues to upward mobility but eventually foundered on contradictions of the market economy; the economic system could not reward the millions of new four-year graduates expecting secure, middle-class employment after finishing school. The contradiction between mass higher education and the corporate economy exploded in the 1970s, a mismatch I examine in my book *Culture Wars*. Currently, the enormous debt incurred by college graduates is the latest gnawing contradiction of higher education attendance. To make the debt conundrum even worse, underemployment exists side by side with large numbers of unfilled job openings. The earlier contradiction of too many graduates for too few well-paying jobs has morphed into a predicament of too many unfilled jobs despite an abundance of collegiate job seekers, especially in the burgeoning high-tech sector, where employers (following Paul Ryan above) complain that college degrees are inappropriate and inadequate preparation for the labor actually required. (More on this shortly.) Badge programs emerged in the midst of these contradictions and quickly gained authority, capital, and enrollees year by year.

Proliferating badge programs are best poised to displace *nonselective and less selective public colleges charging tuition*, from which many students drop out each year without degrees but often with debt. These largely underfunded, sometimes open-access, and mostly public colleges confer degrees that lack distinction in the job market. Selective public university flag-ship campuses (better funded and charging higher tuition), as well as selective high-end private nonprofit colleges, are less threatened by badge programs because their distinctive cre-dentials have strong claims on the college premium in the job market. Low-rank public four-year and two-year campuses—already hollowed out by rising tuition due to state budget cuts and characterized by high drop-out rates—are far more vul-nerable to the entrepreneurial push underway for short-term badge training.

For the millions of undergraduates who dropped out in debt or who face years more of costly coursework or who will graduate into underemployment despite years of study, the badge initiative has obvious appeal, even though much of it is old wine in new bottles. What's new is modular skill training in a cutting-edge industry, IT, which is hungry for labor, awash in cash, and laden with friends in high places. What's old is subcollegiate occupational training in narrow skills. Badges are repackaged technical certificates long offered by community colleges, union apprentice schools, and for-profit commer-cial and industrial institutes. Without a general humanities component, the certificate programs are of course shorter and less costly than AA/AAS or BA/BS degrees and are po-litically appealing to those seeking to erase the curriculum most open to critical social thought, liberal arts.

Organizationally, badge programs are onsite or online in-tensive courses, typically running three to six months, that certify technical competence in a specific skill. Badges can be issued digitally, or attached to baccalaureate or master's tran-scripts; they are portable and "stackable" (certifying succes-sive levels of training completed). Some badge providers ally with public or private colleges to award credits for each badge completed, which down the road can be stamped and stacked on a transcript towards a degree. Other badge programs are for-profit, free-standing enterprises, whose entry-level portals are called "coding bootcamps" for beginners, averaging 14 weeks, though some go six to nine months. Their average starting cost of $13,600 is less than a that for a four-year degree but has to be paid up front. Some boot camps cost more, such as Galvanize at $17,980 and Flatiron at $16,900 (in 2022).[40] For-profit and nonaccredited commercial badge programs do not qualify for Pell Grants or for federal loans, which complicates financing this option. Students must pay out of pocket, or through commercial lenders, or through in-house financial plans offered by the sponsors themselves, which accumulate interest, thus risking debt unless a program is employer subsidized. Coding camps are time-intensive, some requiring six days of study a week, making them a demanding engagement best suited to those who can take weeks off from work and who are not raising children. Entry-level IT positions for badge carriers offer appealing base salaries of $50,000 or more.[41] Having completed a badge program, a student has a singular skill to take to the job market, which is an advantage over having no certified skill, but this advantage can work only as long as that skill is in demand. When a new skill supplants the old one, workers will need to finance re-enrollment, again at their expense, to gain a new badge. The high demand for IT labor is the engine driving this development: "The growing need for tech workers is forcing employers to look beyond traditional recruiting pipelines, like elite universities, to some new sources of talent, including local people without college degrees."[42]

A badge simply and visually signals an achieved skill closely aligned with the names and descriptions of jobs offered by employers. Besides IT, fields especially adaptable to badge programs include health care, industrial processing, materials handling and moving, the building trades, and others whose job descriptions are technically explicit. Badges in the form of short-term occupational certificates also remain on the vocational menus of community colleges. though they have proliferated to multiple other sites: in-house training offered by major corporations (like Google allied with Coursera), free-standing coding camps in the private sector (like the Bloom Institute of Technology), baccalaureate institutions that encourage graduates to add badges so they leave with more than a four-year degree (eCornell offers 120 programs awarding certificates), and even some vocational high schools.[43] According to one academic advocate for this new regime, Ray Schroeder, the "credential train is leaving the station ... with widespread adoption of credentialing that is shorter, less expensive, timelier and more career-centric than traditional full-length degree programs."[44] The *Chronicle of Higher Education* observed that colleges are "entering a new era, one in which some industry and nonacademic certifications are more valuable than degrees ... and colleges are using badges to offer assurances to employers about students' abilities in ways that a degree no longer seems to do.... The explosion in credentials is upending long-held notions about the value of a college degree.... It's also a development laced with confusion."[45]

One major confusion is the sheer number of badge credentials, almost one million in 2021: "The nonprofit Credential Engine has identified 967,734 unique credentials on offer in the US as part of an ongoing effort to catalog degrees, certificates, badges, licenses and apprenticeships. More than half of the nearly one million credentials are offered by nonacademic institutions ... 549,712."[46] Such furious postsecondary non-academic development explains why this project qualifies as a competitive threat to collegiate enrollments and the liberal arts. It also indicates a gold rush stage of development. However, for the moment, too many badges are being offered by too many sites, accredited and unaccredited, which poses a risk to students paying tuition to potentially unreliable sponsors. Accountability is lagging. A shakeout phase will sort the eruption of credentials and providers. When it does, the big players with brand names, developed online assets, and deep pockets will likely monopolize the subsector by eating the smaller ones.

Badge Lunch

Before badge programs began contending with nonselective colleges, computerization took over production, finance, communications, and commerce across the society while also briskly colonizing schools and colleges. On campus, computers occupied more and more physical and curricular space as well as budget lines after 1980. Campuses installed computer science departments and offered computer science degrees while digitizing their operations. They also marketed academic knowledge via MOOCs (massive online open courses) that proved popular and generated revenue. The first full-time online degree-granting institutions were both private: Southern New Hampshire University (SNHU) and Western Governors University (WGU) opened in 1995 and 1997, respectively.[47] Each now enrolls over 100,000 students online, and the two are by far the biggest players in such degree granting. They appeal particularly to adult college dropouts and to members of the armed forces. The huge clientele of these behemoths sets a high bar for new players to get into the game. Universities, facing declining onsite enrollments and reduced state subsidies for public higher education, may decide they must compete by offering online degrees. The online imperative is a competitive pressure, but the revenue lure is also compelling—a potential market of 36 million adults who left college without degrees and are now place-bound by jobs and families but who need or want to finish.[48] Unlike SNHU and WGU, which are way ahead in capturing this market, the City University of New York was planning in 2022 to offer an ambitious array of online degrees, taking advantage of its huge urban footprint and clientele.[49] Capitalization is key because of the high marketing, management, and installation costs of new online ventures.[50] Among the older players, the University of Michigan was an early builder of online college courses and, in partnership with Google, is pioneering the use of XR (extended reality) in training. XR enables virtual hands-on learning designed for job-specific procedures. This amounts to a simulated apprenticeship that is synchronous with the course syllabus. The technology is expensive to develop and implement, but if it works, it will cheapen employers' training costs and lessen their apparent doubts about applicants' "hands-on" experience. The unanswered question here is whether simulated learning can prepare one for real-life situations as well as an onsite on-the-job apprenticeship. Experience is the best teacher; how close can the virtual come to real working life?

College Life versus Badge Programs

The vast economic force of IT has enabled digital dominance in education, production, finance, communications, marketing, and private life. It's a flood only navigable by those with the power and wealth of, say, the billionaire Koch Foundation, which funds Arizona State's redesign.[51] A landmark in the pending transition from degrees to badges as job requirements took place in the aftermath of the 2008 Wall Street collapse. In the financial recovery, banks used the college degree as a hiring filter to selectively bring back staff. According to Bridgette Gray, chief customer officer at the nonprofit Opportunity@Work, college degrees became tools "to screen out workers as employers were struggling to balance the number of applicants they saw. You had degrees being used as a proxy to determine skills in the minds of hiring managers."[52] Employers examined college transcripts as signals for selecting new hires from the deluge of CVs received when business picked back up. Thereafter, however, Gray helped turn the tables on the baccalaureate. She consulted with the state of Maryland to drop the bachelor's degree as a requirement for many jobs. Ultimately, about half of that state's jobs were assessed as not requiring a degree. The nonbaccalaureate hiring policy opened recruitment to larger pools of skilled lower-wage candidates, according to Gray: "They gain their skills through many years of work experience, through a community college or a military service program or even through a workforce training organization. These people make up the bulk of American workers." IBM has also dropped degree requirements for hiring. As Kelli Jordan, director of IBM's career and skills development, explained, the company developed a "new collar" project to deal with the "skills gap": "When we look at the number of jobs that are available— . . . more than 700,000 open technology jobs in the U.S., another half a million over the next decade—it's just not enough coming out of the educational system . . . only something like 60,000 to 70,000 graduating with a computer science degree."[53] Like Gray, Jordan emphasized recruiting people with "different backgrounds . . . community colleges . . . veterans . . . boot camps," and, to an even greater extent than Gray's work with Maryland, IBM will apply the no-degree-required rule to "the vast majority of jobs."

The challenge badges present degrees is legitimized by another claim from IT advocates and employers, mentioned above, the "skills gap." This widely circulating assertion recalls the "Literacy Crisis" of the 1970s, which conservatives promoted to legitimize back-to-basics pedagogy.[54] The "skills gap" is sometimes rendered as a dual predicament: (1) There are too many open jobs in IT with too few qualified applicants being graduated by colleges to meet industry needs; and (2) there is too much unspecific signaling in degree transcripts about exactly what graduates can do, that is, what job-ready skills they bring to an employer. A badge names a specific skill mastered by an applicant, so a prospective employer knows exactly what a candidate has been trained to do. Whereas employers doubt what competencies a college transcript or degree confirms—Ryan Craig called this "hiring friction," which slows hiring—they can see the competency named on the badge awarded by the certifying agent.

Employer disdain for college transcripts was echoed in 2015 by Gunnar Counselman, a founder of the online firm Fidelis, which markets student skill assessment tools for badge programs: "Five years ago, nobody believed the degree was insufficient. . . . The whole skills gap is the result of schools not understanding what employers need."[55] Counselman claimed that students go to school for sixteen years "and you get four freaking data points out of it": the college name, the field of the degree, the year awarded, and a GPA. Sharing this frustration, Craig founded University Venture in 2012 as a private equity fund "for establishing next-generation postsecondary education companies through . . . innovation from within higher education,"[56] but he soon gave up trying to reform collegiate practice from the inside. Instead, he began advocating against vocationalism at community colleges and against four-year degrees as job requirements.[57] The subtitle of Craig's 2018 book, A New U, says it all: "Faster and Cheaper Alternatives to a College Education." Higher education, in his view, takes too long, costs too much, and encumbers students with too much debt. In place of opaque transcripts, he went all in for a variation of short-term badge programs that he called "last-mile training," a pre-employment boot camp tailored to a specific company hiring enrollees directly from the camp itself. Ultrarationalized for producing job-specific skills, such training leaves no daylight between education and occupation. This "last mile" model reveals best, I would say, the instrumental, counterliberal bias of corporate training. The corporate ideal is to produce workers like widgets.

This rising narrow occupationalism recalls John Dewey's sardonic remark that you can train people like animals but you can educate them only as human beings.[58] More than a century ago, Dewey opposed the job training then called industrial education for working-class students (an episode I return to shortly). Current "skills gap" advocates pose coding boot camps instead of broad liberal education at a moment when the college degree is vulnerable. Unemployment among recent graduates is unusually high (13.7 percent as noted above), leaving many with degrees in hand and ready to work but turned away by employers reluctant to hire, while the workforce shows 41 percent of recent graduates in jobs *not* requiring a degree.[59] Badges are becoming the credential business prefers, not mass higher education degrees.

The White House Weighs in on Badges

Momentum for badges also came from the White House in February 2020 at a kickoff for a task force on alternatives to bachelor's degrees. There, Apple CEO Tim Cook boasted, "Once the primary driver of opportunities, the four-year degree is now one of many paths to a successful degree. At Apple, over 50 percent of our employees don't have classic college degrees."[60] Notice that he contrasted "classic college degrees" to "many paths to a successful degree," elevating nonbaccalaureate alternatives to equivalence with four-year degrees. A few months later, Google's senior vice-president for global affairs, Kent Walker, followed Cook's downplaying of the four-year degree: "College degrees are out of reach for many Americans, and you shouldn't need a college diploma to have economic security. We need new, accessible job-training solutions—from enhanced vocational programs to online education to help America recover and rebuild."[61] Walker outflanked college to the left here, posing as a labor advocate by referring to the genuine problem of debt and the insecurity that graduates and nongraduates face—two strong points in the argument for short-term occupational training. He did not argue, however, for general wage increases for noncollege workers, for higher state subsidies to public college campuses to make the degree affordable and less debt inducing.

Two years after the White House kickoff, events finally forced the issue on stagnant and low wages. COVID-19 created a labor supply crisis that reversed the 40-year earnings stagnation. With the economy's stuttering return to normality, workers in lower-wage service sectors were again in great demand, not only in health care but also in hospitality, leisure, warehousing, and customer service, as consumer demand outpaced production and supply. But market forces turned back these labor advances because gains in wages were more than eaten up by raging inflation. "Droves" of workers demanding higher wages began quitting to find higher wages at other employers (in what was dubbed the "Great Resignation" because so many left their jobs).[62] Colleges were also unsettled by COVID, but one thing at least stayed constant in higher education: the continuing decline of liberal arts, that part of the curriculum with the most potential for questioning the status quo and the least friendly to narrow job training.

A War against Questioning the Status Quo

A century ago, a conflict between job-focused training and broad education prefigured the current badge occupationalism. The contention was over the 1917 Smith-Hughes Act, which first proposed federal funding for school-based industrial education, promoted by the National Association of Manufacturers and opposed by the American Federation of Labor. John Dewey called this legislation "the greatest evil now threatening the interests of democracy in education."[63] At a time when the high school movement was opening mass access to secondary education, Dewey thought business domination of public schools would lead to narrow trade education: "Education would then become an instrument for perpetuating unchanged the existing industrial order of society, instead of operating as a means for its transformation."[64] Dewey proposed instead a spacious curriculum that would challenge the status quo by mining the knowledge embedded in occupational themes:

> There is a danger that vocational education will be interpreted in theory and practice as trade education, as a means of securing technical efficiency in specialized future pursuits. . . . An education which acknowledges the full intellectual and social meaning of a vocation would include instruction in the historic background of present conditions; training in science to give intelligence and initiative in dealing with materials and agencies of production; and the study of economics, civics, and politics to bring the future worker in touch with the problems of the day and the various methods proposed for its improvement.[65]

In the next sentence, Dewey concluded with advice on what counted most in a democratic study of occupations: "Above all, it would train power of readaptation to changing conditions so that future workers would not become blindly subject to a fate imposed on them."

"Blindly subject to a fate imposed on them." Apply that caution to the current neoliberal period with its forty years of stagnant wages accompanied by rising prices. To Dewey in 1916, democratic education meant developing autonomy in students so they could become knowledgeable change agents of their society. Sixty-five years later, in 1982, Theodore Sizer was surprised to find academic discussion of "social class" issues absent in school syllabi, even though social class existentially and institutionally pervaded every school he visited. Political exclusion of subjects like "social class and economic inequality" quarantine students from becoming informed and analytic agents of change. Politically unauthorized themes become curricular "desaparecidos." Across the board, this disappearance is repeated in occupational badge programs that ignore civic, critical, and historical matters, issues that collegiate liberal arts are more likely to include.

Moreover, badge schemes disempower the workforce by further segmenting it and extending the lower-wage tier of subcollegiate jobs. Nondegreed labor is easier to pay less with fewer benefits than offered to college graduates, who expect more after their treks to commencement. Many don't get there, of course, and settle for less. Saddled with debt, graduates who expected more, along with indebted dropouts with no degree, are entitled to indignation and resentment, two noncognitive "human" dispositions unproductive at work and potentially destabilizing to the status quo.

Labor resentment is one by-product of working and living in a policy world not of your own design or attentive to your interests. Consider such policies as globalization, deindustrialization, cheap-labor outsourcing, casualization of labor (turning full-time jobs into part-time), privatized health care,

demolition of neighborhoods for highways and gentrifica-
tion, public subsidies for luxury condos and billion-dollar sta-
diums, tax breaks for energy corporations and carmakers in a
time of global warming, destruction of bumper harvests to
artificially raise food prices, no price controls on gas or rent,
defunding of public education and other public services to
open revenue streams for the private sector.[66] The majority—
working-class and middle-class students and families—are
hurt by such market-driven policies. The question of who
benefits from these neoliberal policies was answered by char-
ismatic multibillionaire Warren Buffett in 2006: "There's class
warfare all right, but it's my class, the rich class, that's making
war, and we're winning."[67] Buffett proposed that his millions
in annual earnings be taxed at the higher rate (30 percent, not
17 percent) paid by his own secretary, who was then earning
$60,000 per year. Thirteen years later, billionaire Eli Broad fi-
nally joined Buffett and called for higher taxes on himself and
the super-rich: "I'm not an economist but I have watched my
wealth grow hugely thanks to federal policies that have cut
my tax rates while wages for regular people have stagnated
and poverty rates have increased."[68] Broad's op-ed echoed
Patricia Cohen's report confirming economic inequality: "Corporate profits have rarely swept up a bigger share of the nation's
wealth, and workers have rarely shared a smaller one."[69]

The Algorithm of Class War

The surge in badge and online programs in postsecondary
education has pushed brick-and-mortar institutions into developing virtual baccalaureate and masters options; public
universities now enroll 45 percent of all undergraduates but
only 25 percent of those registered in some 384 online bachelor's programs, so they are playing catch-up to the private
sector.[70] In 2021, in what is called a "watershed moment for

graduate-level business education," online MBA programs enrolled more students than onsite ones, 45,038 to 43,740, as employers tilted toward alternative degrees.[71] The online shift of higher-education degrees may slow down badge programs by competing with them. However, facing debt and wage stagnation, many students and their families as well as working adults will likely choose faster and cheaper online degree and badge programs. These programs will be the downscale options for the majority unless mass opposition from below demands and wins free tuition, open access, and a debt jubilee to invigorate campus enrollments. If current trends are not reversed, inequality will continue shaping postsecondary education, and the affluent young will head to the best four years of their lives on high-end selective campuses, while the majority will attend budget-cut campuses charging more tuition or will enroll in the busiest 12 weeks of their lives offered by for-profit badge programs. This result is what I call the algorithm of class war: incomes produce and predict outcomes.

The income-outcome algorithm underlies the zip code example Ohmann offered. He proposed that applicants to high-end colleges signal their bona fides by various markers, including the zip codes of their costly homes and upscale high schools, the English in their personal essays, the honors and advanced courses indicated in their transcripts, and their SAT scores, which closely track family incomes. These signals help admissions committees sort applicants for those who best fit a high-class campus and curriculum. I mentioned a similar signaling process earlier in referring to banks that, while recovering from the 2008 crash, used college degrees to sort selective graduates from the mountain of CVs received. Ohmann also highlighted such signaling in a review of John Marsh's *Class Dismissed: How We Cannot Teach or Learn Our Way Out of Inequality* (2012). Ohmann foregrounded the income-outcome algorithm when discussing Marsh's view on the college premium:

> Despite his intense criticism of higher education, Marsh was convinced that "[t]he college premium is real. It exists." Therefore, we should advise "every halfway intelligent young person with a pulse [to] go to college." ... I do not believe the earning statistics mean that this advice is correct. ... The premium has been spirited away because of one main, earlier "decision" the student has made—her choice of parents—and by other decisions she had little or no part in making: her parents' income; their choice of neighborhood and of schools for her; their home culture; their choice whether or not to be drunk and violent; their ways of raising the toddler and preschooler she used to be; the extra measures they have taken or not taken to advance her along paths of success. ... The premium is real because class and other realities have made her one kind of chooser and not another, not because of the choice of college itself. Add in that the "college premium" ignores whether the young person is in a position to choose Princeton, or if not maybe Penn State, or maybe the local community college, or perhaps the University of Phoenix. ... Add in this imprecision about "college," and the premium begins to look like the disembodied smile of the Cheshire Cat.[72]

As Ohmann wrote, "Class and other realities have made [the student] one kind of chooser and not another."[73] Even though family incomes are by far the dominant factor in producing education outcomes, some working-class teenagers understand and resist the social limits built into their social position, their race, or their gender; some pull off exceptional academic adaptation despite meager investment in their growth; some receive heroic interventions by teachers, caregivers, or other adult mentors; some are just plain late bloomers. Therefore, in my judgment, for children and teenagers from average-income families, it's inappropriate to interfere with their youthful aspirations; if a young person of low or modest means is determined to reject lower aspirations, their plans are best supported by the grownups in their life, and they should proceed with eyes open—that is, with reasonable cautions about the path ahead. Moreover, college attendance and graduation develop social ways of being, thinking, and doing that elevate aspirations and questioning habits, perhaps helping to explain why collegiate members of the electorate are more likely to vote for liberal candidates.

Aspirations and Outcomes, Then and Now

John Dewey was 86 in 1945, when I was born and when the United States was the only major power whose factories, roads, ports, rail lines, bridges, and communications had not been bombed and degraded by World War II. American businesses found themselves virtually without international competition in meeting surges in domestic and global demands for everything—food, clothing, vehicles, construction equipment and materials, machine tools, and so forth. Also, the war propelled technological advances that then further accelerated because of the Cold War and a burgeoning consumer market (a popular TV commercial in the 1950s boomed, "See the USA in your Chevrolet, America's the greatest land of all!"). Further, labor unions reached a peak membership in the 1950s at over a third of all workers and were a societal force in setting wages, hours, and benefits, while exercising an important social-democratic influence on national policy.[74]

The postwar decades were the best times to be working-class in the United States; economic and political conditions encouraged aspirations. Family incomes rose more for the bottom 80 percent than for the top 20 percent.[75] Rising aspirations also fueled broad political opposition to the status quo;

the 1960s saw progressive movements emerge on and off campuses.[76] By the end of that decade, popular movements had put authorities on the defensive about pursuing the Vietnam War, about racial injustice, about women's inequality, about discrimination against gay people, about authoritarian schooling, and about environmental spoliation. As the stage of history filled with constituencies making progressive demands on authorities, a counterattack began from the top down, an aggressive ideological turn that elsewhere I have named the Conservative Restoration.[77]

Seeds for the Conservative Restoration were planted by Richard Nixon's 1968 campaign. His candidacy activated a conservative bloc to counter the liberal and antiwar climates in politics, on campuses, and in society. Nixon famously anointed this bloc the "silent majority," identifying such voters as the sturdy modest (white) mainstream in contrast to loud unpatriotic protesters on campus and in urban ghettoes.[78] It was these Americans' turn now to take back their country (foreshadowing Trump's MAGA campaign in 2016). Once Nixon's new commissioner of education, Sidney P. Marland, was confirmed in 1970, the president directed him to devise a new vocational initiative. Marland designed a plan he named Career Education, and everything in schooling changed.[79]

Marland proved to be a P. T. Barnum impresario at marketing, and he had to be, because Career Education (prefiguring the occupational Badge programs now under way) was old wine in new bottles. It was repackaged job preparation, which had been unexceptionally around for decades in high schools and community colleges. But, with a new name, a new splashy campaign, and sizable dispersals of federal cash, he made sure it succeeded. To empower low-profile vo-tech advocates in education, Marland and Nixon won extraordinary increases from Congress for the plan; the Federal Vocational Education

Act budget grew astonishingly from $43 million in 1968 to $707 million in 1972 and then to $981 million in 1974.[80] The sound of serious money is a powerful wake-up call. "On this surge of monies occupational education swept into colleges in a fashion dreamed of and pleaded for but never realized by its advocates," according to Arthur Cohen and Florence Brawer.[81] Job training, rebranded as Career Education (and now rebranded again, as badge programs), was sold as a new idea whose time had come. It put liberal arts on the defensive by making administrators an offer they couldn't refuse: rivers of cash for pushing careerism across the curriculum.

Marland used public funds to drive educational policy to serve two political purposes: job prep that would preoccupy and distract students so as to cool down campus protests, for one, and occupationalism to lower economic expectations of students, for the other.[82] He was aware that the hundreds of thousands of new graduates pouring from colleges (thanks to state-subsidized affordable tuition and easy access to nearby campuses) couldn't possibly all be rewarded with college-level employment. The jobs weren't there. So he offered an upbeat vision for depressant Career Education: "We should view the future generations of learners in America as coming to maturity at a time when society may not require all their intellectual and developed capacities in the work force. . . . It is not unlikely that by 1980 we will have table waiters at the Hilton who are MAs in French or nutrition or social science, happily engaged in intellectual, civic, and social pursuits, quite apart from their work lives."[83]

At one large gathering in Houston in 1977, vo-tech educators celebrated Marland as "the father of career education."[84] However, two noted historians of vocationalism, W. Norton Grubb and Marvin Lazerson, did not join the celebration: "Career education is not directed at resolving social problems, developing avenues of upward mobility, or making school and work more satisfying experiences. It is aimed instead at reducing expectations, limiting aspirations, and increasing commitments to the existing social structure."[85] Career Education was the grandfather of the similarly upbeat badge advocates, offering job training instead of college degrees, narrow skills instead of broad liberal arts.

More Restoration: A Second Front Opens to Rescue Capitalism

While Marland spread job preparation nationally, another conservative initiative took wing, this one outside the Nixon administration. Marland had proposed a work-based education reform to lessen student unrest and to lower economic expectations. This second offensive emerged to target radicalism on campus and off, promoted by the US Chamber of Commerce. The Chamber commissioned a prominent power broker from Virginia, Lewis F. Powell, to report on the state of private enterprise in the face of mass protests. On August 23, 1971, Powell issued a panoramic call to arms that became known as the Powell Memorandum. "The assault on the enterprise system is broadly based and consistently pursued. It is gaining momentum and converts." Powell warned. "The ultimate issue may be *survival*—survival of what we call the free enterprise system . . . business and the enterprise system are in deep trouble, and the hour is late."[86] Henry Giroux has called this declaration "the most succinct statement, if not the founding document, for establishing a theoretical framework and a political blueprint for the current assault on the academy."[87]

Powell's declaration was soon followed by his appointment to the Supreme Court. A lawyer by training, Powell's memo issued an alarm that the American system was under attack and required an immediate counteroffensive to survive. (A similar warlike rhetoric of alarm would mark a key report later in the Reagan administration, the 1983 *A Nation at Risk* and would return yet again in Donald Trump's January 2017 inauguration speech, in which he referred to American "carnage.") As Giroux observed, "Powell identified the American college campus as 'the single most dynamic source' for producing and housing intellectuals 'who are unsympathetic to the [free] enterprise system.'"[88] Giroux also noted the systemwide scale of Powell's memorandum "to develop a broad-based strategy not only to counter dissent but also to develop a material and ideological infrastructure with the capability to transform the American public consciousness" by awakening it "to the knowledge, values, ideology, and social relations of the corporate state."[89] The grand reach of Powell's intentions copied the national scale of Marland's plan, perhaps indicating the substantial political fear that opposition movements on campus and in society had generated at top levels of government and corporations. Protest forces then were large and militant but were not yet an insurrectionary challenge to state or capital. Yet key tribunes of the status quo construed them as such as a public relations scare tactic. To turn back the alleged threat, Powell proposed 14 actions business should organize and fund on and off campus. The proposals predated the digital age, so they did not include online tools. Instead, Powell referred to newspapers, magazines, radio, television, campus events, and professional conferences as mass instruments for pro-business advocacy. He urged sending pro-enterprise speakers and authors to campuses and to broadcast channels to counter dissident voices.

Conservative scions, organizations, and foundations responded to his call, gathering momentum year by year; in the 1990s, conservative groups spent a billion dollars ($158.1 million in 1996 alone) to drive public policy, jurisprudence, legislation, news media, and academic discourse to the right.[90] The goals evolved into multiple projects to sway public opinion, to marginalize liberal policies like affirmative action (ended by Trump's Supreme Court majority in 2023), to aggressively advocate anti-tax business perspectives, to unseat liberals and elect conservatives, to reverse state and federal regulation of business, to shrink consumer, labor, and environmental programs and protections, to end abortion rights (finally achieved under the Trump Court in 2022), and to censor textbooks and curricula for hot-button issues like homosexuality, transgender rights, same-sex marriage, or "unpatriotic mentions" of violence against Black people or Indigenous Americans.[91] The silencing of such critical subjects included demonizing words, like "the L-word" (liberal), "the T-word" (taxes), "the A-word" (abortion), and "the G-word" ("global warming," displaced by the bland "climate change"). "Critical race theory" became a notable conservative target later in this culture war, but the Supreme Court's overturning of *Roe v. Wade*, then affirmative action, and earlier ruling that private corporations are "citizens" with constitutional rights were perhaps the most consequential conservative victories of this long "lurch to the right."[92]

Liberal Arts Sinks in the Lurch to the Right

After Powell released his memo, he moved onto the Supreme Court in October 1971. Marland also was rewarded with an appointment in 1975 to head the prestigious College Board. From that post, Marland helped launch further conservative campaigns, such as measures to address the Literacy Crisis, including a national back-to-basics reform plan and intensive grade-by-grade testing (not practiced in any other advanced nation). These associated campaigns intensified the national lurch to the right in education. They proceeded by marshaling the vast institutional and financial power of the status quo against a large, rhetorically strong but organizationally weak protest culture. Careerism—narrow job preparation— and Powell's crusade against liberal policy and campus protests, followed by thunderous back-to-basics advocacy groups inundating schools and colleges along with imposed competency testing to cure alleged illiteracy: all of these, in concert, dramatically narrowed intellectual and political climates, disfavoring the liberal arts. In addition, the job market for liberal arts graduates declined as state support for public K–12 and higher education weakened.

Further, and through a different lens, marginalized liberal arts was vulnerable because it had a high-culture legacy incompatible with business commercialism and narrow job preparation. Historically rooted in belles lettres, philology, classical poetics, rhetoric, and philosophy, liberal studies were luxuries that did not sound like, look like, or fit well with the mass culture and colloquial speech of the non-elite students pouring onto campuses after 1960. Still, academic liberal arts offered open space for questioning the status quo, for syllabi inviting critical study of gender, race, sexuality, class, mass culture, power relations, language use, and literary canons. Until Powell began the stalking of dissent on campuses, schools, media, and society, critical teachers, authors, and scholars tenaciously pursued their disciplines. They were also influential in the radical movements at that time, so this oppositional side of the liberal house drew intense fire from Powell and derivative campaigns afterward, such as Accuracy in Academia.

Since Marland and Powell "saved" capitalism from campus radicals and liberal arts in the 1970s, higher education has been moving steadily in a corporate direction, commercializing collegiate services, delivery systems, degree programs, course offerings, and research facilities.[93] Following the neoliberal quest to monetize everything into private revenue streams, administrations have been transforming colleges into training and marketing centers for business. STEM and business programs now dominate undergraduate majors. Online and onsite MBAs proliferate. Bank branches have opened on many campuses. The humanities have not been able to compete with this pro-business takeover. The marginalization of liberal arts has even included moves to cut some majors altogether.[94] Unsurprisingly, the first two decades of these pacification campaigns became unflatteringly known as the "Big Chill."[95]

Nixon, Powell, and Marland are long gone now, but their neoliberal and conservative policies have left most of the nation's families, schools, and colleges on a steep road downhill. Higher education, for example, pioneered a predatory labor policy—casualization of employment and contingent staffing—increasing the collegiate revenue stream by replacing high-wage full-time faculty with low-wage part-time adjuncts, degrading teaching and learning by marketing a deprofessionalized, cheaper version of "college." The two-tier labor segregation, which soon spread to the rest of the economy, became the shame of an apparently shameless academy.[96]

Shameless Economics: The Stories in the Numbers

Thanks to all of these economic policies, higher education after 1970 offers a gainful story for some and a deficit narrative for the many. Enrollments leveled off from the 1970s through the 1990s, as family wages stagnated and as state subsidies declined, forcing tuition increases that priced out or drove millions into debt. In general, these decades were bad news for working-class families and students, though not uniformly for all. For example, Latinx students increased their collegiate registration by an astonishing 452.1 percent from 1976 to 2020.

Black student registrations rose modestly until 2010, then trailed off. In the case of women, there was a surge of enrollments following the new feminist wave of the 1960s. By 1980, female undergraduates finally outnumbered male students (51.3 percent to 48.7 percent).[97] By 2019, the female majority had risen to 57.9 percent.[98] In 2003, the number of doctorates awarded by US universities to women surpassed the doctorates awarded to men.[99] However, despite a half century of educational gains, women still do not have parity with men in wages or in professions with the highest earnings. The case is the same with Black and Latinx graduates: every indicator shows graduates, employees, and families of color continually lagging white graduates in income, wealth, longevity, employment, and other measures.[100] Regarding women graduates, it remains to be seen if the emerging badge programs will lessen female subordination to men, given that high-tech employees are 75 percent male and embed a notorious male "culture of harassment."[101]

All in all, then, education cannot be and has never been a "great equalizer," as Horace Mann declared more than 150 years ago. In all that time, successive education movements have indeed added layers of formal schooling on top of the ones before. The nation now boasts some 80,000 schools and more than 3,000 colleges, all unable to widely deliver on Mann's bold dream and promise. In the twenty-first century, the nation's racial and gendered inequalities remain steep, and economic differences among social classes are at historic highs.

Higher education copied lower education in reproducing rather than dispelling inequality. Badge initiatives will likely do the same, fortifying inequality. Individual college graduations of persons from disfavored groups will surely continue; those difficult achievements are legitimate occasions for personal and family celebrations. But they are too few, too uncertain, too slow, and too narrow in scale and consequence to transform the formidable long-term structures of inequality in school and society. To build democracy and equality, other kinds of oppositional politics are needed. Such organized opposition would consolidate the majority now losing ground in current power relations, explicitly foregrounding the institutional forces and ideologies sustaining inequality—male domination, white privilege, corporate hegemony, heteronormativity, and imperialism—as the foundational pillars of the status quo. Syllabi as well as campus culture would address these subjugated knowledges and the ways of life, the political formations, the policies, and the pedagogies sustaining them.

Agendas for democratic change, for egalitarian transformation, and for critical learning in education are far easier to propose than are specific plans for gaining the political power needed to win such changes. Nevertheless, the end of the rainbow is a good place to do the impossible math, so here is an agenda: To start, efforts have been under way to change two grossly anti-egalitarian conditions, namely, a campaign to end tuition at public colleges and another to abolish all student debt held by the government. Free tuition at public colleges and debt relief already have mass appeal and support.[102] Tens of millions have a stake in a debt jubilee and in ending tuition. Their numbers need to be consolidated as a political force. Next on the democratic-egalitarian agenda for education would be restoring high levels of state subsidies for public colleges in order to make free tuition possible and to make mass higher education a rich experience with small classes for all, not just for an elite attending high-end campuses. Robust state subsidies would also enable faculty appointments to be universally full-time, ending the gross exploitation of adjunct labor (with all full-time lines available for sharing by cooperating faculty at their choice). Further, regarding the learning process, classroom pedagogy should become interactive, participatory, discussion-based, and problem-posing, including students in course planning and evaluation, moving towards student-centered, project-based, cross-disciplinary inquiry in all courses.

An egalitarian education agenda would also fold community colleges into four-year institutions so as to end the class prejudice and racial segregation supported by the two-year–four-year division. Further, working students with jobs and families would benefit from seven-days-a-week campus operation of classes and facilities. Campuses need childcare, health care, and reproductive services without charge. There should be enhanced provision of mentors, coaches, tutors, and counselors. Vulnerable groups—women, LGBTQIA, students of color, the neuroatypical, immigrants—must have secure and protected participation. Internships should be paid so that all students can afford to gain work experience. The low graduation rates at nonselective colleges, where the majority attend, tell us that such egalitarian policies and investments are badly needed.[103]

Without opposition movements propelling an egalitarian agenda, higher education and the college premium will remain what Carnevale called them, "engines of inequality," and what Paul Tough named "the inequality machine." Against such engines, facing leviathans of authority, humans are strangely clever, resilient, and resourceful, finding ways to slide past, stifle, and work around limits. Human agency is brilliant and dogged; like rust, it never sleeps. Michel de Certeau called this agency "bricolage" ("making do"), while ethnographer James Scott called these oppositional maneuvers "weapons of the weak," that is, furtive, below-the-radar resistance, using the tools, language, bodies, and materials at hand to outwit limits imposed by the strong status quo.[104]

In a strong democracy, all are entitled to the *passion of knowing the world*, as one educator of poor children put it.[105]

That society would use its wealth to enable the fullest human-ity for all—"bread and roses," as workers demanded in the great Lawrence textile strike of 1912.[106] Postsecondary educa-tion aimed at business careerism is perhaps the hegemonic common sense of our time, "learn so you can earn" instead of "learn so you can humanize yourself and democratize your world." Still, disfavored groups in society, long denied equal-ity, have fought for jobs, respect, and access to college, now threatened because education is the tail wagged by the digital dog of dominant business.

Better times are hard to imagine in the worst of times, but they are already visible in pulses: the enormous Women's March protesting Donald Trump's 2017 inauguration; the coast-to-coast mass outrage following George Floyd's 2020 murder; the huge gatherings greeting young environmentalist Greta Thunberg when she traveled for the World Climate Strike; the young throngs cheering socialist Senator Bernie Sanders when he campaigned for president in 2016 and again in 2020; the millions of workers voting with their feet by leav-ing their jobs in the "Great Resignation" of 2022 to seek higher pay and better working conditions; the Me-Too Movements of women exposing pervasive sexual harassment at their workplaces; the pervasive and persistent opposition to the Supreme Court's 2022 *Dobbs* decision reversing *Roe*; Native Americans' sustained protests against construction of oil pipelines on their lands. From these and other pulses, more people will question the status quo until waves of opposition consolidate into a force that turns the tide.

Notes

Introduction. The Myth of the College Premium
and Other Truisms of American Culture

1. The series of essays I've published on this topic include "Brave New University" (*College English*, 1999); "The Pedagogy of Debt" (*College Literature*, 2006), "Student Debt and the Spirit of Indenture" (*Dissent*, 2008), and "The Debt Experience" (in the collection *The Debt Age*, ed. McClennen et al. [New York: Bloomsbury, 2018]), and "Who's Responsible for Student Debt?" (*Salon*, 2021).

2. Samuel Bowles and Herbert Gintis, *Schooling in Capitalist America: Educational Reform and the Contradictions of Economic Life* (New York: Basic Books, 1976); Paul Willis, *Learning to Labor: How Working-Class Kids Get Working-Class Jobs* (1977; reprint, New York: Columbia University Press, 1981).

3. Barbara and John Ehrenreich's "The Professional-Managerial Class" is the lead essay in the volume *Between Labor and Capital*, ed. Pat Walker (Boston: South End Press, 1979), 5–45. It seeks to explain the twentieth-century rise of the class, between the proletariat and the ruling class, that manages and cushions the operation of society yet consists of neither rulers nor proles. That view has been disputed but lends texture to the complications of modern classes. In subsequent work, notably *Fear of Falling: The Inner Life of the Middle Class* (New York: Pantheon, 1989), Barbara Ehrenreich revised the term to "professional-middle class."

4. I take this succinct phrasing from a conversation with Ira Shor.

5. Marcus quoted in the introduction to the revised edition of Ohmann's *English in America*, xxi.

6. Fish, "Anti-Professionalism," in *Doing Things Naturally: Change, Rhetoric, and the Practice of Theory in Literary and Legal Studies* (Durham, NC: Duke University Press, 1989), 215–46.

7. Fish parlayed this view especially in *Professional Correctness: Literary Studies and Political Change* (New York: Oxford University Press, 1995), where he cites Raymond Williams's comment, in *The Country and the City*, that, even in a work as seemingly neutral as a pastoral poem, we have to decide "where

we stand." Williams was speaking about Sir Phillip Sydney's *Arcadia*, a vaunted poem portraying a beautiful park, and he points out that the park was built on the seventeenth-century seizure and enclosure of the commons—land held in common for grazing—by the new aristocracy. Fish holds that this kind of criticism is ineffective, belonging to the political sphere and the job of those in that sphere, whereas literary critics should stick with their profession's "business routines" (45–48).

8. I rehearse Ohmann's path more fully in "The Politics of Career," in "Richard Ohmann: A Retrospective," a special issue of *Works and Days* 23 (2005): 85–96. The statistics on PhDs come from US Bureau of the Census, H 766–787, "Number of Doctorates, by Field: 1920–1970."

9. *How to Do Things with Words* (1962), 2nd ed. (New York: Oxford University Press, 1975).

10. *Is There a Text in This Class? The Authority of Interpretive Communities* (Cambridge, MA: Harvard University Press, 1980).

11. Paul de Man, *Allegories of Reading: Figural Language in Rousseau, Nietzsche, Rilke, and Proust* (New Haven: Yale University Press, 1979), p. 8. It's interesting to look at what de Man pulls out: Ohmann was concerned about the social efficacy of speech acts, which is very different from de Man's vision of the impersonality, indeed inhumanness, of language. So perhaps Ohmann's shift was not entirely a conversion, as he seemed to have a concern with social effects—and after all, even though he dealt with style, Shaw was a major Fabian socialist in England.

12. "*English in America* Updated: An Interview with Richard Ohmann," *Minnesota Review* 45–46 (1996): 58.

13. *The Politics of Literature: Dissenting Essays on the Teaching of English*, ed. Louis Kampf and Paul Lauter (1972; reprint, New York: Vintage, 1973).

14. H. Bruce Franklin, *Prison Literature in America: The Victim as Criminal and Artist* (1978), expanded ed. (New York: Oxford University Press, 1989), xxiii.

15. Davis reported to me that he has "always tried to write fairly directly. The person that influenced me the most was Richard Ohmann. He was on *Radical Teacher*, and his writing was the most clear, almost conversational, in academic writing, and it was a style that I totally admired and tried to follow" (168–69). See Jeffrey J. Williams, "Identity and Ability: An Interview with Lennard J. Davis," *Cultural Politics* 17.2 (2021): 163–74.

Chapter 1. The Costs and Benefits of College Education

1. Margaret Spellings, "An Argument against Free Community College Tuition," *PBS NewsHour*, June 8, 2021; John King, "Why This Former U.S. Education Secretary Believes Community College Should Be Free," *PBS NewsHour*, June 9, 2021. The *NewsHour* anchor, Judy Woodruff, noted that

17 states already have free community college. President Biden's plan to make that free tuition national in all fifty states failed in Congress in the following year.

2. Barack Obama, "Remarks by the President on College Affordability, Ann Arbor, Michigan," The White House—President Barack Obama, January 27, 2012, https://obamawhitehouse.archives.gov/the-press-office /2012/01/27/remarks-president-college-affordability-ann-arbor-michigan. See also Obama, "Remarks by the President on College Affordability, Syracuse NY," August 2, 2013, //obamawhitehouse.archives.gov/.

3. "President Clinton's Call to Action for American Education in the 21st Century," State of the Union Address, 1997.

4. George H. W. Bush, "Message to the Congress Transmitting Proposed Legislation on Educational Excellence," April 5, 1989, American Presidency Project, www.presidency.ucsb.edu/documents/message-the-congress -transmitting-proposed-legislation-educational-excellence.

5. Donald J. Trump, *Great Again: How to Fix Our Crippled America* (New York: Simon and Schuster, 2016), 57–59.

6. Lauren Camera, "Biden Calls for 4 Years of Free College," *U.S. News & World Report*, October 22, 2015, usnews-com/news/articles/2015/10/22 /biden-calls-for-4-years-of-free-college.

7. Adam S. Minsky, "Biden Touts Free College Plan in Speech, but Advocates Want Him to 'Keep His Promises' on Student Loan Forgiveness," *Forbes*, April 29, 2021, https://www.forbes.com/.

8. William G. Bowen and Michael S. McPherson, *Lesson Plan: An Agenda for Change in American Higher Education* (Princeton, NJ: Princeton University Press, 2016), 3.

9. Google's Ngram viewer, s.v. "college wage premium," https://books .google.com/ngrams. The more general, predecessor phrase, "return on investment in education," came into common use in the late 1950s via human capital economics. It referred to primary and secondary schooling as well as higher education.

10. Lyndon B. Johnson, "Remarks at the 200th Anniversary Convocation of Brown University, Providence, RI, September 28, 1964," American Presidency Project, http://www.presidency.ucsb.edu/ws/?pid=26534.

11. Horace Mann, "The Necessity of Education in a Republican Govern-ment" (1839), Voices of Democracy: The U.S. Oratory Project, http:// voicesofdemocracy.umd.edu/.

12. John Marsh presents a strong argument for this position in *Class Dismissed: Why We Cannot Teach or Learn Our Way out of Inequality* (New York: Monthly Review Press, 2011).

13. For a clear discussion of the general point that rapidly changing job markets complicate the hypothesis of the college premium, see Peter Cappelli,

Will College Pay Off? A Guide to the Most Important Financial Decision You Will Ever Make (New York: PublicAffairs, 2015), 41–45. Cappelli takes up many of the topics here and, like me, skeptically assesses the theory of a college wage premium. As his subtitle indicates, he emphasizes the uses and dangers of the idea of the college premium to students and families making practical choices, whereas my themes are largely political and ideological. Still, I learned much from his work and recommend it.

14. "Fordism" was Antonio Gramsci's name for the system of mass production and consumption Henry Ford helped develop. It has become a common name for the period (from about 1900 to 1970) when large, vertically integrated corporations bestrode the economic landscape. "Neoliberalism" has lately taken on a similar role for the period given definition by the politics and practices of Margaret Thatcher and Ronald Reagan and by the ideas of economists such as Milton Friedman. The world began to look more neoliberal than Fordist by the 1980s. While the boundaries of periods and their labels might be debatable, my overarching theme is that the college premium connects to a major historical shift.

15. For a compact account, see Wolfgang Lehmacher, "Don't Blame China for Taking U.S. Jobs," *Fortune*, November 8, 2016.

16. Claire Cain Miller, "The Motherhood Penalty vs. the Fatherhood Bonus," *New York Times*, September 6, 2014; Miller, "A Baby Bust Rooted in Economic Insecurity," *New York Times*, July 6, 2018, B1, B5; Michael S. Teitelbaum and Jay M. Winter, "Bye-Bye, Baby," *New York Times*, April 6, 2014, SR1, SR6–SR7; Nicholas Bakalar, "26.3," *New York Times*, March 1, 2016, D4.

17. Harvey, *The Enigmas of Capital: The Crises of Capitalism* (London: Profile Books, 2011), 243.

18. Randall Collins, *The Credential Society: An Historical Sociology of Education and Stratification* (1979), Legacy ed. (New York: Columbia University Press, 2019). See also Ivar Berg's earlier, widely read study *Education and Jobs: The Great Training Robbery* (New York: Praeger, 1970).

19. Michel Foucault, *Discipline and Punish: The Birth of the Prison*, trans Alan Sheridan (New York: Vintage, 1975), 174–77.

20. Kai-Fu Lee, "The Real Threat of Artificial Intelligence," *New York Times*, June 25, 2017, SR4. Lee chairs a venture capital firm and is president of its Artificial Intelligence Institute.

21. I draw on David Harvey's analysis in *A Brief History of Neoliberalism* (Oxford: Oxford University Press, 2005). He does not include education in the areas of life transformed by neoliberalism, though he includes the University of Chicago as a main incubator of neoliberal theory in the United States. To take but one of Harvey's bracing observations: "The incredible concentrations of wealth and power that now exist in the upper echelons of capitalism have not been seen since the 1920s. The flows of tribute into the

world's major financial centers have been astonishing. What, however, is even more astonishing is the habit of treating all of this as a mere and . . . even unfortunate byproduct of neoliberalization. . . . It has been part of the genius of neoliberal theory to provide a benevolent mask . . . to hide the grim realities of the . . . reconstitution of naked class power" (119). For a prescient analysis of the devaluation of college degrees as they proliferate, see Pierre Bourdieu, *Distinction: A Social Critique of the Judgement of Taste*, trans. Richard Nice (Cambridge, MA: Harvard University Press, 1984), 132–68.

22. See my account in "The Strange Case of Our Vanishing Literacy," in Ohmann, *Politics of Letters* (Middletown, CT: Wesleyan University Press, 1987), 230–35.

23. See Richard Ohmann and Ellen Schrecker, "The Decline of the Professions: Introduction," *Radical Teacher* 99 (Spring 2014): 1–6. This issue of *Radical Teacher* also includes essays on the diminished control of work in historically strong professions (law, medicine), as well as in more marginal ones (K–12 teaching, journalism).

24. Universities are the home site of almost all professions. Whether most members make their livings there, teaching and doing research, or are employed by corporations or governments, or (less and less, these days) are set up in private practice, their making of knowledge, their teaching of it, their admission of new practitioners, their monitoring of careers, and so on happens at or under the auspices of universities. So hard times for universities put professional education, research, and legitimacy under stress.

25. This sharp decline in state funding included the period after the Great Recession of 2008. See "Two Decades of Change in Federal and State Higher Education Funding," Pew, October 15, 2019, pewtrusts/org.en/research-and-analysis-issue-briefs/2019/10; and "Federal and State Funding of Higher Education: A Changing Landscape," Pew, June 11, 2015, esp. figure 4, https://www.pewtrusts.org/en/research-and-analysis/issue-briefs/2015/06/federal-and-state-funding-of-higher-education.

26. Emma Whitford, "Two Decades of Change in Federal and State Higher Education Funding," *Inside Higher Ed*, May 5, 2021.

27. Jennifer Ma and Matea Prender, "Trends in Pricing and Student Aid, 2021," College Board, https://trends.collegeboard.org/college-pricing/figures-tables/average-estimated-undergraduate-budgets-2021.

28. Melanie Hanson, "Total Student Loan Debt," Education Data Initiative, update November 30, 2021, https://educationdata.org/total-student-loan-debt.

29. "Student Debt: Lives on Hold," *Consumer Reports*, June 28, 2016, which is a condensed version of James B. Steele and Lance Williams, "Who Got Rich off the Student Debt Crisis?" The Center for Investigative Reporting, 2016.

30. "Undergraduate Enrollment," National Center for Education Statistics, updated 2023, https://nces.ed.gov/programs/coe/indicator/cha. Percentage

data declines for 2017–21 taken from "Spring 2023: Current Term Enrollment Estimates," National Student Clearinghouse Research Center, May 24, 2023, nscresearchcenter.org/current-term-enrollment-estimates/.

31. Doug Lederman, "The Culling of Higher Ed Begins," *Inside Higher Ed*, July 19, 2017.

32. See Paul Fain, "Deep Partisan Divide on Higher Education," *Inside Higher Ed*, July 11, 2017.

33. Scott Jaschik, "Losing the White Working Class, Too," *Inside Higher Ed*, July 31, 2017. The poll was conducted by Brodnitz/Normington and commissioned by House Majority PAC, whose purpose is to help regain a Democratic majority in the House. The results, published by *Politico*, cover many political issues and, on my reading, suggest the strong influence on respondents of conservative ideas and the waning (though still identifiable) influence of unions.

34. Since more than 40 states have charter school laws, with wide variations in funding rules and educational practices, this is a messy area. But a key point is that kids in charters take public money with them typically via their home district's per capita allotment, which is used there with little public direction or accountability.

35. Sharon Otterman, "Despite Money and Attention, It's Not All A's at 2 Harlem Schools," *New York Times*, October 13, 2010, A20.

36. Michael Bloomberg, "Why I'm Backing Charter Schools," *Wall Street Journal*, December 1, 2021. For a reply to Bloomberg, see Valerie Strauss, Diane Ravitch, and Carol Burris, "The Problem(s) with Bloomberg's $750 Million Investment in Charter Schools," *Washington Post*, December 10, 2021.

37. Eleanor Yang Su, "Public School, Private Donations: The Money Debate," *Huffington Post*, January 19, 2012. Figures are from the Public Policy Institute of California.

38. Motoko Rich, "Nation's Wealthy Places Pour Private Money into Public Schools, Study Finds," *New York Times*, October 22, 2014, A16.

39. Patrick McGeehan, "Pepsi Wins Battle in Cola Wars: $21 Million CUNY Deal," *New York Times*, August 14, 2013, A20.

40. Andrew Martin, "On Campus, New Deals with Banks," *New York Times*, May 31, 2012, B1.

41. Joel E. Meyerson and William F. Massy, *Measuring Institutional Performance in Higher Education* (Princeton, NJ: Peterson's, 1994). I cite these terms not to lament a barbarian takeover of ivied halls but to suggest that as educational administrators were resetting their goals and methods in emulation of for-profit business, they were also importing its jargon.

42. The founding (in the 1990s) and continued success of University Business is itself evidence of the shift in thinking about higher education. At Wesleyan University, where I taught, they paid consultants a goodly sum to develop a brand—"The Alternative Ivy"—which students mocked, I hope into oblivion.

43. See my "Historical Reflections on Accountability," which first appeared in *Radical Teacher* 57 (1999) and is collected in Ohmann, *Politics of Knowledge: The Commercialization of the University, the Professions, and Print Culture* (Middletown, CT: Wesleyan University Press, 2003), 136–49. For the origin of the meme "conservative restoration," see Ira Shor, *Culture Wars: School and Society in the Conservative Restoration, 1969–1991* (Chicago: University of Chicago Press, 1992).

44. Michael Stratford, "White House Pivots to Accountability and Outcomes, and Away from Debt-Free, in Major Duncan Speech," *Inside Higher Ed*, July 27, 2015.

45. Eric Hoover, "Marketing Finds Its Place on the Campus," and "Marketing to Survive: Colleges Hone Their Search for a Competitive Advantage," *Chronicle of Higher Education*, March 4, 2016, B44, B46. The institutions discussed are George Fox University and the University of Alabama at Huntsville.

46. Jeffrey R. Young, "The New Transcript: More Information and a Digital Format Can Empower the 'Quantified Student,'" *Chronicle of Higher Education*," March 4, 2016, B39–B40.

47. Mark Sigelman of Burning Glass Technologies, quoted in Jeffrey R. Young, "Voices from a Credentials 'Summit,'" *Chronicle of Higher Education*, March 4, 2016, B40.

Chapter 2. Does Going to College Raise Lifetime Earnings?

1. Anthony P. Carnevale, Stephen J. Rose, and Ban Cheah, *The College Payoff: Education, Occupations, Lifetime Earnings* (Washington, DC: Georgetown University Center on Education and the Workforce, 2011), 1 (subsequent citations appear as page numbers in the text). "Lifetime earnings" is defined as pay for full-time work from age 25 through age 64. The report adds that the "worth" of a bachelor's degree kept rising, to $2.8 million by 2011. Like the authors of the Georgetown report, I use the colloquial "average" for both "mean" and "median," except when clarity requires differentiating them. A year earlier, the College Board's third iteration of its report "Education Pays" had claimed "much evidence that [college] pays off," according to coauthor and economist Sandy Baum. Baum, "Calculating How Much 'Education Pays,'" *Inside Higher Ed*, September 21, 2010. The College Board's and the Georgetown Center's data were updated and confirmed a decade later; see Michael T. Nietzel, "New Study: College Degree Carries Big Earnings Premium but Other Factors Matter Too," *Forbes*, October 11, 2021.

2. See two *New York Times* reports by Steve Lohr, "A Way Out of Poverty and into an $85,000 Tech Job," March 16, 2019, B1; and "Tech Jobs Are Flocking to New York: Can Workers Snare Them?" February 13, 2020, B5. Lohr follows the Per Scholas training centers opening around New York to

qualify high school graduates for good-paying IT jobs. For a pandemic-era report on the shortage of construction workers despite high wages in that sector, see Madeleine Ngo, "Do We Have the Skills to Build Back Better?" *New York Times*, September 13, 2021, B1, B2.

3. Cecilia Rouse, "Q + A," *Colloquy* (Summer 2012): 9.

4. Claudia Goldin and Lawrence F. Katz, *The Race between Education and Technology* (Cambridge, MA: Harvard University Press, 2008), 325.

5. See, for example, "Hunger on Campus: Pay Tuition or Eat," where Kaya Laterman (*New York Times*, May 14, 2019, NJ1, NJ6) reports that "many college students say they skip meals or take 'poverty naps' because they can't afford to buy food."

6. I have drawn on the discussion of cause, including Mill's third condition, in Richard J. Murnane and John B. Willett, *Methods Matter: Improving Causal Inference in Educational and Social Science Research* (New York: Oxford University Press, 2011), 36–37.

7. A word about my standing in this discussion: I am a literary critic and theorist who came to think of myself as doing cultural studies, as it became a recognized field. That meant bringing historical, sociological, and other ideas and perspectives to bear on culture, very broadly conceived. My professional reach does not extend to formal economics. For example, I do not understand all of the mathematics that go into some of the methods and conclusions I discuss here. Thus, I am limited in my assessment of some arguments, especially of some economists, to considering how well their formulations of research questions capture what they and the rest of us would like to find out, and how they deal with the social contexts of causal links. In other words, I focus on how well they meet Mill's third condition when arguing for the college premium. Needless to say, "they" do not all share a single view. But many economists and educational researchers, as well as many other people who care about higher education, think the college premium and related hypotheses are reliable guides to thinking and acting in the real world. I have my doubts, which is what this book is about.

8. See Murnane and Willett, *Methods Matter*, esp. 36–38, 71–74.

9. Of course, few parents are social science researchers, but almost all are graduates of various levels and types of schooling, from affluent to poor public districts, from high-cost nonsectarian private to low-cost religious, and so on. The common parental self-advocacy for their own children that includes seeking smaller classes is thus not research based but rather experiential or intuitive or peer-sourced knowledge.

10. Murnane and Willett, *Methods Matter*, 36–37, 70–74. There were other failures of randomness, too. For instance, only large elementary schools met the requirements of the experimental design, so the better performance of students in small classes might have owed in part to the large-school environment.

11. Murnane and Willett, *Methods Matter*, 34–35.

12. Nor could participants' interests have been taken out of the picture by double-blind (or triple- or more) protocols like those often used in in medical experiments. There's no way to conceal from teachers, parents, and administrators which treatment is the new "medication" and which is the "placebo."

13. Murnane and Willett and many social scientists use "quasi-experiment" as the term encompassing such studies. A subcategory of the quasi-experiment, in this usage, is the "natural experiment," in which comparison groups are created by a nonhuman force, such as a flood or earthquake. For my purposes, the critical distinction is between planned experiments aiming for scientific rigor and the sorting of people into groups in order to move toward a practical goal. In everyday understanding, the latter are not experiments at all. Another term I put into play is "counterfactual," though it is theoretically crucial to the search for causality in human affairs in which the challenge is (at one level) how to know what would have happened to the people who received a particular treatment if they had not received it.

14. A nonrandom difference between the two groups has to do with the fact that large schools with lots of students in each grade were more common in cities, where families were relatively prosperous, than in poorer rural areas. Hence, children from prosperous families were more likely to be assigned to the small classes that subdivision had produced. Murnane and Willett show how statistical analysis can minimize the risk of trouble with Mill's third condition here. Their whole discussion is far more complex than my comment indicates (*Methods Matter*, 166–85). The study on which they base their analysis is Joshua D. Angrist and Victor Lavy, "Using Maimonides' Rule to Estimate the Effect of Class Size on Scholastic Achievement," *Quarterly Journal of Economics* 114.2 (1999).

15. Joshua D. Angrist, "Lifetime Earnings and the Vietnam-Era Draft Lottery: Evidence from Social Security Administrative Records," *American Economic Review* 80.3 (1990): 331.

16. See Joshua D. Angrist and Stacey H. Chen, "Schooling and the Vietnam Era's GI Bill: Evidence from the Draft Lottery," *American Economic Journal: Applied Economics* 3 (2011): 96–119. Specifically, GI Bill benefits reduced the wage penalty of the affected cohort by about 15 percent and hence "did not come close to offsetting the full costs of conscription borne by draftees" (116). In adapting Angrist's work to my purposes, I have omitted some analytic details, including that the second study measured earnings after twice as many years in the workforce as did the first, by which time both the wage penalty and the wage premium had flattened out.

17. Angrist and Chen, 99, 111, 116.

18. Andy Mager, "'We Ain't Marching Anymore': Draft and Military Resistance to the Vietnam War," *Nonviolent Activist, The Magazine of the War Resisters League* (March–April 2000).

19. One available choice steered clear of both military service and lawbreaking: conscientious objection, which became more popular as the war went on. In 1972, there were more conscientious objectors than draftees (Mager, "We Ain't Marching Anymore").

20. I've slid past a thicket of ethical complexities here. For instance, given that almost everyone thought small classes better than large ones *before* the STAR project, was it fair to assign thousands of children in Tennessee to large classes for three years just to confirm this bit of received truth?

21. Murnane and Willett say violating some ground rules for good research makes a "defensible causal inference" impossible; "violating other tenets does not threaten the ability to make a causal inference, but does limit the ability to determine to whom the results of the study apply" (*Method Matters*, 27). I have framed my discussion of designed and quasi-experiments in some of their terms, though I have deployed them more informally. Clearly, they would not accept my critique of some particular quasi-experiments.

22. A longitudinal observational study by epidemiologist Michael Marmot, reported and analyzed in *The Status Syndrome: How Social Standing Affects Our Health and Longevity* (New York: Henry Holt, 2004), links education as a risk factor insofar as achieving higher social status through education correlates with better health and longer life for graduates as well as for their immediate families.

23. This is not to say that breakfasting regularly on Bob's Red Mill Muesli could not correlate with high earnings and that the connection could not be causal. In fact, I hypothesize that someone who favors a cereal brand with no sugar in it and with only one or two ingredients is knowledgeable about food production, thoughtful, and perhaps more attractive to employers than a job candidate who eats more highly processed, sweetened, and chemically preserved products—not, of course, because of having impressed an interviewer by smart answers to questions about breakfast food but because the qualities of mind revealed in those answers might signal the kind of practical intelligence an employer would value. Of course, that kind of intelligence might have been sharpened by a college education. You, reader, can probably follow this line of analysis back to the complexities of causality in real life.

24. Chitra Ramaswamy, "Do Tall People Really Deserve to Earn More?" *The Guardian*, April 29, 2015; Nick Collins, "Blondes Paid More than Other Women," *The Telegraph*, April 4, 2010; Diane Kurtzleben, "Seven Ways Your Looks Affect Your Economic Well-Being," *Vox*, June 2, 2014; Suzanne McGee, "For Women, Being 13 Pounds Overweight Means Losing $9,000 a Year in

Salary," *The Guardian*, October 30, 2014. There is a voluminous literature on IQ and earnings; unsurprisingly, IQ correlates closely with SAT scores, success in school and college, and usefulness to employers. Finally, one investigator claims to have found that being a Virgo, Libra, or Taurus is a predictor of high earnings. That would clearly be pertinent to questions of merit and success, but I decline to pursue the astrological branch of this issue.

25. For an extended critique of mainstream economics along these lines, see Fred Block, *Post-industrial Possibilities: A Critique of Economic Discourse* (Berkeley and Los Angeles: University of California Press, 1990). An earlier analysis from the left, specifically of human capital theory, is found in Samuel Bowles and Herbert Gintis, "The Problem with Human Capital Theory: A Marxian Critique," *American Economic Review* 65.2 (1975): 74–82.

26. Murnane and Willett, *Methods Matter*, 136.

27. In addition to Vietnam lottery studies, Murnane and Willett analyze one that was enabled when, in 1981, Congress eliminated a program of the Social Security Administration that offered college financial aid to 18- to 22-year-olds whose fathers had died. This action allowed comparison of two groups that differed only in having received or not received the offer. Significantly more of those who received it enrolled in college (*Methods Matter*, 141–64). The finding contributes hard knowledge to the study of investment in college, which would, however, progress very slowly indeed if fed only by such windfalls from natural experiments.

28. Carnevale, Rose, and Cheah, *The College Payoff*, 3 (figure 1). Having a doctoral degree comes out second highest in the levels of educational attainment because median earnings for PhDs are lower than median earnings for MBAs, MDs, and the like, lumped together as professionals. Apparently, educational attainment and earnings are not covariates at the top levels. That's odd.

Chapter 3. What Makes People "Well-Off"—or Not?

1. For an account of how human capital theory took root, see Pedro Nuno Teixeira, "Gary Becker's Early Work on Human Capital—Collaborations and Distinctiveness," *IZA Journal of Labor Economics* (2014): 3–12, https://link .springer.com/content/pdf/10.1186/s40172-014-0012-2.pdf. Becker's *Human Capital* (New York: Columbia University Press, 1964) has strongly influenced the vast body of research since then about education as an investment.

2. The social construction of human subjects has been a long-term interest in sociology, philosophy. and education, in the works of John Dewey, Alfred North Whitehead, Shirley Brice Heath, Judith Butler, Jean Anyon, Pierre Bourdieu, and many others. One study of curriculum for developing compliant adults was historically situated by Amy Wan in

Producing Good Citizens (Pittsburgh: University of Pittsburgh Press, 2014), which examines government literacy programs for immigrants around the time of World War I.

3. Unsurprisingly, estimates of their political positions vary widely depending on how "liberal" is defined and on which practical or philosophical issues are taken as indicators. Most estimates I've seen classify around 70 percent of academic economists as liberal. Voter registration is easier to pin down. In 2016, more than 80 percent of economists at forty "leading U.S. universities" were registered Democrats (Mitchell Langbert, Anthony J. Quain, and Daniel B. Klein, "Faculty Voter Registration in Economics, History, Journalism, Law, and Psychology," *Economics Journal Watch* 13.3 (2016): 422–51.

4. For data on unequal family investments in children especially under six, see Sabino Kornrich, "Inequalities in Parental Spending on Young Children, 1972–2010," *AERA Open* 2.2 (2016), https://doi.org/10.1177/2332858416644180. A compelling ethnography that compares family investment in and influence on child development is Annette Lareau, *Unequal Childhoods: Class, Race, and Family Life* (Berkeley: University of California Press, 2003).

5. Payback is a product of the advertising firm McKinney. See "Payback: Online Game by McKinney for Next Gen Personal Finance Helps College-bound Students Manage College Debt," Cision PR Newswire, October 3, 2017, http://www.prnewswire.com/news-releases/payback-online-game-by -mckinney-for-next-gen-personal-finance-helps-college-bound-students -manage-college-debt-300528384.html. See also Ron Lieber, "A Game to Help Students Pay the Right Price for College," *New York Times*, September 29, 2017.

6. "K–12 and College Completion Rates Set Record," *Education Week* 32.12 (2012): 5.

7. The same can be said of K–12 in the United States. Instead of a singular "American schooling," school in the United States is systemically divided and unequal like higher education. The main division is between public schools and tuition-charging private schools. This division is further stratified into traditional public schools, accountable to local and state authorities, versus charter schools financed by public funds but subsidized by private sources and not as accountable to public oversight as traditional schools. Then there is the distinction between private religious and private nonsectarian, as separate subsystems of schooling. In addition, public schools are also differentiated by location: urban versus suburban versus rural as one distinction, with further differences depending on race and class (inner city low-income public schools serving minority students versus urban middle-income and high-income schools serving mostly white students in more affluent neighborhoods). The tradition of financing public schools by local property taxes especially privileges white families in high-tax residential suburbs while public schools

in multiracial towns and cities typically deploy "catchment" subdistricts to install racist assignments of students to local units.

8. Doug Lederman, "College Isn't Worth a Million Dollars," *Inside Higher Ed*, April 7, 2008.

9. Alan Benson, Raimundo Esteva, and Frank S. Levy, "Dropouts, Taxes, and Risk: The Economic Return to College under Realistic Assumptions," *Social Science Research Network*, January 26, 2015, https://ssrn.com/abstract =2325657. The authors hold that the advantages of a first-tier education in California apply broadly in other state systems. Their study points to an additional rejoinder to a uniform college payoff: the return for women was consistently higher than that for men at both California tiers. In fact, a man starting a CSU education in 1980, a time of high inflation and hence costly student loans, would have done better financially by taking his high school diploma straight into the job market.

10. At Harvard, Yale, and Princeton, for example, the four-year graduation rate is about 97 percent. A brief look at the College Scorecard (https:// collegescorecard.ed.gov/) shows how extreme the variation is across institutions.

11. In addition to these four assumptions, the authors write of a fifth that leads to high estimates of the economic return on investment: the reckoning of both college costs and eventual earnings in pretax figures—whereas families actually use after-tax assets to finance college costs.

12. A 2005 survey of 24 studies concluded that going to a prestigious and expensive university had a statistically significant but "very small effect on earnings." Liang Zhang, *Does Quality Pay? Benefits of Attending a High-Cost, Prestigious College* (London: Routledge, 2009), 2.

13. Dirk Witteveen and Paul Attewell, "The Earnings Payoff from Attending a Selective College," *Social Science Research* 66 (January 30, 2017): 154–69. This more recent study is theoretically sophisticated and method-ologically advanced. I base the following discussion on its results, though without implying that the authors would endorse my inferences.

14. To be sure, colleges differ in how they measure and report selectivity. No doubt some of them define "application" more broadly than others, and it is possible and legal to swell a pool of applicants by encouraging many who have little chance of acceptance. The percentage of applicants accepted is not so firm a number as average SAT score or rank in class.

15. Mark Schneider, "How Much Is That Bachelor's Degree Really Worth? The Million Dollar Misunderstanding," *Education Outlook* (American Enterprise Institute for Public Policy Research), no. 5 (May 2009). These figures do not take into account tuition, fees, and other costs, but those do not differ much between the most selective private institutions and the group just below them.

16. Elizabeth A. Harris and Josh Katz, "Why Are New York's Schools Segregated? It's Not as Simple as Housing," *New York Times*, May 2, 2018.

17. And *securing* the educational rewards of this investment may require continued parental vigilance and the badgering of school administrators. For a striking example, featuring a yearlong fight against a redistricting plan in one such suburb, see Annette Lareau, Elliot B. Weininger, and Amanda Barrett Cox, "How Entitled Parents Hurt Schools," *New York Times*, June 24, 2018.

18. There are of course contingencies that complicate the family's planning: Will their college student receive financial aid? How much will he or she work for pay during the academic year and summer vacations? How much debt will the student assume? And so on. Life brings surprises and changes of mind; most models do not take those into account.

19. "Income and Wealth in the United States: An Overview of Recent Data" (drawing on data from US Census reports), Peter G. Peterson Foundation, November 9, 2022, https://www.pgpf.org/blog/2023/02/income-and-wealth-in-the-united-states-an-overview-of-recent-data. Income inequality by race was reported for 2020 by Peterson to be $67,521 for white households, compared to $45,870 for Blacks and $55,321 for Hispanics. Asian households topped the list at a $94,903 median income for 2020.

20. There were nine colleges in the United States in 1776, including seven of the eight present-day Ivy League schools (all but Cornell). After Harvard's founding in 1636, no other college existed in Massachusetts until Bowdoin was founded in 1794, 26 years before Maine became a separate state. Robert Samuel Fletcher, author of *A History of Oberlin College from Its Foundation through the Civil War* (Oberlin, OH: Oberlin College, 1943), thought that in 1860 Oberlin was probably the largest college or university in the United States, with about 400 students. So I remember from his introductory class in American history, which I took in 1949. For a brief account of the stagnation of the American college during the first two-thirds of the nineteenth century, see the early chapters of Lawrence R. Veysey, *The Emergence of the American University* (Chicago: University of Chicago Press, 1965).

21. Similarly, when Horace Mann saluted education for turning wilderness into farmland, forests into ships, and so on (see chapter 1), he knew that these socially valuable projects would make some individuals rich, but he celebrated education as a national investment, not a personal one.

22. Christopher Jencks and David Riesman, *The Academic Revolution* (1968; reprint, London: Transaction, 2002), 1.

23. On race, see "Age Distribution of College Students 14 Years Old and Over by Sex, 1949 to 2019, Table A-6," and "Population 18 and 19 Years Old by School Enrollment Status, Sex, Race, and Hispanic Origin, October 1967 to 2019, Table A5b," US Census Bureau, February 2, 2021, Washington, DC. Foundational histories of community colleges include Arthur M. Cohen and

Florence B. Brawer, *The American Community College* (San Francisco: Jossey-Bass, 1982); Steven Brint and Jerome Karabel, *The Diverted Dream: Community Colleges and the Promise of Educational Opportunity in America, 1900–1985* (New York: Oxford University Press, 1989); and Kevin J. Dougherty, *The Contradictory College: The Conflicting Origins, Impacts, and Futures of the Community College* (Albany: SUNY Press, 1994). The seminal study on the conflicted roles of the community college was Burton R. Clark, "The 'Cooling-Out' Function in Higher Education," *American Journal of Sociology* 65.6 (1960): 569–576.

24. "A Losing Legacy," *Harvard Crimson*, May 28, 2015 (commencement issue), https://www.thecrimson.com/article/2015/5/28/staff-losing-legacy -admissions/. As the *Crimson* editorial notes, many applicants with no Harvard parent have had schooling and fine-tuning comparable to those of legacies. The picture should be glossed as one of class privilege more than of Harvard inbreeding.

25. Timothy J. Bartik and Brad J. Hershbein, "Degrees of Poverty: The Relationship between Family Income Background and the Returns to Education," Upjohn Institute Working Paper (Kalamazoo, MI: W. E. Upjohn Institute for Employment Research, 2018), 18–284.

Chapter 4. Education for Jobs and Careers

1. Not that they lack interest in those matters or want to shut down lines of inquiry that might foster criticism of the status quo. Most economists, sociologists, and professors of education are liberals who consider extreme inequality a social ill and view generationally transmitted inequality as an impediment to well-functioning markets (see chapter 3, note 3).

2. The pandemic's enhancement of choices especially for lower-wage and noncollege labor has been widely noted. See, for example, Noam Scheiber's feature report "How the Pandemic Has Given Workers New Leverage," *New York Times*, November 2, 2021, B1, B4. However, this pandemic wage bump was largely negated by galloping price inflation in 2021–22, as well as by the inability of part-time workers to force employers to regularize their "just-in-time" erratic work scheduling. See Scheiber's subsequent report "Few Gains for Part-Time Workers," *New York Times*, February 4, 2022, B1, B3.

3. I have noted that "choice" is an odd term for what takes students to college. For many raised in families above the median income, it's a little like the choice to be 18 years old after being 17. College is an obligatory chapter in their life scripts. "Selection bias" is fine as a term of art for scholars but is odd in the same way, if it references life as lived. Upper-class infants are not born with abilities that lead them to select college, so much as they are *raised* to have the abilities that will let them be students at Stanford or Princeton one day.

4. For an interview with Diane Auer Jones about the Trump administration's strategies and philosophy, see Andrew Kreighbaum, "DeVos to Announce New Push for Deregulation, Innovation," *Inside Higher Ed*, July 29, 2018, https://www.insidehighered.com/news/2018/07/30/trump-administration -official-describes-plan-rethink-higher-education-through. Enrollment in for-profit universities more than quadrupled from 2000 to 2010; then fell by almost 50%, according to the National Center for Education Statistics, "The Condition of Education; Letter from the Commissioner," 2018, *https://nces.ed .gov/programs/coe/indicator_cha.asp*.

5. See Madeline Ngo, "After Dropping Free Community College Plan, Democrats Explore Their Options," *New York Times*, October 23, 2021, A19; and Katie Rogers, "Free Community College Excluded from Spending Bill, First Lady Says," *New York Times*, February 8, 2022, A13.

6. Richard Arum and Josipa Roksa, *Academically Adrift: Limited Learning on College Campuses* (Chicago: University of Chicago Press, 2011), 35–36.

7. Mary Grigsby, *College Life through the Eyes of Students* (Albany: State University of New York Press, 2009), 117.

8. Arum and Roksa, *Academically Adrift*, 4.

9. Rebekah Nathan, *My Freshman Year: What a Professor Learned by Becoming a Student* (New York: Penguin, 2005), 113.

10. David F. Labaree, *How to Succeed in School without Really Learning: The Credentials Race in American Education* (New Haven: Yale University Press, 1997), 259, quoted in Arum and Roksa, *Academically Adrift*, 17.

11. Bryan Caplan, "The World Might Be Better-Off without College," *Atlantic* (January–February 2018), 3.

12. Joel Spring, *The Sorting Machine: National Education Policy since 1945*, rev. ed. (New York: Addison-Wesley Longman, 1988).

13. The degree may also signal out-of-class achievements—impressing mentors, staying out of serious academic and legal trouble, living apart from nurturing or nagging parents, captaining the field hockey team, being a student tutor in the writing lab, and so on. Such behavioral development also takes place through classroom delivery of curriculum. Traditional pedagogy transfers standard canons of required and approved subject matters. John Dewey broadly opposed the academic abstractness of school curricula whereby teacher-centered instruction detached knowledge making from student experience, feeling, and participation.

14. Nick Collins, "Oxbridge Students' MA 'Degrees' under Threat," *London Telegraph*, February 12, 2011. Note that almost all Oxford students graduate with honors of one grade or another.

15. Bryan Caplan, *The Case against Education: Why the System Is a Waste of Time and Money* (Princeton, NJ: Princeton University Press, 2018), 215. Caplan has some fun with his objections to human capital purism. For

instance, one can get the "best education in the world" (at Princeton) for nothing. Just "show up and start attending classes. No one will stop you. . . . Gorge yourself at Princeton's all-you-can-eat buffet of the mind. After four years you'll have a college education but no BA. If you are a paying student, you can skip the education but have a diploma. Which will be more use on the job market?" (26–27). In spite of quips like this, his book is a handy guide to signaling.

16. See Basil Bernstein's *Class, Codes, and Control*, vol. 1: *Theoretical Studies towards a Sociology of Language* (London: Routledge & Kegan Paul, 1971). Doubtless, the elaborated code has changed a lot in 50 years, not to mention cross-Atlantic differences in class and language. But the bonding force of dialect remains strong, and a college degree sends a signal that the applicant talks like "us."

17. For an ethnography documenting class and race differences in the development of children at school and in the home, see Annette Lareau, *Unequal Childhoods: Class, Race, and Family Life*, 2nd ed. (Berkeley: University of California Press, 2011). For a feminist counter to Paul Willis's report on working-class "lads," see Angela McRobbie, "Settling Accounts with Subcultures: A Feminist Critique," *Screen Education* 34 (1980); and McRobbie, *Feminism and Youth Culture: From Jackie to Just Seventeen* (Boston: Unwin, 1991).

18. Two critical overviews of the research that share many of my concerns, but not my overall assessment, are Michael Hout, "Social and Economic Returns to College Education in the United States," *Annual Review of Sociology* 38 (2012): 379–400; and Philip Oreopoulos and Uros Petronijevic, "Making College Worth It: A Review of Research on the Returns to Higher Education," *Future of Children* 23.1 (May 2013): 41–65.

19. Sophie Quinton (Stateline.org), "Why Universities Charge Extra for Specialized Degrees," Government Technology, June 1, 2017, https://www.govtech.com/education/higher-ed/why-universities-charge-extra-for-specialized-degrees.html.

20. Lizette Alvarez, "Florida May Reduce Tuition for Select Majors," *New York Times*, December 9, 2012.

21. Anthony P. Carnevale, Jeff Strohl, and Michelle Melton, *What's It Worth? The Economic Value of College Majors* (Washington, DC: Georgetown University Center on Education and the Workforce, 2013), 6. These figures are median annual incomes for all full-time workers with terminal bachelors' degrees in the named majors, not lifetime returns on having chosen those majors—"major premia," as it were. They cannot be, because choosing a major is usually not independent of the initial investment in "college." Saying, as these authors do, that choosing a major has greater economic consequences than getting a college degree muddies the conceptual waters. Choosing a

major is not separable from choosing college; rather, it is one step toward getting that degree and one opportunity that comes with having chosen college. Of course, for some students, that initial decision was driven by the wish to major in, say, accounting or music and then be an accountant or clarinetist. That many students change their fields of study while in college might count as a further benefit of the initial investment in college.

To generalize: going to college is a choice that carries with it various freedoms unavailable to high school grads who go right into the job market. Another freedom is that of changing one's plans for education and career; another is choosing to study hard, or hardly at all. We might think of such flexibility in young adulthood as another form of class privilege. True, it is available to a few students from working-class backgrounds who receive enough scholarship support to attend elite four-year colleges without having to work large numbers of hours or accrue large amounts of debt, and without having to spread their undergraduate studies over five, six, or more years. That track is one way class mobility happens.

22. The disconnect between graduates' employment and the fields in which they majored was critically studied decades ago in two-year colleges by Fred Pincus, in "The False Promises of Community Colleges: Class Conflict and Vocational Education," *Harvard Educational Review* 50.4 (August 1980). Several years earlier, W. Norton Grubb and Marvin Lazerson critiqued the unexamined assumption that collegiate vocationalism pays off. "Rally 'Round the Workplace: Continuities and Fallacies in Career Education," *Harvard Educational Review* 45.4 (November 1975). Even earlier, focused on the payoff of four-year degrees, Ivar Berg and Sherry Gorelick marshaled data to question such a connection in their humorously subtitled book, *Education and Jobs: The Great Training Robbery* (Boston: Beacon Press, 1971). At that time, a demographic crisis overwhelmed the job market. Large numbers of baby boomers were graduating in a national job market unable to absorb them. The large surplus of unemployed college grads enabled employers to demand college degrees for employment in jobs previously requiring high school diplomas, a practice then referred to as "credentialism." The persistent underemployment of college grads and employer demand for higher academic credentials than required for a job spilled into the twenty-first century, when economists renamed it "degree inflation." See, for example, Catherine Rampell, "It Takes a B.A. to Find a Job as a File Clerk," *New York Times*, February 20, 2013, A1, A3.

23. Yasser Al-Saleh, "Why Engineers Make Great CEOs," *Forbes*, May 29, 2014; Patricia M. Flynn and Michael A. Quinn, "Economics: Good Choice of Major for Future CEOs," *American Economist* 55.1 (2010): 58–72, https://journals.sagepub.com/doi/10.1177/056943451005500107. Al-Saleh refers to the *Fortune* 500; Flynn and Quinn to the S&P.

24. The majority of K–12 teachers, especially in grades K–5, are women, as are registered nurses; that they choose dependable but middling salaries in the helping professions is consonant with the traditionally gendered system of labor, which is unfriendly to women who choose male-dominated fields like tech and science. On that, see Katie Benner, "Women in Tech Reveal Culture of Harassment," *New York Times*, July 1, 2017, A1, A16; and Claire Cain Miller, "Tech's Man Problem," *New York Times*, April 16, 2014, BU1, BU6–BU7. A presupposition undergirding the research is that students and their families make educational choices primarily on economic grounds. The hope of high pay does help explain some recent trends, such as the flow of undergraduates into STEM fields and vocational programs in recent years, though it doesn't account for this gender bias. Economic rationality might include a wish for predictable outcomes and incur little risk, but the deeply gendered choices of major leading to employment tracks women into lifelong lower earnings. On the rising proportion of college students majoring in STEM fields before the pandemic, see "Science & Engineering Degree Attainment, 2017," National Student Clearinghouse Research Center, April 11, 2017), https://nscresearchcenter.org/snapshotreport-science-and-engineering-degree-completion-by-gender/.

25. "BME Jobs Expected to Grow 6%," UC Davis Biomedical Engineering newsletter, April 13, 2022, https://bme.ucdavis.edu/news/bme-jobs-expected-grow-72-percent.

26. "Occupational Employment and Wages, 2006," Bureau of Labor Statistics, May 17, 2017, https://www.bls.gov/news.release/archives/ocwage_05172007.pdf; "Nuclear Engineers" in Bureau of Labor Statistics, *Occupational Outlook Handbook*, accessed April 13, 2018, https://www.bls.gov/ooh/architecture-and-engineering/nuclear-engineers.htm?view_full.

27. Tom DiChristopher and John W. Schoen, "Petroleum Engineering Degrees Seen Going from Boom to Bust," CNBC, December 4, 2015, https://www.cnbc.com/2015/12/04/petroleum-engineering-degrees-seen-going-from-boom-to-bust.html (citing Lloyd Heinze, U.S. Association of Petroleum Department Heads).

28. "Petroleum Engineers," in Bureau of Labor Statistics, *Occupational Outlook Handbook*, 2021, https://www.bls.gov/ooh/architectural-and-engineering/petroleum-engineers.

29. Peter Cappelli, *Will College Pay Off? A Guide to the Most Important Financial Decision You Will Ever Make* (New York: PublicAffairs, 2015), 42. The BLS in 2021was more bullish for "computer and information technology" degree holders than it was for petroleum engineers. The bureau predicted a 13 percent jump in job openings in that field for the 2020s due to growth in cloud computing, big data collection and storage, and information security. "Petroleum Engineers."

30. Harry Braverman, *Labor and Monopoly Capital: The Degradation of Work in the Twentieth Century* (1974; reprint, New York: Monthly Review Press, 1998). The deskilling and dispossession of labor articulated by Braverman was incorporated into and superseded after 1980 by twin policies of neoliberalism and globalization, which now dominate education and economic life in general, as David Harvey explains in *A Brief History of Neoliberalism* (New York: Oxford University Press, 2005).

31. For my detailed adaptation of Gramsci's idea of hegemony to an earlier and deep social and economic transformation, see *Selling Culture: Magazines, Markets, and Class at the Turn of the Century* (New York: Verso, 1996).

32. Carnevale, Strohl, and Melton, *What's It's Worth?* 6, 119, 170.

33. Cappelli, *Will College Pay Off?* 34–35.

34. See "Careers in Turf Management: Job Options and Requirements," *Best Accredited College*, October 20, 2021, https://bestaccreditedcolleges.org /articles/careers-in-turf-management-job-options-and-requirements.html.

35. I did the aggregation, working from *What's It Worth?* and four other studies: Joseph Altongi, Erica Blom, and Costas Meghir, "Heterogeneity in Human Capital Investments: High School Curriculum, College Major, and Careers," NBER Working Paper 17985, National Bureau of Economic Research (2012); Chang Hwan Kim, Christopher R. Tamborini, and Arthur Sakamoto, "Field of Study in College and Lifetime Earnings in the United States," *Sociology of Education* 88.4 (October 2015): 320–39, DOI 10.1177/0038040715602132; Kate Zaback, Andy Carlson, and Matt Crellin, *The Economic Benefit of Postsecondary Degrees: A State and National Level Analysis* (State Higher Education Executive Officers, 2012); Stephanie Owen and Isabel Sawhill, "Should Everyone Go to College?" CCF Brief 50, Center on Children and Families, Brookings Institution, (2013). These studies used categories similar to or the same as mine. I assigned outlying majors to one or another of the groups by commonsensical criteria. The ordering of groups by monetary outcomes was consistent across all five studies: STEM majors were at the top and education majors at the bottom, with minor irregularities in between.

36. Richard Hoggart, *The Uses of Literacy: Aspects of Working-Class Life with Special References to Publications and Entertainments* (1957; reprint, London: Routledge, 1998).

37. According to Cappelli, surveys of managers "report that only about 10 percent of the knowledge, skills, and abilities they use on the job were learned in any classroom experience" (*Will College Pay Off?* 39). But perhaps they were learned in the interstices of "college"? Cappelli supplies no reference. A lot of CEOs (nine of those leading the top ten corporations) majored in business or engineering fields, but history, pharmacy, economics, and many other majors are on the resumes of the *Fortune* 500. As Steve Jobs said in an interview, "A lot of people in our industry haven't had very diverse experiences. So they don't

have enough dots to connect, and they end up with very linear solutions without a broad perspective on the problem. The broader one's understanding of the human experience, the better design we will have." Quoted in Gary Wolf, "The Next Insanely Great Thing," *Wired*, February 1, 1996.

Chapter 5. The Payoff of College Education for the United States

1. Mann expressed his legendary claim thus: "Education then, beyond all other devices of human origin, is the great equalizer of the conditions of men, the balance-wheel of the social machinery." *Twelfth Annual Report on Education*, delivered 1848, printed 1849, State Library of Massachusetts, accessed July 9, 2023, https://archives.lib.state.ma.us./handle/2452/204731. Herbert Gintis and Samuel Bowles, *Schooling in Capitalist America* (New York: Basic Books, 1976); John Marsh, *Class Dismissed: How We Cannot Teach or Learn Our Way out of Inequality* (New York: Monthly Review Press, 2011). Perhaps the most famous brief rejection of class cooperation was the first sentence of the constitution of the Industrial Workers of the World (1905): "The Employing Class and the Working Class have nothing in common." Facsimile of the original constitution available online at IWW, accessed July 6, 2023, https://www.iww.org/resources/constitution/. On the IWW, see Melvyn Dubofsky, *We Shall Be All: A History of the Industrial Workers of the World* (1969; reprint, Urbana: University of Illinois Press, 2000).

2. Wilson's remark about GM's and America's congruent interests has a fascinating backstory. Nominated as secretary of defense by President-Elect Eisenhower in December 1952, Wilson was called the Senate confirmation hearing the next month, which was closed to the press, but his remarks were leaked to the press through eyewitness accounts. Wilson, the powerful and wealthy GM chief known as "Engine Charlie," claimed he was misquoted, and transcripts later had him putting country before company in his testimony, but the first quote stuck. See Justin Hyde, "GM's 'Engine Charlie' Wilson Learned to Live with a Misquote," *Detroit Free Press*, September 14, 2008.

3. See Ann Carrns, "Will That College Degree Pay Off?" *New York Times*, August 14, 2021, B5; Erica Green, "For-Profit Colleges Preyed on Black and Female Students, Suit Says," *New York Times*, April 12, 2022, A14; Rick Seltzer, "Analysis Finds Benefits to Attending a Selective College and Penalties for Attending a For-Profit," *Inside Higher Ed*, September 6, 2018; Ashley A. Smith, "For-Profit College Attendance Linked to Poor Financial Outcomes," *Inside Higher Ed*, October 23, 2013.

4. Quoted in Maurice R. Berube, *American Presidents and Education* (Westport, CT: Greenwood Press, 1991), 96.

5. Zolan Kanno-Younger, Alon Rappoport, and Emily Cochrane, "Biden's Budget Tilts Priorities toward Center," *New York Times*, March 29, 2022, A14, A16.

6. See table 1, "Numbers of Public and Private Two-Year Colleges, 1900–1978," in Arthur M. Cohen and Florence B. Brawer, *The American Community College* (San Francisco: Jossey-Bass, 1982), 10.

7. See, for example, earlier texts on the already-recognized predicament of too many graduates chasing too few jobs, including Richard B. Freeman, *The Overeducated American* (New York: Academic Press, 1976): Sidney P. Marland, *Career Education: A Proposal for Reform* (New York: McGraw-Hill, 1974); and Ivar Berg, *Education and Jobs: The Great Training Robbery* (1971; New York: Percheron Press, 2003).

8. Karl Marx and Friedrich Engels, *The German Ideology, Including Theses on Feuerbach and Introduction to a Critique of Political Economy* (Amherst, NY: Prometheus Books, 1998).

9. Karl Marx, *Capital: A Critique of Political Economy*, vol. 1, trans. Ben Fowkes (London: Penguin, 1992).

10. Claudia Goldin and Lawrence F. Katz, *The Race between Education and Technology* (Cambridge, MA: Belknap Press of Harvard University Press, 2008).

11. Although Katrina was an act of nature and the draft lottery was an act of Congress, both qualify as natural *experiments* in that they were not driven by a wish to create groups so that economists might study the economic effects of different educational "treatments" on their lifetime earnings.

12. See Laurent Belsie, "The Rise and Fall of the College Graduate Wage Premium," *The Digest* (National Bureau of Economic Research), no. 1 (January 2008), https://www.nber.org/digest/jan08/rise-and-fall-college -graduate-wage-premium.

13. Goldin and Katz, *The Race between Education and Technology*, 1–2. Subsequent citations to this work appear by page in the text.

14. I omit analysis of the role played in their story by "skill-biased technological change," illuminating though it is. See their chapter 3 (89–125). But read it with caution: their argument is couched in the language and ideology of technological determinism. For instance: "New technologies alter the relative demand for different types of labor." Their chief example is the computer—which of course did not just drop from the sky and begin altering the demand for skilled labor. It was conceived over a long period, going back theoretically at least to Alan Turing but arguably to Jeremy Bentham. It was shaped as a technology partly through funding by the US military. Then, companies such as Google, Amazon, and Facebook took charge of the internet with the aim of profiting from sales of users' attention (stimulating and directing consumption through advertising) and of data about them (collecting and selling customer data to efficiently target marketing). Compare the similar story of television, as told by Raymond Williams in *Television: Technology and Cultural Form* (London: Fontana, 1974). Such

technologies have naturally been shaped by those who have the resources to use and adapt the technology—with increasingly concrete visions of their profitability and their impact on social relations. It's enough to make citizens pull for a victory of education over technology, sooner rather than later. But that's another story.

15. Long after New England towns were fully settled, property lines, rights, and values were a major concern of the owners. Farmers built the thousands of miles of stone fences that run through untended woodlands to mark the boundaries of real estate. For a study of how colonial New Englanders altered the landscape to suit their agrarian needs once they had dispossessed the indigenous populations, see William Cronon, *Changes in the Land: Indians, Colonists, and the Ecology of New England* (New York: Hill and Wang, 2003).

16. See Gillian Brockell, "'A republic, if you can keep it': Did Ben Franklin Really Say Impeachment Day's Favorite Quote?" *Washington Post*, December 18, 2019.

17. William Giles Atkins, *History of the Town of Hawley, Franklin County, Massachusetts, from Its First Settlement in 1771 to 1887* (West Cummington, MA: privately printed, 1887), 37, 16. I infer that the six months of free public schooling required by law ran from November through April. These were one-room schoolhouses. Some of them were still in use in the early 1920s, and I spoke in the 1980s with a woman who, just after high school, served as the last teacher at one near my house. She walked two and a half miles to get there each morning and, after stoking up the wood stove, taught at most nine students and at fewest five. She was basically a tutor for two farm families. One should keep such conditions in mind when weighing the role of public schooling in human capital development. Besides Atkins's history, I also draw on an unfinished manuscript by Harrison Parker, the town's most recent historian, who tells the story of the Cooley family's luck in having iron ore under their "worthless" land (photocopied pages, "The Sons and Daughters of Hawley").

18. Marshall Sahlins, *Stone Age Economics* (1972; reprinted, New York: Routledge, 2017), esp. ch. 3, "The Domestic Mode of Production."

19. Atkins, *History of the Town of Hawley*, 37.

20. In 1966, 80 years after the 1886 survey of Hawley's wealth, I bought 150 acres of field and forest for less than $100 an acre. Since then, 50 years or more, the price has risen at about the same pace as inflation—in other words, with no further return on investment. Two or three traditional farms remain out of 107 in 1886. A few boutique farmers sell organic yogurt, grass-fed beef, and such. A land trust preserves some open farmland and a lot of woodland. A state forest comprises 8,000 acres. Less than half the land is in private hands and potentially salable. Hawley has no stores or gas stations, no post office or police department, one cross-country ski resort. Its population is a little more than

300, many of them exurbanites or retired people. Five years passed recently without a birth, and Hawley has no school of its own. Nonetheless, it's been a great place to live and puzzle over the return on investment in education.

21. Goldin and Katz, *The Race between Education and Technology*, 11.

22. There were brief variations on and departures from this trajectory; Goldin and Katz's chapter 5, "Economic Foundations of the High School Movement," is a wide-ranging and perspicuous exploration of interplay between markets and education.

Chapter 6. At the End of the College Rainbow

1. J. Cheeseman Day and E. C. Newburger, "The Big Payoff: Educational Attainment and Synthetic Estimates of Work-Life Earnings," Current Population Reports (23-210), US Census Bureau (July 2002), https://www .census.gov/prod/2002pubs/p23-210.pdf. This publication is the first data source indicating a million-dollar payoff for the college degree.

2. See John Miller, "Dangerous Talk about Education and Economic Mobility," *Dollars and Sense* (July–August 2019): 9–14. Miller cites the college premium in the first two decades of this century as stable at around 70 percent.

3. On the selective increase in the premium, especially the larger median earnings gap between high school and college graduates from 1979 to 2012 (differentiated here by gender as well), see David H. Autor, "Skills, Education, and the Rise of Earnings Inequality among 'the Other 99 Percent,'" *Science* 23 (May 2014): 3–5, 14, 17. Of many reports on student debt, see Tara Siegel Bernard, "No Degree, but Saddled with Debt," *New York Times*, June 7, 2020, B1, B5; and "Student Debt Is Crushing, Canceling: It Is Still Bad Policy," *New York Times*, May 15, 2022, SR10. On Biden's long-promised loan forgiveness plan, see Michael D. Shear, Jim Tankersley, and Zolan Kanno-Youngs, "Dogged Push for Biden's Ear on Loan Debt," *New York Times*, August 27, 2022, A1, A14. The plan proposed "canceling $10,000 in debt for those earning less than $125,000 a year and $20,000 for those for low-income students. [Biden's] plan also reduces payments for federal student borrowers for years to come" (A14). To date the executive action has been blocked in court by lawsuits filed by Republican congressional leaders.

4. Jeanna Smialek, "The Dark Side of the White-Hot Labor Market," *New York Times*, June 7, 2022, A1, A15; Lydia DePillis, "Job Openings Drop Slightly, but Workers Remain Scarce," *New York Times*, July 7, 2022, B4.

5. Table 3, "College Enrollment and Work Activity of Recent High School and College Graduates," Bureau of Labor Statistics, 2021, www.bls.gov/news .release/hsgec.nrO.htm; Elizabeth Redden, "41% of Recent Grads Work in Jobs Not Requiring a Degree," *Inside Higher Ed*, February 17, 2020, https:// www.insidehighered.com/quicktakes/2020/02/18/41-recent-grads-work-jobs -not-requiring-degree; Don Troop, "Here's Your Diploma. Now Here's Your

Mop," *Chronicle of Higher Education*, October 22, 2010, A6; Patricia Cohen, "Long Road to Adulthood Is Growing Even Longer," *New York Times*, June 13, 2010, 26; Catherine Rampell, "Many with New College Degree Find the Job Market Humbling," *New York Times*, May 19, 2011, A1, A4; Rampell, "It Takes a B.A. to Find a Job as a File Clerk," *New York Times*, February 20, 2013, A1, A3; Rachel Swarns, "Degree? Check. Enthusiasm? Check. Job? Not So Fast," *New York Times*, June 9, 2014, A12; Ann Carrns, "Your Money Advisor: Will That College Degree Pay Off?" *New York Times*, August 14, 2021, B5.

6. "Net Worth of U.S. Billionaires Soared by $1 Trillion—to Total of $4 Trillion—since Pandemic Began," Americans for Tax Fairness, December 8, 2020, https://americansfortaxfairness.org/issue/net-worth-u-s-billionaires-soared-1-trillion-total-4-trillion-since-pandemic-began/. For the 2023 *Forbes* list, see "Forbes World's Billionaires List 2023: The Top 200," *Forbes*, July 7, 2023, https://www.forbes.com/sites/forbeswealthteam/2023/07/07/forbes-worlds-billionaires-list-2023-the-top-200/?sh=6dc71493224e. See also Stephen Gandel, "C.E.O. Earnings Soar, Widening the Pay Gap," *New York Times*, June 8, 2022, B4; Patricia Cohen, "A Bigger Pie, but Uneven Slices: Research Shows Slim Gains for the Bottom 50%," *New York Times*, December 7, 2016, B1, B3; and Patricia Cohen, "Profits Swell, but Laborers See No Relief," *New York Times*, July 14, 2018, A1, A16. As David H. Autor notes, "Between 1979 and 2012, the share of all household income accruing to the to the top percentile of U.S. households rose from 10.0% to 22.5%" ("Skills, Education, and the Rise of Earnings Inequality," 3–4).

7. Jeanna Smialek, "Soaring Inflation Tightens Squeeze on U.S. Consumers," *New York Times*, July 14, 2022, A1, A16.

8. Patricia Cohen noted that "since the 1950s, three-quarters of working Americans have seen no change in lifetime income" ("Why the Pain Persists Even as Incomes Rise," *New York Times*, September 16, 2017, BU1). See also Emily Badger and Eve Washington, "Across U.S., It's Getting Harder to Find a Home," *New York Times*, July 15, 2022, A1, A14. On the decline in state funding for higher education, see Thomas G. Mortenson, "Budget and Appropriations: State Funding: A Race to the Bottom," *American Council on Education Journal* (Winter 2012). Mortenson wrote: "Based on the trends since 1980, average state fiscal support for higher education will reach zero by 2059. . . . Public higher education is gradually being privatized." Men's median wages were basically flat from 1973 ($58,412 in 2020 dollars) to 2019 ($58,173 in 2020 dollars), though women's wages rose gradually in those years from about $33,000 to about $47,000 (Women's Bureau, "Median Annual Earnings by Sex, Race, and Hispanic Ethnicity, 1960–2020," US Department of Labor, accessed June 27, 2023, https://www.dol.gov/agencies/wb/data/earnings/median-annual-sex-race-hispanic-ethnicity). Also, median family income was flat from 1989 ($69,152) to 2012 ($70,300), according to US Census Bureau data.

9. Josh Moody, "A 5th Straight Semester of Enrollment Declines," *Inside Higher Ed*, May 26, 2022. See also Emma Whitford, "Millions Cancel and Change Education Plans in Response to the Pandemic," *Inside Higher Ed*, April 30, 2020.

10. Scott Jaschik, "Decline in Male, Black, and Latino Students Planning on College," *Inside Higher Ed*, May 23, 2022; "College Students Are Not OK," *New York Times*, May 24, 2022, SR6; Chuck Collins, "The Wealthy Kids Are All Right," *American Prospect*, May 28, 2013; Scott Jaschik, "More than a Third of Prospective College Students Are Reconsidering Higher Education," *Inside Higher Ed*, December 3, 2020.

11. Kate Stoltzfus, "Paul Tough on Fixing Higher Education's Broken System," *Educational Leadership* (May 2022): 12–17.

12. For gender inequalities in lifetime earnings in the top 14 majors chosen by men and women, see "Choice of College Major Influences Lifetime Earnings More than Simply Getting a Degree" (University of Kansas press release), *EurekAlert!* September 16, 2015, https://www.eurekalert.org/news-releases. Also, Anthony P. Carnevale, Jeff Strohl, and Michelle Melton provide data on the gender bias toward females in student majors with highest earnings. They use a percentage rather than a dollar figure to emphasize the college premium, claiming an 84 percent boost in lifetime earnings for college graduates (*What's It Worth? The Economic Value of College Majors* [Washington, DC: Georgetown University Center on Education and the Workforce, 2013]). See also Carolyn Sloane, Erik Hurst, and Dan Black, "A Cross-Cohort Analysis of Human Capital Specialization and the College Gender Wage Gap," National Bureau of Economic Research, revised February 2020, nber.org/papers/w26348; and the works cited in note 6, above.

13. Scholars have critiqued this function of education to reproduce existing unequal hierarchies. Herbert Gintis and Samuel Bowles, in *Schooling in Capitalist America* (1976), named it the "correspondence principle," and Joel Spring similarly described it in *The Sorting Machine*, 2nd ed. (1988). See also Jeannie Oakes, *Keeping Track*, rev. ed. (2005); and John Marsh, *Class Dismissed* (2012).

14. Doug Lederman, "Report Documents How Higher Education Exacerbates Racial Inequities," *Inside Higher Ed*, July 31, 2013. Lederman quotes Anthony Carnevale and Jeff Strohl from their study *Separate and Unequal: How Higher Education Reinforces the Intergenerational Reproduction of White Racial Privilege* (Washington, DC: Georgetown University Center on Education and the Workforce, 2013), released the same day.

15. Tressie McMillan Cottom, *Lower Ed: The Troubling Rise of For-Profit Colleges in the New Economy* (New York: New Press, 2017).

16. Doug Lederman, "College Isn't Worth a Million Dollars," *Inside Higher Ed*, April 7, 2008.

17. See Day and Newberger, "The Big Payoff." Five years later, Mark Kantrowitz updated the estimate to $1.2 million, in "The Financial Value of a Higher Education," *NAFSAA: Journal of Student Financial Aid*, 37.1 (2007): 19–27.

18. Sources regarding the million-dollar claim include Philip Oreopoulos and Uros Petronijevic, "Making College Worth It: A Review of Research on the Returns to Higher Education," Working Paper 19053, National Bureau of Economic Research, May 2013, http://www.nber.org/papers/w19053; and Mark Schneider, "How Much Is That Bachelor's Degree Really Worth? The Million-Dollar Misunderstanding," *AEI* (American Enterprise Institute for Public Policy Research), no. 5 (May 2009): 1–7.

19. For a neo-Weberian analysis of persistent social class inequities involving parental status and income that examines "asset hoarding" by the skilled and privileged who endeavor to pass on their advantages only to their own families, see D. Witteveen and P. Attewell, "The Earnings Payoff from Attending a Selective College," *Social Science Research* 66 (2017): 154–69. The authors find that degrees from selective colleges pay off with higher earnings than do degrees from nonselective colleges, especially 4–10 years after graduation, though women graduates of selective colleges earn less than their male peers.

20. Carnevale, Strohl, and Melton, *What's It Worth?*

21. Ohmann, "The Literacy Crisis Is a Fiction If Not a Hoax," *Chronicle of Higher Education*, October 25, 1976, 32. Later, Ohmann took on another sacred cow of dominant culture—technology—which began invading schools and colleges, at great cost, with promises of enhanced student learning. See "Literacy, Technology, and Monopoly Capital," *College English* (December 1979), reprinted in *Politics of Letters* (Middletown, CT: Wesleyan University Press, 1987), 215–29.

22. See Ira Shor, *Culture Wars: School and Society in the Conservative Restoration, 1969–1984* (Chicago: University of Chicago Press, 1986), esp. ch. 3, "Settling for Less, 1975–1982: The War on 'Illiteracy.'"

23. Merrill Shiels, "Why Johnny Can't Write," *Newsweek*, December 8, 1975. This cover story showed a white elementary schoolboy laboring with pencil and paper, and the article featured eminent conservative luminaries prophesying a national cultural collapse. Paul Tough discredits the decline, in Paul Tough, *The Inequality Machine: How College Divides Us* (New York: Houghton-Mifflin Harcourt, 2021), ch. 3, "Fixing the Test."

24. Shor, *Culture Wars*, 58–62. See also Education Commission of the States, *Writing Achievement, 1969–1979*, National Assessment of Educational Progress (Denver, December 1980); and Education Commission of the States, *Three National Assessments of Reading: Changes in Performance, 1970–1980* (Denver, April 1981).

25. Christopher Jencks and Meredith Phillips, eds., *The Black-White Test Score Gap* (Washington, DC: Brookings Institution Press, 1998), esp. chs. 5 and 6.

26. Data on different variables affecting the college payoff can be found in Stephanie Owen and Isabel Sawhill, *Should Everyone Go to College?* (Washington, DC: Brookings Institution, 2013); Carnevale, Strohl, and Melton, *What's It Worth?*; Sandy Baum, Jennifer Ma, and Kathleen Payea, *Education Pays: The Benefits of Higher Education for Individuals and Society* (New York: College Board, 2013); ChanHwan Kim, Christopher R. Tamborini, and Arthur Sakamoto, "Field of Study in College and Lifetime Earnings in the United States," *Sociology of Education* 21 (2015): 1–20; and Rick Seltzer, "Analysis Finds Benefits to Attending a Selective College and Penalties for Attending a For-Profit," *Inside Higher Ed*, September 6, 2018.

27. Sabino Kornrich, "Inequalities in Parental Spending on Young Children, 1972–2010," *AERAOpen* 2.2 (June 2016). See also Sean F. Reardon, "No Rich Child Left Behind," *New York Times*, April 28, 2013, SR6.

28. Annette Lareau, *Unequal Childhoods: Class, Race, and Family Life*, 2nd ed. (Berkeley: University of California Press, 2011), 1–13, 165–97.

29. Sabrina Tavernise, "Education Gap Grows between Rich and Poor, Studies Show," *New York Times*, February 9, 2012; Thomas B. Edsall, "The Reproduction of Privilege," *New York Times*, March 12, 2012. On the class effects of unpaid internships for affluent students, see Ron Lieber, "Internships That Aid All but Interns," *New York Times*, June 11, 2022, B1, B5.

30. Richard Hoggart, *The Uses of Literacy* (London: Chatto Windus, 1956).

31. Stephanie Saul, "Top Colleges Cling to Favoring Alumni's Children," *New York Times*, July 14, 2022, A1, A19.

32. See Kevin Carey, "How Much Does Getting into an Elite College Actually Matter?" *New York Times*, March 15, 2019.

33. Anemona Hartocollis, "Getting into Harvard Is Hard; Here Are 4 Ways to Get an Edge," *New York Times*, November 8, 2018, A13.

34. Theodore Sizer, *Horace's Compromise: The Dilemmas of the American High School* (Boston: Houghton-Mifflin, 1984), 6. Sizer at that time was part of an influential liberal triumvirate of education reformers, including John Goodlad and Ernest Boyer. Oppositional scholars who studied the institutional settings producing biased effects include Michelle Fine (author of *Framing Dropouts*), Jonathan Kozol (*Death at an Early Age* and *Savage Inequalities*), and Herb Kohl (*"I Won't Learn That from You."* In mass higher education, an early and widely debated analysis of postsecondary failure was Burton Clark, "The Cooling-Out Function in Higher Education," *American Journal of Sociology* 65.6 (1960): 569–76. See also Clark's retrospective review in "The Cooling-Out Function Revisited," *New Directions for Community Colleges* 32 (Winter 1980): 15–31.

35. Michel Foucault, *"Society Must Be Defended": Lectures at the College De France, 1975–1976*, trans. David Macey (New York: Picador, 2003), 7–11.

36. See Jacques Steinberg, "Plan B: Skip College," *New York Times*, May 15, 2010, WK1, which quotes an economist from American University declaring that "some high school graduates would be better served by being taught how to behave and communicate in the workplace." Steinberg reports that in one survey of 2,000 businesses in Washington State, "employers said entry-level workers appeared to be most deficient in being able to 'solve problems and make decisions,' 'resolve conflict and negotiate,' 'cooperate with others,' and 'listen actively.'"

37. School disruptions during the pandemic generated much discussion of "learning losses" among students and how to address them once onsite classes resumed. For a discussion of reputed learning losses in cognitive and noncognitive skills, see Claire Cain Miller and Bianca Pallaro, "362 School Counselors on Pandemic's Harm," and Miller, "Tips for Helping Students Recover from Pandemic Stress," both in the *New York Times*, June 20, 2022, A15.

38. The liberal arts–technical version of the "T-shaped" graduate was articulated by Brandon Busteed, chief partnership officer and global head of learn-work innovations at Kaplan University, in Doug Lederman, "Dropping the Degree as a Hiring Requirement" (interview), *Inside Higher Ed*, June 3, 2022. On version 1, see Lindsay McKenzie, "Closing the Skills Gap with Digital Badges," *Inside Higher Ed*, September 26, 2018.

39. "Q&A with Ryan Craig, Author of New Book on Faster, Cheaper College Alternatives," *Inside Higher Ed*, August 22, 2018.

40. For data comparisons of short-term badge programs, see James Gallagher and Adolfo Perez-Gascon, "How to Pay for a Coding Bootcamp in 2023: The Definitive Guide," Career Karma, June 2023, careerkarma.com/blog/how-to-pay-for-coding-bootcamps.

41. For a report on earnings of tech program graduates in the high-wage New York City area at a time when demand for tech employees was high, see Steve Lohr, "A Way Out of Poverty and into an $85,000 Tech Job," *New York Times*, March 16, 2019, B1.

42. Steve Lohr, "Training Gap for Tech Jobs, but a Study Finds Hope," *New York Times*, February 2, 2020. *Fortune* magazine claimed in 2022 that 715,000 jobs in cybersecurity alone were then open. Sydney Lake, "Companies Are Desperate for Cybersecurity Workers—More than 700k Positions Need to Be Filled," *Fortune*, June 30, 2022, https://fortune.com/education/business/articles/2022/06/30/companies-are-desperate-for-cybersecurity-workers-more-than-700k-positions-need-to-be-filled/.

43. Paul Fain, "Alternative Credentials on the rise," *Inside Higher Ed*, August 27, 2020.

44. Ray Schroeder, "Credential Train Is Leaving the Station—Get on Board," *Inside Higher Ed*, May 25, 2022.

45. Goldie Blumenstyk, "When a Degree Is Just the Beginning," *Chronicle of Higher Education*, September 18, 2015, B5.

46. Lindsay McKenzie, "Credential Count Approaches 1 million," *Inside Higher Ed*, February 11, 2021.

47. In 2022 *Forbes* online issued its "College Ranking: Best Online Universities for Return on Investment," compiled by Lucie Lapowski, which listed 325 degree-granting institutions (https://www.forbes.com/sites /lucielapovsky/2021/12/27/college-ranking-best-online-universities-for -return-on-investment/?sh=77eebcb56614).

48. Paul Fain, "New Data on the 36 Million Americans Who Left College without a Degree," *Inside Higher Ed*, October 31, 2019.

49. Steven Mintz, "Can CUNY Successfully Bring the 'Wolves in Sheep's Clothing' into the Fold?" *Inside Higher Ed*, March 31, 2022.

50. See Doug Lederman, "Arkansas's Winding Path to Building an Online University," *Inside Higher Ed*, June 14, 2022, which reported that a relatively low capitalization, at $7 million, held back this merger of a public and a private operation.

51. Paul Fain, "Koch Foundation and Others Fund ASU's Higher Ed 'Redesign,'" *Inside Higher Ed*, September 9, 2020.

52. Doug Lederman, "Dropping the Degree as a Hiring Requirement," *Inside Higher Ed*, June 3, 2022. The National Student Clearinghouse Research Center puts the number of adults aged 25–64 who never finished college at 39 million. "Some College, No Credential Student Outcomes: Annual Progress Report— Academic Year 2021–22," National Student Clearinghouse Research Center, April 25, 2023, https://nscresearchcenter.org/some-college-no-credential/.

53. Paul Fain, "Interview with IBM Official about the Company's 'New Collar' Push to Look beyond College Degrees," *Inside Higher Ed*, October 29, 2019.

54. See Shor, *Culture Wars*, ch. 3, "The War on Illiteracy." Goldie Blumenstyk called into question the corporate claim, calling it "the so-called skills gap, or the apparent mismatch between the skills employers say they want in job candidates and what they see—in recent college graduates" ("When a Degree Is Just the Beginning: Today's Employers Want More, Say Providers of Alternative Credentials," *Chronicle of Higher Education*, September 18, 2015, B5).

55. Quoted in Blumenstyk, "When a Degree Is Just the Beginning," B6.

56. "Q&A with Ryan Craig, Author of a New Book on Faster, Cheaper College Alternatives," *Inside Higher Ed*, August 22, 2018.

57. Ryan Craig, "Community Colleges Rely Too Much on Low-Value Associate Degrees That Don't Lead to Transfer," *Inside Higher Ed*, October 19,

2018. The piece dovetails with Craig's book, *A New U: Faster + Cheaper Alternatives to College* (Dallas: BenBella Books, 2018).

58. John Dewey, *Democracy and Education* (1916; reprint, New York: Free Press, 1967), 13.

59. See Lindsay McKenzie, "Closing the Skills Gap with Digital Badges," *Inside Higher Ed*, September 26, 2018; Elizabeth Redden, "41% of Recent Grads Work in Jobs Not Requiring a Degree," *Inside Higher Ed*, February 18, 2020.

60. Paul Fain, "Ad Council Campaign from White House Task Force Will Tout Alternatives to Bachelor's Degree," *Inside Higher Ed*, February 24, 2020. See also Fain, "Alternative Credentials on the Rise," *Inside Higher Ed*, August 27, 2020.

61. Paul Fain, "Alternative Credentials on the Rise," *Inside Higher Ed*, August 27, 2020.

62. Dana Rubinstein and Emma G. Fitzsimmons, "New York City Workers Are Quitting in Droves," *New York Times*, July 14, 2022, A1, A20.

63. John Dewey, "An Undemocratic Proposal," in *American Education and Vocationalism: A Documentary History, 1870–1970*, edited by W. Norton Grubb and Marvin Lazerson (New York: Columbia University Press, 1974), 144.

64. Dewey, *Democracy and Education*, 316.

65. Dewey, *Democracy and Education*, 318–19.

66. A good example of secretive policy making is New York governor Kathy Hochul's shoving through billion-dollar subsidies to chip makers and to the Buffalo Bills football team for a new stadium after she took office, while promising transparency in government. See Jay Root, "Hochul's Transparency Vow Hits a Snag: Hochul," *New York Times*, July 12, 2022, A1, A15.

67. Ben Stein, "In Class Warfare, Guess Which Class Is Winning?" *New York Times*, November 26, 2006, BU3. See also Tom Snowden, "Buffett Blasts System That Lets Him Pay Less Tax than Secretary," *London Times*, June 28, 2007; Warren Buffett, "Stop Coddling the Super-Rich," *New York Times*, Aug. 15, 2011, A21.

68. Eli Broad, "Please Raise My Taxes," *New York Times*, June 26, 2019, A31.

69. Cohen, "Profits Swell, but Laborers See No Relief."

70. According to *US News & World Report*'s 2022 rankings, "Best Online Bachelor's Programs," usnews.com/education/online-education/bachelors/rankings.

71. Liam Knox, "Online M.B.A.s Overtake Residential Programs," *Inside Higher Ed*, May 17, 2022.

72. Richard Ohmann, "Review of *Class Dismissed*," *Radical Teacher*, 94 (Fall 2012): 63–72.

73. This is what Pierre Bourdieu called the *habitus*, the historical condition in and through which an individual undergoes the social construction of themselves as a hierarchically differentiated human subject. See his master-

work, *Distinction: A Social Critique of the Judgement of Taste* (Cambridge, MA: Harvard University Press, 1984).

74. Michael Zweig, *The Working-Class Majority: America's Best-Kept Secret* (Ithaca, NY: Cornell University Press, 2000), 122.

75. Robert Reich, "The Limping Middle Class," *New York Times*, September 4, 2011, SR6.

76. See Henry A. Giroux, *Neoliberalism's War on Higher Education* (Chicago: Haymarket Books, 2019); and Giroux, *Against the Terror of Neoliberalism: Politics beyond the Age of Greed* (Baltimore: Paradigm, 2008).

77. See Shor, *Culture Wars*.

78. "Nixon's Silent Majority Speech: The Day the 60s Died," PBS Learning Media, accessed June 27, 2023, https://www.pbslearningmedia.org/resource/23784e9a-e7c1-a64c-80aaa6e522f6e/nixons-silent-majority-speech-the-day-the-60s-died/. Nixon's televised speech was broadcast November 3, 1969. The unflattering media reception led Vice-President Agnew to make his famous televised "nattering nabobs of negativity" rebuttal speech on November 13, 1969.

79. See Shor, *Culture Wars*, ch. 2, "Settling for Less, 1971–1975: The War for 'Careerism'—Career Education Depresses Activism and Aspirations." See also Sidney P. Marland, *Career Education* (New York: McGraw-Hill, 1974).

80. Arthur M. Cohen and Florence B. Brawer, *The American Community College* (San Francisco: Jossey-Bass, 1982), 192.

81. Cohen and Brawer, 192.

82. Marland, *Career Education*, 40–41.

83. Marland, 42.

84. Shor, *Culture Wars*, 31.

85. W. Norton Grubb and Marvin Lazerson, "Rally 'Round the Workplace: Continuities and Fallacies in Career Education," *Harvard Educational Review* 45.4 (1975): 353.

86. Lewis F. Powell Jr., "The Powell Memorandum," August 23, 1971, Scholarly Commons, accessed June 27, 2023, https://scholarlycommons.law.wlu.edu/powellmemo/1/.

87. Henry Giroux, *The University in Chains: Confronting the Military-Industrial-Academic Complex* (Boulder, CO: Paradigm, 2007), 142.

88. Giroux, 142.

89. Giroux, 142.

90. David Callahan, "$1 Billion for Ideas: Conservative Think Tanks in the 1990s," National Committee for Responsive Philanthropy, March 18, 1999, https://www.ncrp.org/wp-content/uploads/2016/11/1BillionForIdeas-lowres-1.pdf. See also Jacob S. Hacker and Paul Pierson, *Winner-Take-All Politics: How Washington Made the Rich Richer—and Turned Its Back on the Middle Class* (New York: Simon and Schuster, 2010), excerpted in "The Powell Memo: A Call-to-Arms for Corporations," *Moyers & Company*, September 14,

2012, https://billmoyers.com/content/the-powell-memo-a-call-to-arms-for
-corporations; and "Noam Chomsky on Powell Memorandum," YouTube,
September 24, 2015, https://www.youtube.com/watch?v=T9T3w6vrUis.

91. On the proliferation of political restrictions on curricula, see Jacey
Fortin and Giulia Heyward, "Teaching Black History Month, under New
Limits," *New York Times*, February 13, 2022, 14. On conservative restrictions on
policy outside education, see Lisa Friedman, "Tackling Environmental
Racism without Mentioning Race," *New York Times*, February 13, 2022, A13.
And on the state of Florida's prohibition against teaching critical race theory,
see Colleen Flaherty's "Mixed Message," *Inside Higher Ed*, May 9, 2022.

92. Adam Liptak, "Justices Curb E.P.A. Power over Emissions: Ruling on
Final Day of Court's Term Solidifies Lurch to the Right," *New York Times*,
July 1, 2022, A1, A17.

93. See, for example, Joshua Hunt, *University of Nike: How Corporate
Cash Bought American Higher Education* (New York: Melville House, 2018);
Ohmann's *Politics of Knowledge: The Commercialization of the University, the
Professions, and Print Culture* (Middletown, CT: Wesleyan University Press,
2003), esp. chs. 3 and 7; Henry A. Giroux and Susan Searls Giroux, *Take Back
Higher Education* (New York: Palgrave Macmillan, 2004), 264–76; Giroux,
The University in Chains; and Derek Bok, *Universities in the Marketplace*
(Princeton, NJ: Princeton University Press, 2003).

94. Lizette Alavarez, "Florida May Reduce Tuition for Select Majors," *New
York Times*, December 9, 2012; Scott Jaschik, "Kentucky's Governor vs. French
Literature," *Inside Higher Ed*, February 1, 2016; Rick Seltzer, "Kentucky's
Governor Says Universities Should Think about Cutting Programs with Poor
Job Prospects," *Inside Higher Ed*, September 14, 2017; Colleen Flaherty,
"Faculty Members at Wisconsin Stevens Point React to Plan to Cut 13 Majors,"
Inside Higher Ed, March 13, 2018; Colleen Flaherty, "U of Vermont to Cut 12
Majors, 11 Minors," *Inside Higher Ed*, December 4, 2020.

95. The phrase comes from the popular film *The Big Chill* (Lawrence
Kasdan, director, 1983), about the reunion of college friends from the 1960s,
more than a decade after graduation, for the funeral of a member of their
group who had committed suicide. An earlier and lower-budget film, John
Sayles's *The Return of the Secaucus Seven* (1980) anticipated "the big chill"
theme with deeper political insight. Perhaps the most telling feature film in
this genre was the 1975 *Jonah Who Will Be Twenty-Five in the Year 2000* (Alain
Tanner, director; Tanner and John Berger, cowriters).

96. See Ohmann's comments in his interview with Jeffrey Williams,
reprinted in Ohmann, *Politics of Knowledge*, ch. 15, esp. 247–50.

97. Melanie Hanson, "College Enrollments and Student Demographic
Statistics," Education Data Initiative, updated July 26, 2022, https://
educationdata.org/college-enrollment-statistics.

98. National Center for Education Statistics, *Digest of Education Statistics*, 2019.

99. Scott Smallwood, "American Women Surpass Men in Earning Doctorates," *Chronicle of Higher Ed*, December 12, 2003, A10.

100. Patricia Cohen, "Racial Wealth Gap Persists despite Degree, Study Says," *New York Times*, August 16, 2015.

101. Katie Benner, "Women in Tech Reveal Culture of Harassment," *New York Times*, July 1, 2017, A1, A16; Claire Cain Miller, "Tech's Man Problem," *New York Times*, April 6. 2014, BU1, BU6–BU7.

102. Meghan Brink, "Debt Relief Has Public Support," *Inside Higher Ed*, May 27, 2022. Several initiatives to end tuition have been proposed by Senator Bernie Sanders; Mario Cuomo, the late former governor of New York, and the state of Arizona.

103. "Only 61 percent of first-time, full-time students at four-year colleges complete their college degree within eight years, which is twice the normal time. . . . A college degree provides a boost to earnings and employment, but much of the gains come from completion of the degree . . . college dropouts forgo the majority of the benefits of higher education." Sophia Koropeckyj, Chris Lafakis, and Adam Ozimek, "Executive Summary," in *The Economic Impact of Increasing College Completion* (Cambridge, MA: American Academy of Arts and Sciences, 2017).

104. Michel de Certeau, *The Practice of Everyday Life* (1984), trans. by Steven Rendall (Berkeley: University of California Press, 2011); James Scott, *Weapons of the Weak: Everyday Forms of Peasant Resistance* (New Haven, CT: Yale University Press, 1987).

105. *A Passion for Knowing the World* is the title of a book written by Paulo Freire's eldest daughter, Maddalena, that recounts her experience teaching poor children in Brazil.

106. "Bread and Roses" is a song that emerged from the Lawrence strike. The lyrics originated in a poem by James Oppenheim published in the *American Magazine* in 1911. Oppenheim adapted it from a slogan he heard from striking women in the West. It has been put to music in recent times by several artists, including Judy Collins and Mimi Farina. See the Zinn Education Project for more background and books on this song and the strike.

Index

Academically Adrift (Arum and Roksa), 134

academic labor: casualization of, 47–48, 223; crisis of, 42–43, 44; demonization of, 48; disruptive change to, 44–45; political views and, 240n3; tenure-track, 43

accounting majors, 156

Accuracy in Academia, 222

adjunct faculty positions, 140

advanced degree, 131

Agnew, Spiro T., 260n78

Allegories of Reading (de Man), 14

"Alternative Ivy, The" brand, 234n42

Alverno College, 110

American Association of University Professors (AAUP), 44

"American Family Plan," 22

American Federation of Labor, 211

Angrist, Joshua D., 71, 237n14, 237n16

anti-tax movements, 153–54

Anyon, Jean, 239n2

Apple, Inc.: employees' education at, 209–10

artificial intelligence "revolution," 40

Arum, Richard, 134, 135, 136

Atkins, William Giles, 185, 186

Atlantic Monthly (magazine), 11

Attewell, Paul, 114

Austin, J. L.: *How to Do Things with Words,* 14

automation, 37–38, 39–40

automobile industry, 32, 36

Autor, David H., 253n6

bachelor's degree: economic effect of, 58–59, 61–62, 77–78, 91, 94–95, 128, 235n1, 245n21; online, 213; price tag, 190–91; on résumé, 136–37, 141, 207

badge programs: accountability of, 205; benefits of, 209; boot camps, 203, 209; clientele of, 201, 202, 205–6; college life *vs.,* 206–9; cost of, 203; impact on higher education, 190, 192–93, 204–5; inequality and, 224; occupationalism of, 209; organizational structure of, 202–3; popularity of, 201–2, 214; types of, 203–4

Barnum, P. T., 217

Bartik, Timothy J., 124

Baum, Sandy, 235n1

Bayh-Dole Act of 1980, 29, 52

Bennett, William, 41

Benson, Alan, 112, 113

Berg, Ivar, 246n22

Biden, Joseph R., 21–22, 49, 133, 165, 231n1, 252n3

"Big Chill," 223, 261n95

biomedical engineering, 149

Birmingham School of cultural studies, 10

Black Lives Matter, 44, 49

Black veterans, 71, 72–73

Bloomberg, Michael R., 51

Bloom Institute of Technology, 204

Blumenstyk, Goldie, 258n54

Borough of Manhattan Community College, 110–11

Bourdieu, Pierre, 239n2, 259n73

Bowen, William G., 22

Bowles, Samuel, 7; *Schooling in Capitalist America*, 163, 254n13
Braverman, Harry, 248n30; *Labor and Monopoly Capital*, 152
Brawer, Florence, 218
"Bread and Roses" (song), 227, 262n106
Brill, Dale A., 144
Broad, Eli, 213
Brooklyn College, 110
Brown University, 198
Brown v. Board of Education of Topeka, 24
Buffett, Warren, 213
"Build Back Better" bill, 49, 133, 165, 166
Bureau of Labor Statistics (BLS), 151, 247n29
Bush, George H. W., 21
business major, 145–46, 148
Busteed, Brandon, 257n38
Butler, Judith, 239n2

California: first-tier education in, 241n9; public universities, 112–13; school system, 51
California State University (CSU), 112
Cambridge University: "complimentary" MA degree, 139
campus: franchises on, 52; social movements on, 129–30; social services, 226
capital mobility, 34, 35, 36
Caplan, Bryan, 136, 137, 141, 244n15; *The Case against Education*, 140
Cappelli, Peter, 151, 152, 156, 232n13, 248n37
Career Education plan, 217, 218, 219
careerism, 218, 222, 227
Carnevale, Anthony P., 61, 62, 155, 195, 226, 254n12; *The College Payoff*, 85, 93, 94
Case against Education, The (Caplan), 140
causality, 11–12, 75, 96
causal research: alternative strategies, 77–78; criticism of, 68, 95–97; economists' approach to, 93, 97; instrumental-variables estimation method, 92–93; in medicine, 83–84, 96; natural experiments, 237n13; observational studies,

78, 83–87; planned experiments, 66–67, 78, 79, 238n21; quasi-experiments, 69–73, 76, 78, 90–91, 237n13, 238n21; random assignments, 66–69; representative groups, 80–81
cause and effect: philosophical studies of, 64–65
Census Bureau: American Community Survey, 77; data collections, 83, 84; study of lifetime earnings, 59
Century (magazine), 11
CEOs, education of, 248n37
Certeau, Michel de, 226
charter schools, 27, 50–51, 68, 198, 234n34, 240n7
Cheah, Ban, 93
chemistry majors, 147
Cheney, Lynne, 41
children's education, 196–97, 236n9
choice of college: academic factor of, 104; interactive tools for, 104–5; living conditions and, 104; personal factors of, 103, 104–5; rational approach to, 102–3, 106; types of institution and, 103–4
Chomsky, Noam, 13
City University of New York, 52, 111, 206
Class Dismissed (Marsh), 163, 214
class war, algorithm of, 213–16
Clinton, Bill, 21
Clinton, Hillary, 37, 49
Cohen, Arthur, 218
Cohen, Patricia, 213, 253n8
college: benefits of, 20; as black box, 107–8, 111; budget cuts, 44, 53; business thinking in, 54; categories of, 109; as cause, 60–65; communications of, 205; competition for students, 56; consumer information about, 54–55; corporate interests and, 3; deals with banks, 52–53; enrollment priorities, 4, 113–14; evolution of, 120, 242n20; faith in economic benefits of, 132; freedoms of, 246n21; loans, 21; marketing strategies, 56–57; military infrastructure and, 15; online courses, 205–6; practice of contracting out work, 53; preparation

for, 136; privatization of, 52; purpose of, 3, 5; quality measurement, 114–15; ranking of, 55, 111–12, 114; reproduction of inequality, 41; retention and graduation rates, 195, 197, 202, 241n10, 258n52; return on investment, 106, 115, 116; selective, 202; sources of income, 52; statistics, 224; studies of, 17–18; transformation into universities, 120; types of, 103–4. *See also* community colleges

college admission: allocation of funds for, 119; family background and, 196–97; gender and, 224; legacy, 197; priorities, 113–14; race and, 195, 223–24; relocation to suburbs for, 118–19; selectivity in, 114–17, 136, 138, 241n14, 241n15, 243n3; token, 197

College Board, 221, 235n1

college education: assumptions about, 113; barriers to, 87; as commodity, 110; cost and benefits of, 22–23, 41; criticism of, 140–41, 244–45n15; devaluation of, 210; extracurricular activities, 244n13; globalization and, 31–32; Great Recession and, 31; as hiring filter, 136–37, 206–7; human capital theory and, 128; ideology and, 129–30, 162–63; lifetime earnings and, 60–61, 64–65, 124, 125, 133–34, 160, 239n28; parents' investment in, 123; perceived benefits of, 31, 102, 162, 169; practical intelligence and, 238n23; reputability of, 119–20; return on investment in, 30, 33, 45, 122, 131–32, 138, 165, 169–70; social status and, 119–20; as "sorting machine," 136; taxation and, 165, 166; time of completion, 262n103; traditional connotations, 120–21

College English (journal), 16

"College for All" idea, 5, 108, 133, 164, 166, 167–69, 170–71, 176

college graduates: earnings of, 35, 59, 95, 103, 106, 193–94; ethnicity of, 224; job market for, 33, 39–40, 56–57, 148–49, 191, 192, 209, 246n22; occupational preparation of, 35–36; skills of, 134

"College Movement," 201

College Payoff, The (Carnevale), 77, 85, 87, 91, 92, 93, 94–95, 97

college premium: age and, 130; businesses and, 3–4, 35; changes in, 37, 190; contradiction of, 192; correlation to risk factor, 84; cultural dimension of, 86; as cure for inequality, 29–30, 31; economic arguments for, 190, 236n7; evolution of, 35; free market discourse of, 141; gender factor, 85, 130; human capital hypothesis, 158; hypotheses about, 133; level of income and, 3; measurement of, 108, 143; myth of, 1–2, 23, 28, 58–59, 108, 110, 128, 232n13; as payoff for intelligence, 86, 160–61; as penalty, 125; politics and, 50; precollege skills and, 136, 138, 139, 142; promotion of, 21–22, 86–87; public opinion about, 49; quantitative metrics of, 129; race and, 130; reality of, 215; selection biases, 130–31; signaling hypothesis, 141, 158, 159, 160; skepticism about, 31; studies of, 83, 123–24; theoretical perspective, 99; unequal distribution of, 193, 225; upward mobility and, 34–35

colleges, proprietary, 133

College Scorecard, 54–55, 105, 106, 107

Collins, Judy, 262n106

common school revival movement, 179

community colleges, 133, 204, 208, 231n1

computer programming major, 147

Conservative Restoration, 217

Cook, Tim, 209, 210

Cooley, Noah, 182

corporate interests, 35, 163, 165, 204

correspondence principle, 254n13

Cosmopolitan (magazine), 11

Cottom, Tressie, 193

Counselman, Gunnar, 208

Country and the City, The (Williams), 229n7

COVID-19 pandemic: education and, 41–42, 257n37; labor market and, 33–34, 191, 210; wage bump, 243n2

Craig, Ryan: *A New U,* 200, 208
Credential Engine, 204
credentialism, 39, 204, 246n22
critical race theory, 41, 221
cultural capital, 121
culture: capitalist industry and, 10–12
Culture and Society (Williams), 10
culture war, 48
Culture Wars (Shor), 201
Cuomo, Mario, 261n95, 262n102
curricula: exclusion of humanities subjects
  from, 202; ideological frames, 198–99,
  212; overregulation of, 198

Davis, Lennard J., 17, 230n15
degree-plus, 191
de Man, Paul, 13, 230n11; *Allegories of
  Reading,* 14
democratic education, 212
demographic trends, 38
DeVos, Betsy, 51
Dewey, John, 209, 211–12, 216, 239n2,
  244n13
dissident learning, 41, 49
Duncan, Arne, 55, 108

economic capital, 121
economic inequality, 40, 191–92, 232n21,
  242n19, 243n1, 253n6
eCornell, 204
Edison Schools, 50
education: as answer to national problems, 25–26; automation in, 39–40;
  benefits of, 242n21; capitalism and,
  36–37; demand for, 177, 178; democracy
  and, 226–27; economic value of, 63,
  88–89; as equalizer, 224, 249n1; family
  strategies for, 122; human capital
  theory and, 87–88, 89; investment in,
  177–78, 181; policymaking, 93, 133,
  217–20; popular assumptions about,
  1–2, 3, 5; problem-solution approach,
  27; proposed reform of, 219; quality of,
  111, 122; "reproduction theory" of, 7, 8,
  254n13; social mobility and, 2–3, 198,
  238n22; technological development

and, 188; *vs.* trade training, 209; trans-
  formation of, 211–12; working-class
  families, 142. *See also* higher education
Education and Jobs (Berg and Gorelick),
  246n22
Ehrenreich, Barbara, 8, 229n3
Ehrenreich, John, 8
Eisenhower, Dwight D., 163, 249n2
elementary education, 183, 184
employees: free market choices, 128;
  training of, 163, 174–75
Engels, Friedrich, 12, 38
engineering majors, 31–32, 147, 149
*English in America: A Radical View of the
  Profession* (Ohmann), 6, 7, 9, 12–13
Erie Canal, 187
Esteva, Raimundo, 112, 113

fallacy of division, 62, 63
family income: return on education and,
  124–25, 126
Farina, Mimi, 262n106
Federal Vocational Education Act,
  217–18
Fish, Stanley, 13, 14, 229n7
Floyd, George, 227
Ford, Henry, 232n14
Fordism, 37, 232n14
for-profit universities, 29, 43, 46–47
Foucault, Michel, 39, 198
Framingham Heart Study, 83, 84
Franklin, Benjamin, 185
Franklin, Bruce, 17
Friedman, Milton, 232n14
Fuller, Margaret, 99

General Motors (GM), 163, 165, 249n2
Georgetown University Center for
  Education and the Workforce, 59, 60,
  93, 145, 235n1
GI Bill (Servicemen's Readjustment Act),
  24, 71–72, 237n16
Gintis, Herbert, 7, 8; *Schooling in
  Capitalist America,* 163, 254n13
Giroux, Henry, 7, 219, 220
globalization, 31–33, 37

Goldin, Claudia: on demand for school-
ing, 180, 183, 185; on economic value of
education, 63, 181, 187, 195; hypothesis
of evolution of education, 177, 178,
188; *The Race between Education and
Technology*, 176, 188, 192; on social value
of education, 201
Gorelick, Sherry, 246n22
"Graduate Students, Professionals,
Intellectuals" (Ohmann), 9
Gramsci, Antonio, 12, 232n14, 248n31
Gray, Bridgette, 207
Great Resignation, 210, 227
greenskeeper job, 156–57
gross domestic product (GDP), 172–73
Grubb, W. Norton, 218, 246n22

habitus, notion of, 259n73
Harvard University: admission practices,
121; founding of, 242n20; graduation
rate, 241n10; legacies, 121, 243n24;
wealthy families and, 119, 121
Harvey, David, 39, 232n21
Hawley, MA: decline of, 187; domestic
mode of production, 187; foundation
of, 181–82; history of, 251n17; land
value in, 186, 187, 251n20; mandatory
schooling in, 184; population of, 185, 187
heart health studies, 83–84
Heath, Shirley Brice, 239n2
hegemony, concept of, 12, 154, 248n31
Hershbein, Brad J., 124
higher education: call for reform of,
225–26; campaign to defund, 48; civic
and cultural benefits of, 23–24; commercialization of, 201, 222–23; crisis of,
208–9; criticism of, 4–5, 215; decline
of public support for, 153; development
of national system of, 120; economic
outcomes of, 21, 89–90, 100, 162; egalitarian agenda, 226, 227; employment
and, 154–55; enrollments, 223; evolution of, 144, 164, 214; funding of,
44–45, 51–52, 53; government investment in, 40–41, 48; growth of, 188; as
investment, 21; as job training, 3–4;

labor policy, 154, 223; policymaking,
164, 166–68; in political discourse,
24, 48–49; power relations and, 196;
public debates on, 23; reproduction of
inequality, 40–41, 193, 224–25; state
support of, 222, 253n8; studies of, 8
high school graduates: *vs.* college graduates, 59–60; earnings of, 59, 63, 91,
94, 95, 103; prospects of, 39; skills of,
257n36
"High School Movement," 179, 201
high schools, statistics of, 189
hiring friction, 208
Hochul, Kathy, 259n66
Hoggart, Richard, 160
Howe, Florence, 16
How to Do Things with Words (Austin), 14
human agency, 226
human capital: definition of, 88;
investment in, 177
human capital theory: explanation of
prosperity, 186–87; inquiry into college
payoff, 87–89, 99–100, 128–29, 133, 135,
143, 175; limitations of, 143, 178; main
idea of, 174; quantitative approach of, 175
humanities majors, 147
human skills. *See* soft skills
human subjects: studies of social
construction of, 239n2
Hume, David, 64
Hurricane Katrina, 176, 250n11

IBM, hiring practices, 207
ideology, 30, 96
income-outcome algorithm, 214–16
industrial jobs, 32–33, 34, 37
instrumental-variables estimation (IVE),
92–93, 95
IQ level, 239n24
Is There a Text in This Class? (Fish), 14
IT sector: badge programs and, 207;
coding camps, 203; college degrees
and, 152; job openings in, 154, 203,
207–8, 247n29; outsourcing of work
in, 152; salaries, 62, 152, 154, 203, 236n2
Ivy League schools, 116–17, 242n20

Jayapal, Pramila, 166, 167, 168
Jefferson, Thomas, 23, 24, 179
Jobs, Steve, 248n37
job skills, 199–200, 206
Johnson, Lyndon B., 24, 25, 164
Jordan, Kelli, 207

K-12 schools: decline of state support of, 222; donors of, 51; inequality across, 26, 27–28, 193, 198, 240n7; management of, 27; privatizing of, 21, 28, 29, 50, 51; teachers in, 247n24
Kampf, Louis, 16
Katz, Lawrence F.: on demand for schooling, 180, 181, 183, 185; on economic value of education, 63, 181, 187, 195; hypothesis of evolution of education, 177, 178, 188; *The Race between Education and Technology*, 176, 188, 192; on social value of education, 201
Koch Foundation, 206

labor: demand for non-college, 33–34; deskilling and dispossession of, 153, 248n30; gendered system of, 85, 247n24; monopoly capitalism and, 152–53; new technologies and, 250n14; outsourcing of, 153; training costs of, 153; transformation of, 171
Labor and Monopoly Capital (Braverman), 152
labor market: automation and, 37–38; changing conditions of, 150, 151; COVID-19 pandemic and, 33–34, 191, 210, 243n2; destabilizing factors, 212–13; for low-wage workers, 191; neoliberalism and, 38–39; wage gap, 34
labor unions, 216
Land Ordinance of 1785, 179
Lareau, Annette, 196
Lauter, Paul, 16
Lavy, Victor, 237n14
Lawrence strike, 227, 262n106
Lazerson, Marvin, 218, 246n22
learning, 133–34, 135–36, 142, 143, 154, 156
Learning to Labor (Willis), 8

Lederman, Doug, 193
Lee, Kai-Fu, 40
legacy students, 197
Levy, Frank S., 112, 113
liberal arts, 144, 210, 222, 223
Lieber, Ron, 104
lifetime earnings: definition of, 235n1; educational attainment and, 59, 60–65, 85, 91–94, 124, 239n28; gender factor, 92, 94, 99, 194, 224, 254n12; individual characteristics and, 62, 85–86, 99, 239n24; occupation and, 62, 92, 94; race factor, 92, 94; selectivity in admissions and, 114–15, 116–17; social determinants of, 95, 194; studies of, 59, 124; variations of, 61, 62
literacy crisis, 194, 195, 208, 221–22
literary training, 6–7
Lohr, Steve, 235n2

MA degrees, 139
Maimonides's class size rule, 70
Manchin, Joe, 22, 133
Mann, Horace, 24, 129, 163, 180, 224, 242n21, 249n1
Marcus, Steven, 12
"Market-Driven Higher Education" conference, 54
Marland, Sidney P., 217, 218, 219, 220, 221, 222, 223
Marsh, John, 215; *Class Dismissed*, 163, 214
Marx, Karl, 38, 172
Massachusetts: early colleges in, 242n20; farming in, 183; land speculation in, 181–82, 186; public schooling in, 184
mass education, 180–81, 201
massive online open courses (MOOCs), 205
MBA programs, 214, 223
McPherson, Michael S., 22
Measuring Institutional Performance in Higher Education (Meyerson and Massy), 54
Melton, Michelle, 254n12
meritocracy, 4
Me-Too Movements, 227

Mill, John Stuart, 64, 65, 66, 78, 82, 96, 237n14
Modern Language Association (MLA), 16, 42–43
modular skill training, 202
monopoly capitalism, 152–53
Montessori schools, 122
Mortenson, Thomas G., 253n8
Murnane, Richard J., 68–69, 70, 237n13, 237n14, 238n21, 239n27
myths of American culture, 6–12

National Association of Manufacturers, 211
National Council of Teachers of English, 16
National Defense Education Act, 24, 25
natural experiments, 237n13, 250n11
neoliberalism, 50, 232n14
New England: early settlers, 251n15; farming in, 183; human and cultural capital, 183; investment in schooling, 181; waterways, 187
New Orleans public schools, 176
New U: Faster + Cheaper Alternatives to College, A (Craig), 200, 208
New York City: college admission, 118; schools in, 117
Nixon, Richard M., 79, 217, 219, 223, 260n78
No Child Left Behind Act, 24, 25
North American Free Trade Agreement (NAFTA), 32, 37
nuclear engineers, 149–50
nursing majors, 146

Obama, Barack, 21, 54, 55, 105, 133
Oberlin College, 242n20
observational studies, 83–87
occupational education, 199, 217–19
Occupy Wall Street protest, 46
Ohmann, Richard: academic career, 14–15; background and education, 13–14; on college premium, 1, 2, 215; critique of higher education, 4–5, 6, 7–8, 13–14, 190; on culture and capitalist system, 10–12; editorial work, 16; on income-outcome algorithm, 214–15;

influence of, 230n15; on literacy crisis, 194, 195; political activism, 15–16; publications of, 6, 9, 14, 18–19; research interests, 16–17; on speech acts, 230n11
oil and gas industry, 150–51
Old Deluder Satan Act, 184
online education, 205–6, 213–14
Oppenheim, James, 262n106
Opportunity@Work, 207
Organization of the Petroleum Exporting Countries, 150
overlap phenomenon, 94
Oxford University: "complimentary" MA degree, 139

Paris Climate Accord, 37
Parker, Harrison, 251n17
pauper schools, 179
"Payback" (interactive simulation game), 103–5
PBS NewsHour, 20
pedagogy of debt, 7
Pell Grant, 105
Per Scholas training centers, 235n2
Peterson, Peter G., 242n19
petroleum engineers: earnings of, 151, 155; job market for, 150–51
pharmacology major, 145
PhDs: earnings for, 239n28; job market for new, 42, 43; overproduction of, 43
Philadelphia school system, 50
planned experiments, 66–67, 78, 79, 91, 237n13, 238n21
political correctness, 41, 49, 140
Politics and Letters (Williams), 10
Politics of Knowledge (Ohmann), 9
Politics of Literature, The (Kampf and Lauter), 16
popular movements, 217
postgraduate degrees, 190–91
Powell, Lewis F., 219–20, 221, 222, 223
Powell Memorandum, 219, 220
precollege investments, 127
primitive accumulation, 183
Princeton University: admission to, 243n3; graduation rate, 241n10

private tutoring, 117–18

Professional Correctness (Fish), 229n7

professional-managerial class (PMC), 8, 9–10, 40–41, 229n3

Project STAR (Student-Teacher Achievement Ratio): parents' influence on, 67–68, 236n9; participants, 67, 69; problem of attrition, 69; random assignments, 67–68, 69, 74, 78–79, 236n10, 237n12, 237n14, 238n20; results of, 67; school administration influence on, 68–69; teachers' self-interest in, 68

prosperity: competing causes of, 130; external conditions for, 98; higher education as path to, 100; inheritance as factor of, 101; personal abilities and, 98–99

public policy, conservative turn, 220–21

public schools: competition with charter schools, 51; desegregation of, 24, 25, 50; establishment of, 24; funding of, 26, 51, 179, 240n7; inequality across, 27–28; legal and economic arrangements for, 179; quality of, 26; reform of, 28; statistics, 50

Puritan religion, and value of education, 184–85

quasi-experiments, 69–73, 76, 78, 79, 82, 90–92, 237n13, 238n21

race: college access and, 195; income inequality and, 242n19

Race between Education and Technology, The (Goldin and Katz), 176, 188, 192

Radical Caucus, 16

radical pedagogy movement, 7

Radical Teacher (journal), 16

random assignments, 66–68, 75, 76–77, 90–91, 236n10

randomized studies, 69, 70

reader response theory, 14

Reagan, Ronald, 220, 232n14

registered nurses, 156, 247n24

"Relation between Family Income Background and the Returns to Education, The," 124

research universities, 143–44

"Rethinking College" broadcast, 20

return on investment in education: common use of the phrase, 231n9; family income and, 124–25, 126; GDP as measure of, 172–73; hypotheses about, 138–39; nation's payoff from, 173, 174; racial disparities, 126; social impact of, 174; studies of, 138, 172

Rockefeller family, 121

Roe v. Wade, 221

Roksa, Josipa, 134, 135, 136

Rose, Stephen J., 93

Rouse, Cecilia, 62, 63

Ryan, Paul, 201

Said, Edward, 5, 13

Sanders, Bernie, 5, 37, 49, 166, 167, 168, 227, 262n102

Sayles, John, 261n95

Scholastic Aptitude Test (SAT), 117, 194–95

schooling: class size rule, 70; curricula, 244n13; division between schools, 240n7; funding of, 180, 181, 189; history of, 176–77; introduction of mandatory, 184, 185; liberal view of, 129; postelementary, 179; "problem" of poor, 26–27; prosperity and, 188; public demand for, 184, 185, 188–89; regulations, 184–85, 251n17; return on investment in, 185–86; social construction and, 197–99; spread of, 180, 224; studies of, 236n9

Schooling in Capitalist America (Bowles and Gintis), 163, 254n13

Scott, James, 226

Scott, Rick, 144

Selling Culture (Ohmann), 6, 10–11, 17

"Shaping of a Canon, The" (Ohmann), 6, 9–10

Shaw, George Bernard, 9

Shor, Ira, 2, 3, 7, 16
Sidney, Philip: *Arcadia*, 230n7
signaling hypothesis, 136, 139, 140, 141
Sinema, Kyrsten, 133
Sizer, Theodore, 198, 212
skilled workforce, 128
"skills gap," 191, 207–8, 209, 258n54
Smith, Adam, 87, 88, 89
Smith-Hughes Act, 211
social capital, 121
social class system, 39–40, 128, 160, 198, 229n3
social mobility, 1, 3, 34–35
social reproduction, 36–37
soft skills, 199, 200
Southern New Hampshire University (SNHU), 205, 206
speech act theory, 14, 230n11
Spring, Joel, 136
Stanford University: admission to, 243n3; payoff, 139
Steinberg, Jacques, 257n36
STEM fields: business interests and, 3, 26, 223; career trajectory, 147; earnings, 157; students' choice of, 101–2, 247n24; subsidies for, 144
Strohl, Jeff, 254n12
student debt, 7, 8, 29, 31, 45–46, 110, 125, 190, 252n3
students: average age of, 105; commitment to learning, 135, 136; as customers, 55–56; ethnic composition, 223–24; financial aid to, 56, 105, 239n27; gender composition, 120, 224; legacy, 56; marketable skills, 57; part-time, 154; poverty of, 236n5; race disparity, 120; subject choice, 137; from upper-income families, 101–2, 103; from vulnerable groups, 226
subjugated knowledge, 198, 199
suburban high schools, 118

Tea Party movement, 132
tenure-track positions, 140
textile industry, 32

Thatcher, Margaret, 53, 161, 232n14
Three Mile Island disaster, 149
Thunberg, Greta, 227
Tough, Paul, 192, 226, 255n23
Trump, Donald J.: education policy, 21, 27–28, 51; inauguration speech, 220, 227; political rhetoric, 37, 217; tax reform, 165
Trump University, 29
"T-shaped worker," 200, 257n38
tuition and fees, 45, 48, 52, 117, 132, 225, 231n1, 262n102
turf management degree, 156–57
Turing, Alan, 250n14

undergraduate majors: career trajectory and, 146–48; choice of, 245–46n21; economic value of, 145, 155; marketing of, 143–45; most popular, 145, 146; predicted earnings, 148; ranking of, 248n35; salary gap, 148; studies on payoffs of, 158; unemployment rates and, 148–49; vocationally oriented, 154–55, 156, 157, 159
United States, Mexico, and Canada Agreement (USMCA), 36
universal basic income, 40
universities: business approach, 54, 234n41; categorization of, 109, 112; competition for students, 56; complimentary bachelor's degree, 139–40; corporate interests and, 41; enrollment in, 244n4; for-profit, 132–33, 163; graduation rate, 241n10; history of, 242n20; marketing strategies, 56–57; online courses, 205–6; privatization schemes, 52; purpose of, 233n24; regulations of, 133; vocational training in, 163–64
University Business, 54, 234n42
University of California (UC), 112, 149
University of Chicago, 232n21
University of Michigan, 206
University of Phoenix, 110
University Venture, 200, 208

veterans, 24, 25, 71–72, 74
Vietnam-era draft lottery: college atten-
    dance and, 82, 176; designers of, 79;
    opting out of, 74; as quasi-experiment,
    79, 80; as random assignment process,
    70–71, 72–73, 75–77, 78, 79, 80, 81–82,
    237n16; representative groups, 80;
    resistance to, 4; targeted population,
    80–81
Vietnam War: college infrastructure and,
    15; deserters, 75; enlistments, 75, 76;
    resisters and exiles, 73, 74, 75
vocational education, 137, 153, 158, 159, 211,
    247n24
Volvo, 35, 175

wage gaps, 34
wage statistics, 253n8
Walker, Kent, 210
Wan, Amy, 239n2
"we" as homogeneous concept, 28–30
Wesleyan University, 234n42

Western Governors University (WGU),
    205, 206
Whitehead, Alfred North, 239n2
"Why Johnny Can't Write" cover story,
    42, 195, 255n23
Willett, John B., 68–69, 70, 237n13,
    237n14, 238n21, 239n27
Williams, Raymond, 10, 229n7,
    250n14
Willis, Paul, 142; Learning to Labor, 8
Wilson, Charles E., 163, 249n2
Witteveen, Dirk, 114
Women's March, 227
Woodruff, Judy, 230n1
World Climate Strike, 227
World Health Organization, 37

XR (extended reality), 206

Y2K problem, 151, 152
Yale University: graduation rate, 241n10
Yang, Andrew, 40